Dante's Interpretive Journey

RELIGION AND POSTMODERNISM
A SERIES EDITED BY MARK C. TAYLOR

Dante's Interpretive Journey

WILLIAM FRANKE

THE UNIVERSITY OF CHICAGO PRESS

CHICAGO AND LONDON

William Franke is assistant professor of comparative litera-
ture and Italian at Vanderbilt University. He has published
articles in *Romanische Forschungen*, *Religion and Literature*,
Comparative Literature Studies, and *Italian Quarterly*.

The University of Chicago Press, Chicago 60637
The University of Chicago Press, Ltd., London
©1996 by The University of Chicago
All rights reserved. Published 1996
Printed in the United States of America

05 04 03 02 01 00 99 98 97 96 1 2 3 4 5

ISBN: 0-226-25997-8 (cloth)
     0-226-25998-6 (paper)

Library of Congress Cataloging-in-Publication Data

Franke, William.
    Dante's interpretive journey/William Franke.
       p.   cm.—(Religion and postmodernism)
    Includes bibliographical references and index.
    1. Dante Alighieri, 1265–1321.   Divina commedia. 2. Dante
Alighieri, 1265–1321—Religion. 3. Christianity in literature.
    4. Hermeneutics—Religious aspects—Christianity. I. Title.
    II. Series.
PQ4417.F73   1996
851'.1—dc20

                                              95-35966
                                                 CIP

♾ The paper used in this publication meets the minimum
requirements of the American National Standard for Infor-
mation Sciences—Permanence of Paper for Printed Library
Materials, ANSI Z39.48-1984.

A Daniela Ridenti
Un pensiero, in compenso

Contents

Preface

It will be evident to whoever is acquainted with scholarship on Dante, and particularly with its North American offshoot, how the present understanding of Dante grows from the soil of American Dante criticism, borrowing insight especially from John Freccero and Giuseppe Mazzotta, among many other heirs of Charles Singleton. At the same time, it would be misleading not to avow that the present work brings quite a different agenda and a different sort of sensibility to the study of Dante. My purpose is not to replace anything existing in Dante studies but to offer another, separate witness to the astonishing rediscovery of Dante that has come about in our time. If an ambition of in some way surpassing previous work motivates the present effort, it is to be found in the direction of raising to a level of general relevance for literary studies and other humanities disciplines some of the principles of poetic interpretation that have been emerging with such éclat from recent critical study of Dante especially in North America and, more broadly, in the English-speaking world.

The work is hybrid and eclectic by its nature. I expect it to be fruitfully approached out of many different backgrounds and types of interest. Though certain of its arguments are bound to prove controversial, this ought not to impede some aspects of the work from being found useful or illuminating for all sorts of readers, from those uninterested in the philosophical project to those whose interest is specifically theoretical. Accordingly, it is not intended that the book necessarily be read sequentially from beginning to end. Chapter 1, for example, contains a bulk of theoretical reflections that attach themselves to the phenomenon of the address to the reader explored in the first section of that chapter. They need not delay proceeding to substantive criticism of the poem, especially in chapters 2 and 5. They are collocated according to a systematic ordering of the project, not with a view to prescribing a single itinerary for its assimilation by all readers. Chapters 2 and 3 interlock and form a central axis of the work as a whole. Not by accident were they the project's genetic core, and in some sense, as so frequently in Dante's own works, the significance of the whole may best be understood as emanating from this center.

Since, then, the book does not read in pseudonarrative sequence like a story, a brief synopsis, however inadequate, indicating main lines in the organization of the ensemble is in order. It may not be fully intelligible in advance of sustained reading but can serve as an aid during and after some direct acquaintance with parts of the text in relating these to the rest.

The major premise of the work, at once speculative and critical in nature, is that the medieval, theological perspectives on interpretation that are built into the *Divine Comedy,* not unique certainly to Dante but given incomparable expression in his poem, can be (in fact, cannot help but be, whether consciously or not) revealingly brought into dialogue with the very different assumptions about interpretation which have fundamentally determined the cast of modern thought. The theoretical issues raised in the introduction, concerning poetic interpretation as an event of truth disclosing potentially both human existence and divinity, are brought to focus in chapter 1 in a discussion of the ontological implications of Dante's discourse of direct address to a reader. The first extensive exegetical segment of the work, chapter 2, deals with the address to the reader in *Inferno* IX as key to defining Dante's interpretive poetics. Chapter 3 reflects theoretically on the temporal dimension of the interpretive act—understood as a response and ultimately as conversion to what addresses one—before returning in its conclusion to the tensions inscribed in *Inferno* IX as made manifest by irresolvably contrasting readings of the canto.

Chapter 4 explains the meaning of a hermeneutic approach to Dante in terms that engage more specifically the history of scholarship focused on the issue of the poem's truth claims. These claims, it is emphasized, concern an existential truth, hence one intrinsically addressed to a reader/interpreter. The chapter enfolds a case in point in the form of a reading of *Purgatorio* X as illustrative of a truth not of realistic mimesis but of existential engagement. It then suggests how Dante's experience of theological truth is neither just a fiction nor purely mystical, but rather is interpretive in character and as such embraces both of these seeming alternatives. The possibility of even a revealed truth's being mediated by the accidents and misprisions of tradition is explored in chapter 5 in an extended treatment of Dante's Statius. This meditation too demonstrates the way truth addresses a reader in a specific historical situation, transposing it in this case from a pagan to a Christian cultural context. The chapter culminates in a challenge to contemporary hermeneutic thinking by defending the possibility of an eternal truth. This concludes the critique of modern and postmodern theories of interpretation in the light of

Dante's poetic praxis and theological vision, which emerges as the over-arching argument of the book.

An earlier, shorter version of chapter 4, section 1 (with some splicing from 2), appeared in *Lectura Dantis: A Forum for Dante Research and Inter-pretation* 12 (1993): 34–52; and a shorter version of chapter 5, section I, is due to appear in *Quaderni d'italianistica*. Part of chapter 2 was published in *Religion and Literature* 26/2 (1994): 1–26, and an earlier approximation in chapter 1, section 1, came out in the *MLN* 109 (1994): 117–27. The latter had been delivered in the form of a paper called "Dante's Address to the Reader and Its Resonance with Contemporary Theories of Inter-pretation" at the University of Tulsa's Symposium in Comparative Liter-ature: "Dante and Modernism," in March 1992. A paper entitled "Dante and the Poetics of Religious Revelation," based on materials from the introduction, was given at the 1993 MLA convention in Toronto and subsequently requested for publication in *Symplokē: A Journal for the Inter-mingling of Literary, Cultural and Theoretical Scholarship* 2/2 (1994). To all editors concerned, thanks for permission to reprint.

In writing this work I became personally indebted to a number of Dantists, Italianists, and medievalists, especially to Jeffrey Schnapp, John Freccero, Sepp Gumbrecht, Robert Harrison, Zygmunt Barański, Ra-chel Jacoff, Allen Mandelbaum, and Giuseppe Mazzotta. I am grateful as well to John Sallis and Charles Scott for pertinent philosophical discus-sion and for opportunities to participate in the Collegium Phaenomeno-logicum in Perugia, for which the Vanderbilt University Research Council provided me with generous support. Donald Marshall was an-other invaluable philosophical and theoretical interlocutor, as were Mark C. Taylor, Gian Balsamo, and Joel Weinsheimer. For vigilant, stylistically sensitive copyediting I thank Madeleine Avirov. Finally I wish to thank my colleagues in Comparative Literature and in French and Italian at Vanderbilt, especially Margaret Doody, Patricia Ward, Barbara Bowen, and Luigi Monga for supporting me and for helpful readings of parts of the manuscript. The final preparation of the manuscript was assisted by a fellowship from the Alexander von Humboldt Stiftung.

Piacenza   W. F.

INTRODUCTION

Truth and Interpretation in the Divine Comedy

"*I*nterpretation" has become a watchword in contemporary Dante studies. In concert with intensified interest in theories of interpretation across a broad range of disciplines over the last few decades, critical approaches to Dante have increasingly played up the dominance of interpretive techniques in his works. The roles of reading and interpretation especially in the *Divine Comedy,* perhaps always recognized more or less as important, have more recently appeared to afford a baton for orchestrating the poem as a whole. The understanding of Dante's art as fundamentally an art of interpretation has expressed itself particularly in renewed interest in Dantesque allegory.[1] It has been encouraged by a general renovation of the notion of allegory, in consequence of trends in literary criticism and theory privileging indirection and "otherness" in the way language can, or is constrained to, signify its meanings.[2]

1. For a sampling, see essays collected in *Dante e le forme dell'allegoresi,* ed. Michelangelo Picone.

2. An important catalyst in this general reevaluation of allegory, which received a decisive impulse from Walter Benjamin's *Ursprung des deutschen Trauerspiels* (1928; reprint, Frankfurt: Suhrkamp, 1963) was Paul de Man's essay "The Rhetoric of Temporality," first published in *Interpretation,* ed. C. Singleton (Baltimore: Johns Hopkins University Press, 1969). Already, however, a conception of allegory that essentially equated it with interpretation had been formulated influentially by Northrop Frye in *Anatomy of Criticism: Four Essays* (Princeton: Princeton University Press, 1957), where allegory was described as a kind of internal commentary of a work upon itself, an implicit interpretation folded back into the composition by which the author "tries to indicate how a commentary on him should proceed" (pp. 89–90). Angus Fletcher, in *Allegory: The Theory of a Symbolic Mode* (Ithaca: Cornell University Press, 1964), developed this idea into the view that "Whenever a literary work is dominated by its theme, it is likely to be called an allegory" (pp. 220–21), for the theme and its significance exert a control that imposes an interpretation on whatever is narrated. For discussion of these and other treatments of the interpretive character of allegory, see Morton W. Bloomfield, "Allegory as Interpretation," *New Literary History* 3 (1972), and his argument that "allegory is that which is established by interpretation, or the interpretive process itself" (p. 302). A challenging application of specifically psychoanalytical interpretation in defining the nature of allegory is Joel Fineman's "The Structure of Allegorical Desire" in *Allegory and Representation,* ed. Stephen Greenblatt (Baltimore: Johns Hopkins University Press, 1981), pp. 26–60; a sociological variation is elaborated by Romano Luperini in *L'Allegoria del moderno: Saggi sull'allegorismo come forma artistica del moderno e come metodo di conoscenza* (Rome: Riuniti, 1990).

1

This increased interpretive self-consciousness in approaching Dante has far-reaching philosophical significance and incalculable consequences for reading the *Commedia*. It can render intelligible and even possible once again the sort of experience of truth in which art like Dante's originates, for the theological revelation that Dante takes over as his own and humanity's truth can be made to be experienced in an originary fashion, as convincingly true, by the interpretive mediation of poetry. Precisely because poetry affords opportunities for interpreting—that is, experiencing and appropriating—truth, it can enable truth to occur as truth, as the compelling disclosure of an order of significance and being, rather than only as a trace or remnant of itself in the form of philological object or cultural artifact. Again, this possibility for understanding Dante opens up in conjunction with contemporary theorization, specifically of the experience of truth in art. In particular, Martin Heidegger's thought on truth as originating (in) the work of art and its elaboration by Hans-Georg Gadamer, together with numerous diversely inspired efforts along similar and diverging lines, has redefined truth and placed it back in the center of the experience of art and, I maintain, illuminated something of the essence of an experience such as that of Dante, along with his potential reader, in the *Divine Comedy*.[3]

To begin to approach this sort of perspective on truth and its intrinsic relation to interpretation, it may be helpful first of all to consider a generality. Characteristically, the hermeneutic approach takes the interpreter and interpretation itself as integral to whatever is being interpreted. Rather than being characterized by objective detachment and an attitude of disinterestedness, which have come to be prized as distinguishing qualities of true knowledge in a scientific age, knowledge understood hermeneutically as interpretation turns precisely upon structures of involvement—be they existential, literary, or religious—whereby every kind of knowing is understood as also a way of being, specifically of being involved with what is being known. Etymologically, *inter-praestare* alludes to a condition of mutual indebtedness.[4] A mutual claim or belonging

---

3. Martin Heidegger, *Der Ursprung des Kunstwerkes* (originally a 1935–36 lecture collected in *Holzwege*, 1950, translated under the title "The Origin of the Work of Art"). For Gadamer, see *Wahrheit und Methode* (1960), translated as *Truth and Method*, and especially part 1: "Freilegung der Wahrheitsfrage an der Erfahrung der Kunst" (The question of truth as it emerges in the experience of art). For attempts, embracing these and other figures, to describe historically the emergence of this way of thinking about truth in poetic art, see Gianni Vattimo, *Poesia e ontologia* (Milan: Mursia, 1985) and Michael Murray, "The new Hermeneutic and the Interpretation of Poetry," in *Contemporary Hermeneutics and Interpretation of Classical Texts* (Ottawa: Ottawa University Press, 1981).

4. Cognates familiar to students of romance letters are the French *prêter*, to lend, and the Italian *prestito*, loan. Reference to this etymology, one among many that could be evoked, is found in Julia Kristeva, "Psychoanalysis and the Polis," in *Transforming the Heremeneutic Context:*

affords interpretation and interpreter alike their purchase on what is interpreted, and conversely makes them beholden to it.

The investment of oneself in one's world, and vice versa, that underwrites all interpretive enterprises, finds what has become in many important ways a normative expression for Western intellectual tradition in the *Divine Comedy*. For self-investment in the interest of paying its due to what is given in instances of inspiration, history, dogma, and cosmos, Dante perhaps has no equal. Precisely the interestedness of Dante's representations not only of his own but even of the other world, their acutely personal, passionate, prejudiced character and charisma, has helped earn them consideration as great poetry, without eliminating a certain taste of scandal attaching to so audaciously self-centered and self-willed an outlook on such a megalomaniac scale.

Dante's taking his own life—not just the autobiographical form but his own historical existence built up also from collateral texts—as the fulcrum for his Christian didactic poem and epic fiction or history foregrounds this work's standing as an interpretive undertaking. The complex identity of the first-person speaker in the poetic narrative with the historical Dante Alighieri involves the author in his text in a way that extends beyond the scope of any merely or strictly literary convention. Every poetic production is, of course, indebted to some historically existing individual(s)—and in this generic sense all are interpretive—just as individuals in all historical periods would appear to be indebted to poetic fictions in their being what and as they are. But Dante's poem programmatically places this ineluctable structural condition center-stage of the fiction itself, blurring the boundary between fact and fiction in reaching toward their common origin in interpretation,[5] in this instance in the

---

From *Nietzsche to Nancy,* ed. G. Ormiston and A. Schrift (Albany: State University of New York Press, 1990), p. 92.

5. For an introduction to this problematic from a broadly Kantian perspective, see Louis O. Mink, "History and Fiction as Modes of Comprehension," *New Literary History* 1 (1970): 541–58; see also Michael Riffaterre, *Fictional Truth* (Baltimore: Johns Hopkins University Press, 1990). The centrality of this issue as it pertains to Dante and in particular to his *Vita nuova* is suggested by María Rosa Menocal, *Writing in Dante's Cult of Truth: From Borges to Boccaccio* (Durham: Duke University Press, 1991). Menocal points out the inadequacy of "that positivist dichotomy of fact versus fiction with which we perforce operate in our times and in our culture. In the new life, when the old gods and the first loves are dead, Truth is strange, and it is everywhere to be read, and poetry is its handmaiden" (p. 50). This is so because "What is true, in a text such as the *Vita nuova* . . . is that which lies between the pedestrian and ultimately meaningless 'facts' of any possible encounters with a Bice Portinari—or any other woman, for that matter—and what renders such facts true and meaningful" (p. 49). These remarks, however suggestive, leave everything yet to be gained by understanding truth as it figures in the *Commedia* from a specifically hermeneutic point of view, which it will be the burden of this essay to develop. Such a perspective also remains philosophically undeveloped in another treatment that nevertheless recognizes truth as the central issue posed by Dante's poetry, Teodolinda Barolini's

mutual belonging of Dante as literary invention and as historical person-
age together, since the one would not be what it is at all without the
other.

Dante presents the supreme and absolute truth of Christianity, which
his poem would propound, in a way that makes it indissociable from the
story of his own individual search and journey. The way of understanding
put in practice in Dante's work, as in all works of interpretation, consists
in finding oneself in the midst of what is to be understood and so under-
standing oneself and it in relation to each other. We can say along with
one contemporary school of hermeneutic theory that interpretation al-
ways consists in the application of what is being understood to oneself:
"Alles Verstehen ist Anwendung des Verstandenen auf uns selbst." ("All
understanding is the application of what is understood to ourselves").[6]
Dante dramatizes on an epic scale this basic principle of interpretation,
which only makes itself felt indirectly in academic studies like this
one, for example, where the author's own involvement generally is not
represented or figured as such. In this, as in so many other respects,
which may be seen to follow one another consequentially, Dante's
work is exemplary and revelatory of the phenomenon of interpreta-
tion in general.

The following study and reflection is ventured on a wager that Dante's
epoch-making work of interpretation can illuminate some of the major
questions in and around "hermeneutics" today, and that conversely cer-
tain theoretical instruments and insights offered by contemporary specu-
lation in this area can be illuminating aids in pondering Dante's poem.
The synergism between interpretation theory and Dante's interpretive
practice, if this wager wins, will vindicate a way of proceeding that
otherwise could be dismissed as anachronistic by the canons of histori-
cist criticism. To this extent, the essay participates in a debate over the
nature and possibility of historical understanding, coming in on the side
of those who maintain that our every access to the past passes through
the present, as the site for the ongoing happening of the past, rather

---

Dante's Poets: Textuality and Truth in the Comedy (Princeton: Princeton University Press, 1984).
The question of truth and its history in Dante criticism will be taken up in detail in chapter 4.

6. This formula, taken from Gadamer, is rehearsed as a continuing refrain throughout Horst
Jürgen Gerigk's *Unterwegs zur Interpretation: Hinweise zu einer Theorie der Literatur in Auseinanderset-
zung mit Gadamers 'Wahrheit und Methode'* (Stuttgart: Guido Pressler, 1989). Or to compare the
formulation of another strand of hermeneutic thought, that of Paul Ricoeur, interpretation of
a text aims to "incorporer son sens à la compréhension présente qu'un homme peut prendre de
lui-même" ("incorporate its sense into the present understanding that a man can reach of him-
self"). *Le conflit des interprétations: Essais d'herméneutique I*, p. 8. Throughout this book, where no
English editions of works written in other languages are cited, I have done the translating—as
literally as possible—myself.

than being achieved in spite of the present and by methodically filtering it away.[7]

This essay, then, equally speculative and critical in intent, aims to make a contribution simultaneously to the understanding of Dante's poem and to the theory of interpretation, specifically to existential hermeneutics, a field, however, to be redefined from within a horizon of thought of the poem's own projection.[8] It will suggest that an inexhaustible mystery probed in Dante's poem is the nature of interpretation itself, where interpretation is not understood reductively as just a human activity or, even more reductively, as a self-transparent operation of an epistemological subject, but may possibly involve—or be involved in—an event of world, truth, or even divinity. It will ask what models of interpretation, what effectual practices and malpractices, with what success and consequence, Dante's poem, itself a model of poetic interpretation in Western cultural tradition, embodies. And most importantly it will challenge current assumptions and theories about interpretation in the interest of helping to clear a space of possibility for the event of the poem to occur.

1. HISTORICITY OF TRUTH

"... colui che 'n terra adusse
la verità che tanto ci soblima ..."
(*Paradiso* XXII. 41–42)

Considered historically—for, indeed, interpretation, far from excluding history, includes it as in its essence interpretive—the cultural project of

---

7. The most fully developed theoretical statement of this position is Gadamer's previously cited *Truth and Method*. See, e.g., p. 328: "The truth is that historical understanding always implies that the tradition reaching us speaks into the present and must be understood in this mediation—indeed *as* this mediation." Gadamer's thought and terminology are adapted to the study of medieval literature by Hans Robert Jauss, *Alterität und Modernität der mittelalterlichen Literatur: Gesammelte Werke 1956–76* (Munich: Fink, 1977). See especially pp. 9–26. For a further, thought-provoking challenge to historicist paradigms in medieval studies cognizant of recent developments in the theory of textual criticism and making claims for the "transhistorical value" of the poetic text, see Lee Patterson, *Negotiating the Past* (Madison: University of Wisconsin Press, 1987).

8. "Existentialism," having become passé as a movement, is acutely assessed with regard to the reasons for its enduring intellectual validity by Luigi Pareyson in "Rettifiche sull' esistenzialismo," in *Scritti in onore di G. Bontadini* (Milan: Vita e Pensiero, 1975), pp. 227–47. Theological versions of what I am calling "existential hermeneutics" include the work of Rudolph Bultmann, Karl Barth, and Paul Tillich, from which the present work is distinguished inter alia by its thinking through poetry and by its literary-critical approach to the hermeneutic question, which by its nature resists systematic-theological as well as direct philosophical treatment. Taking Dante's poem as the field for designing an existential, theological hermeneutic (or theory of interpretation) enacts a movement of "deregionalization" of the sort that Paul Ricoeur considers

Dante parallels in provocative ways the currents in modern thought that have culminated in "philosophical hermeneutics."[9] Both may be described as radicalizations of the thinking of the historical conditionedness of all knowledge and culture. This development in German thought may be traced from the protohistoricism of Johann Gottfried von Herder, with his recognition that each historical epoch has an individuality that is incommensurable with that of others and so can be comprehended only in its own historically specific terms, through the variously historical hermeneutics of Friedrich Schleiermacher, Johann Gustave Droysen, and Wilhelm Dilthey, to Heidegger's analysis of the historical character of understanding as built directly into the structure of existence in the world. With this last thinker, lucid awareness is achieved of the historicity not only of every possible object of understanding but also of understanding itself, that is, of its being in every instance situated within determinate limitations and partialities, remote from the bird's-eye view of so-called historical science. Denied the illusion of being able to project oneself without residue into the past so as to understand its particularities exclusively from their own perspective, historians rather must recognize that they always only fuse their own inescapable horizon of understanding with that of the past world they wish to study. That historical understanding is always just such a "fusion of horizons" ("Horizontverschmelzung") is the thesis in which Gadamer has attempted to bring the whole modern development of hermeneutics to consummation as a philosophical theory.[10]

This opening up and exposing of rational and dogmatic knowledge to the crosscurrents of history, which begins taking place toward the end of the eighteenth century with the challenge to Enlightenment paradigms, recapitulates in crucial respects a break with Scholastic knowledge based on ahistorical essences of which Dante deserves to be hailed as a perhaps unwitting protagonist.[11] Dante's bringing the knowledge of his age into the midst of historical flux, most simply but decisively by his opting for

---

necessary for the movement of hermeneutics from what at first must be concrete areas of knowledge toward its goal of universality. See *Du texte à l'action: Essais d'herméneutique II,* p. 350.

9. Of this putative revolution in thought, *Wahrheit und Methode* has become a sort of manifesto. The major breakthroughs, however, are found in the works, early and late, of Gadamer's teacher, Martin Heidegger, as will be made evident throughout this study by its allusions and citations.

10. On the history of the development of hermeneutic philosophy centered on this problematic, leading up to and including Gadamer's contribution, see Franco Bianchi, *Storicismo ed ermeneutica* (Rome: Bulzoni, 1974).

11. See especially Hans Urs von Balthasar, *Herrlichkeit: Eine theologische Ästhetik,* vol. 2 (Einsiedeln, Switzerland: Johannes, 1962), particularly section 1 on Dante's conversion ("Wendung") to the vernacular, to secularism, and to history. The master design and momentous historical significance of Dante's works are often more overtly appreciated by nonspecialized scholarship, which views Dante in broader synthetic contexts. See also Karl-Otto Apel, *Die Idee*

the vernacular, defined in his treatise on the subject by its mutability in contrast to unchanging, rule-governed, "grammatical" language, was motivated not by a spirit of epistemological critique so much as by a prophetic spirit, bent on seeing true ideals become effectual on a broad historical basis, hence in the lives of the laity. From the time of the *Convivio,* Dante took upon himself the task of vulgarizing clerical knowledge and so of placing the nourishment of a divine *scientia* as well as of human wisdom, theretofore reserved largely for sterile fruition by the few learned in a dead language, on tables for general cultural consumption by all whose natural desire to know had survived uncorrupted.[12] Dante's championing of the vernacular, especially in his choosing it for his poem of the highest doctrinal intent and content, constitutes an emblematic gesture and a program for rendering the timeless verities of philosophy and dogmatic religion effective in history.

Dante need not be seen as an absolute innovator here. Historical consciousness had become manifest in a variety of forms in medieval Europe even centuries before Dante's time. Questions raised—often rather nervously—by theologians about the human *auctores* of various books of the Bible, for example, had generated reflection upon the possibility of some sort of historical mediation even of the sacred truth of Scripture.[13] Nevertheless, Dante's imaginative enactment of a revelation of religious truth in convincingly historical terms, bringing timeless dogma into intrinsic contact with corruptible matters of fact and language, and with the historical existence of a reader, constituted a major provocation regarding the issue of truth and history,[14] as it still does today.

It is perhaps no exaggeration to sum up the direction and import of Dante's whole life's work as a writer under the concept of *divulgazione,* which in a precise sense indicates translation into the vernacular, but also carries along in its train a thoroughgoing cultural revolution. The incidence of knowledge upon history, even were the body of knowledge

---

der Sprache in der Tradition des Humanismus von Dante bis Vico (Bonn: Bouvier, 1975), especially pp. 104–29.

12. "Oh beati quelli pochi che seggiono a quella mensa dove lo pane de li angeli si manuca! . . . E io adunque, che non seggio a la beata mensa, ma fuggito de la pastura del vulgo, a' piedi di coloro che seggiono ricolgo di quello che da loro cade, e conosco la misera vita di quelli che dietro m'ho lasciati. . . . Per che ora volendo loro apparecchiare, intendo fare un *generale convivio*" (*Convivio* I. i. 7–11; emphasis mine).

13. See A. J. Minnis, *Medieval Theory of Authorship* (London: Scholar Press, 1984).

14. This registers, for example, in Zygmunt Barański's discussions of "authority and challenge" with regard to this poetry "'truer' than history" and of Dante's compulsion to innovate generically in "'Primo tra Cotanto Seno': Dante and the Latin Comic Tradition," *Italian Studies* 46 (1991): pp. 7–8, as well as in "La lezione esegetica di *Inferno* I: Allegoria, storia e letteratura nella *Commedia*"; for background, see R. H. C. Davis and J. M. Wallace-Hadrill, *The Writing of History in the Middle Ages* (Oxford: Clarendon Press, 1991).

vulgarized to remain self-identical (which it does not), is thereby made not a secondary effect but the primary thrust of such knowing and culture as Dante disseminates. Not knowledge per se, as an abstract, ahistorical system, but its appropriation, its event in and as originating history (what we will find it useful to think about in terms of Heideggerian "Ereignis"), becomes paramount. The very figure of the "convito" or banquet of knowledge as a "bread of angels" suggests how it is through assimilation, literally digestion, that the knowledge Dante wishes to be shared first comes into its own.

Dante attempted in his treatises to bring the medieval world's most precious reserves of knowledge into the stream of history, where their value could be exploited for the world-historical reform his prophetic sense envisioned. But the divulgation-dissemination of truth as something already fixed and finished, like the dogma of an institutionalized religion, being brought into a historical world likewise already constituted in its supporting structures and foundations, was not likely to originate fundamental change. Indeed, Dante's treatises remained for the most part uncompleted. What Dante discovered in his poem, on the other hand, was an approach to truth and to rendering it active, that is, to making it happen historically, of quite another order of power and significance. He discovered the capability of the work of art, as the site of a coming to be of truth, to open the world anew and give a new sense to history, actually founding an order of significances, or in other words a world, and originating a determinate historical dispensation. With this discovery, Dante's operative notion of truth was revolutionized.[15]

To divulgate or spread the truth is not just to make knowledge of what is taken to be true more widely available. More importantly, divulgation means actualizing truth, putting it to work. For truth becomes effectual only by happening as an event. The course of history may be influenced as intrahistorical forces are directed or redirected in consequence of the application of knowledge, by definition (presumably), knowledge of truth. But, more radically, the advent of truth in history impinges not on the component pieces of history, its separate materials and players, as it were, but on the fundamental dispensation and organizing framework of the historical world. And certainly the knowledge of truth that Dante proposes to divulgate is intended to make the world fundamentally different.

15. I have described Dante's poem as an effort to set up truth in originating a world and by it to institute history in terms borrowed from Heidegger's theory of art: "Die Kunst ist das Ins-Werk-Setzen der Wahrheit. . . . Das ist so, weil die Kunst in ihrem Wesen ein Ursprung ist: eine ausgezeichnete Weise wie Wahrheit seiend, d. h. geschichtlich wird" ("Art is the setting-into-work of truth. . . . This is so because art is in its essence an origin: an outstanding way in which truth comes to be, which means becomes historical"—*Ursprung*, pp. 79–80).

Like the *Convivio* and his other theoretical writings, Dante's *Commedia* is a massive work of appropriation. The highest and holiest offerings of classical and Christian culture are harmonized, or at least amalgamated, into an ensemble that may be entered into experientially, in the wake of the first-person experience of the protagonist. In this, the poem goes quantum leaps beyond the treatise in its receptiveness to the historicity of truth. Although continuity with the *Convivio*'s project of vulgarization is underscored by the reprise in *Paradiso* II of the figure of the "pan de li angeli" ("bread of angels"), truth is nevertheless no longer taken only as a particular "something," a metaphysical substance (an effect perhaps of "veritas" being a grammatical substantive) to be dished out and shared like "vivande" on a banquet table.

The poem is indeed full of metaphysical doctrines put forward with a paraenetic force and often staged with an artistry that promotes Dante's principles as fixed truths. But the truth Dante serves as poet rather than as ideologue, letting it occur in his poem, has rather the character of an event of disclosure. He imagines the truth about each individual as happening *in nuce* as he meets them in the eternal world. By form and gesture, position and surrounding circumstances, as well as by utterance, Dante epitomizes the true and eternal being of the personages he encounters, the "status animarum post mortem" (Epistle to Can Grande, sec. 8), exposed for what it really is, allowing also for concealment as a background of shadow to the truth that comes to light. The essence of each individual unfolds visibly and audibly in the encounter with Dante-protagonist, being made manifest in sensory phenomena and palpable images of punishment, penance, or radiance. In this staggering act of imagination Dante apprehends truth, understood as the ultimate secret and eternal destiny of a human being, in the form of an event, a perceptible happening. Far in advance, presumably, of his own theoretical consciousness,[16] Dante's imagination grasps the eventhood of truth. Indeed, only with the present century will theoretical articulation of the intrinsic historicity of truth, here so compellingly envisioned, be fully achieved.

Although Dante still one-sidedly rehearses the rhetoric of truth as transcendental and timeless, which was handed down to him in the cul-

---

16. There are some indications of a theory of truth in the Letter to Can Grande (sec. 8). The truth of a thing ("veritas de re") is conceived as truth only to the extent that it exists in a subject ("que in veritate consistit tanquam in subiecto"). This is to make truth an attribute of conceptions or propositions existing in conscious subjects rather than of the things themselves. Truth may be defined, then, in accordance with the conventional Scholastic formula (*aedequatio intellectus et rei*) as a correspondence of the ideas of the subject to their object ("similitudo perfecta rei sicut est"). Nevertheless, an understanding of truth as "alētheia" (unconcealment) would not necessarily have been inaccessible to Dante: it finds a key source text in Aristotle's *Nichomachean Ethics* (VI. 3, 4: 1140a). According to this theory, that beings be disclosed as what they are is the precondition of our being able to make true affirmations about them.

tural heritage of the Middle Ages, his poetry nevertheless embodies the radical historicity of the truth of each individual as it is revealed in the immediacy of their encounters with Dante-pilgrim. It is in what happens to the *Commedia's* characters in the present of their appearance in the poem, which essentially recapitulates the decisive event(s) of their earthly historical existence, now seen, however, in the light of an eschatological dawn, that the truth about them, the essence of their being in the sight and judgment of God, is revealed. In this sense it is in the form of history, as realized in sequences of phenomenal events, that the poem proffers its truth, in addition to the metaphysical and doctrinal truth that is also propounded in mixed discursive forms.

Dante's treating truth as disclosure in history has been famously expounded by Erich Auerbach. For Auerbach, Dante is the pivotal figure in a rejuvenation of Western culture that recuperates the earthly, historical lives and fates of humans as united with their true essences. Dante rediscovered "man as we know him in his living historical reality . . . and in that he has been followed by all subsequent portrayers of man, regardless of whether they treated a historical or a mythical or a religious subject, for after Dante myth and legend also became history."[17] The representation of the other, the true, world in images and events that epitomize and eschatologically perfect individuals as they exist in this world constitutes the characteristic procedure of Dante as "Dichter der irdischen Welt" ("poet of the secular world").

Revisiting the argument developed under this title some twenty years later, Auerbach explained that he had taken over ideas broached first by Hegel, making them the basis of his own reading of the *Commedia*.[18] Hegel had written of the "changeless existence" of the denizens of the other world into which Dante "plunges the living world of human action and endurance and more especially of individual deeds and destinies."[19] Deeds, destinies, and action are of course the stuff of human history. But in the *Commedia* they represent not merely the brute fact of what actually happens: they reveal a definitive truth, that is, the divine judgment upon the individuals concerned. Dante undertakes, in Auerbach's words, "to set forth the divine judgment, to unearth the complete truth about individual historical men, and consequently to reveal the whole character and personality" (Auerbach, *Dante als Dichter,* p. 175).

The basic Hegelian insight found another powerful exponent, enor-

---

17. Auerbach, *Dante: Poet of the Secular World,* pp. 19, 175; originally published as *Dante als Dichter der irdischen Welt* (1929).

18. Auerbach, "Farinata and Cavalcante," in *Mimesis: The Representation of Reality in Western Literature,* trans. W. Trask (1953; reprint, Princeton: Princeton University Press, 1968), p. 191.

19. Georg Wilhelm Friedrich Hegel, *Hegel's Aesthetics,* trans. T. M. Knox (Oxford: Oxford University Press, 1975), p. 1103.

mously influential especially for Italian criticism, in Francesco De Sanctis. De Sanctis celebrated the "inimitable individuality" of the *Commedia* in comparison with other medieval representations of the other world, underlining in Dante "the drama of this life represented in the other world, without detriment to its reality and gaining in grandeur" ("il dramma di questa vita rappresentato nell'altro mondo, senza scapitare di realtà e guadagnando d'altezza").[20] De Sanctis too honors Hegel as a paladin of historically incarnate truth—"Nessuno più di lui [Hegel] ti parla d'individuo e d'incarnazione, sente che là è il vero" (p. 340)—even while complaining that his disciples erroneously made form merely instrumental to the manifestation of idea.

The boldly historical nature of Dante's mode of poetic representation can be made evident, for example, by comparing the *Commedia* with other medieval works, for instance Alain de Lille's *Anticlaudianus,* an earlier poetic work with a similarly exalted claim to revealing a divine truth. Alain's celestial theophany is played out by such characters as Natura and Phronesis, abstract and remote from the historically dense and specific personages that so strongly distinguish the work of Dante.[21] To take just one example, even as abbreviated a cameo appearance as that of Pia dei Tolomei is stamped with the indelible marks of an irreducibly historical existence. Geographical place-names specify her earthly origin and terminus, while reference to the single, fatal event of her marriage suffices to adumbrate her whole life story:

> "ricorditi di me che son la Pia:
>   Siena mi fé; disfecemi Maremma:
>   salsi colui che 'nnanellata pria
> disposando m'avea con la sua gemma."
>
> (Purgatorio V. 130–36)

> ("remember me who am Pia:
>   Siena made me; Maremma undid me:
>   he knows it who having first betrothed me
> wedded me with his gem.")

Formally, the poem positions its journey at a precise historical date in 1300, the middle of Dante's life and a year of crisis in the political history of Florence, Italy, Europe. In content, it burgeons with historical personages, so that virtually all the characters, whether they are cast as human or not, are treated as historical. It deals extensively *ad seriatem* with the various regions and rulers, families and cities, of Italy and beyond. The

20. Francesco De Sanctis, *Lezioni sulla* Divina Commedia (1854; reprint, Bari: Laterza, 1955), p. 16.

21. Cf. Peter Dronke, *Dante and Medieval Traditions* (Cambridge: Cambridge University Press, 1986), pp. 8–14.

two great powers of universal history are relentlessly evoked and evaluated, and each receives a concentrated historical review in a prophetic perspective: the Church, especially in the allegorical representations of the Earthly Paradise in *Purgatorio* XXXII; and the Empire, most exhaustively in Justinian's narration of the vicissitudes of the sign of the eagle in *Paradiso* VI.

The historical character and consistency of Dante's poem has received extensive notice and has been widely recognized as key to Dante's significance in the history of culture. As handed down from the Auerbachian paradigm, this emphasis upon the historicity of Dante's narrative has been variously developed especially within the American school of Dante criticism. In one way or another, virtually all the most notable criticism since Singleton acknowledges the historicity of Dante's vision as its radically determinative element. In John Freccero's reading, the *Commedia* begins from Dante's break with the *Convivio*'s Neoplatonic unguided ascent of the mind to truth, conceived as an escape from the body and its imprisonment in a temporal order. Dante is impeded from ascending directly toward the light over the mountain of the prologue scene by beasts representing various passions not fully sublatable into pure intellect. The "piè fermo," that is, the left foot, remains always lower, inasmuch as the will is always weaker than the intellect and drags it back from its purely intellectual love. Dante must get to the top of Purgatory by way of an "altro viaggio." For Christian conversion engages the whole human being in its full historicity, including the body and all that is least conformable to the intellectual ideals of Platonism. Thus Dante's truth cannot be reached except through a recapitulation of his whole personal and cultural history, in order that he be converted not only in his mind but in the full historical amplitude of his existence toward God. Such is the precondition for the whole journey and for its successful consummation.[22]

Even more directly, Giuseppe Mazzotta has recognized that "history is the question that lies at the very heart of the text" of the *Divine Comedy*, and he means history in a sense that makes it indissociable from the particular situatedness of interpretation, in the sense, that is, of a "theology of history" that "emphasizes, in a forceful way, the problematical character of every individual with his irreducible fund of experience and values."[23] Touching in a more oblique but interesting way on the issue, Eugene Vance's work on the history of theories of translation recognizes Dante as unique in the whole of the Middle Ages for having been open

22. John Freccero, *The Poetics of Conversion*. See especially chapters 1 and 2, "The Prologue Scene" and "The Firm Foot on a Journey without a Guide."

23. Giuseppe Mazzotta, *Dante. Poet of the Desert: History and Allegory in the "Divine Comedy,"* pp. 3, 5.

to historical change and contingency as a possible source of enrichment rather than of inevitable loss and decline.[24] And again, Jeffrey Schnapp has shown in convincing detail for cantos XIV to XVIII of the *Paradiso* how, for all its vertical thrust, the *Commedia* always passes through history toward transcendence, transfiguring rather than annulling or escaping from the conditions of history.[25]

A common point of departure, then, for numerous major treatments of the poetics of the *Divine Comedy,* both old ones and especially the newer, has been found in the conspicuous historicity of the poem's content and form. The dense historical allusivity of the poem marks its individuality for many critics, not only specialists but those who view it in bold outline as well, for example, George Steiner.[26] Even textbook histories of literature commonly marvel at how direct and "realistic" Dante's representations of historical personages, places, and predicaments are, finding them to be quite without precedent and emphasizing the radical difference of Dante's poem from poems in the didactic-allegorical genre from which it emerges, precisely on grounds of its reversal of their ahistoricity.

In more ways than are easily reckoned, the undeniable primacy historicity assumes in Dante's interpretation of truth has been fully acknowledged. The present study aims at a more concentrated theoretical development of what, until now, has come to light as truly distinctive about Dante's poetic work primarily through the evidence of particular exegetical instances. In other words, it seeks to interrogate the philosophico-theological presuppositions and underpinnings of Dante's realization of the historicity of truth. Such a philosophical *approfondimento* can help us understand the truth Dante proposes as the correlative of interpretation rather than only as a confessional given, something to be either swallowed whole or indulged as Dante's personal *pazzia,* but in either case opaque and unpersuasive to those who do not happen to share Dante's religious beliefs.[27]

We can, of course, simply accept as part of the fiction that Dante has

24. Eugene Vance, *Mervelous Signals: Poetics and Sign Theory in the Middle Ages* (Lincoln: University of Nebraska Press, 1986), chap. 10 and p. 262. Some decades earlier, Bruno Nardi, in "Il linguaggio," chap. 4 in *Dante e la cultura medievale,* had brought out the originality of the view that Dante had gradually developed of language as in its essence historically evolving.

25. Jeffrey Schnapp, *The Transfiguration of History at the Center of Dante's "Paradise"* (Princeton: Princeton University Press, 1986).

26. See Steiner's discussion of how "context presses on text with the weight of shaping life" (p. 167) in "Dante Now: The Gossip of Eternity," in *On Difficulty & Other Essays* (Oxford: Oxford University Press, 1972).

27. This problem is focused particularly by T. S. Eliot, *Dante* (London: Faber & Faber, 1929), and is further probed by I. A. Richards, *Beyond* (New York: Harcourt Brace Jovanovich, 1974), pp. 107–8.

some sort of direct, privileged access to truth normally unavailable to mortals. This view seems especially easy to adopt in an era when we feel fairly immune to the "truths" Dante is advocating anyway. Yet to treat the truth claims as just a private madness of Dante's that may have enhanced or hampered his poetry, depending on how well we think poetry and theology mix, diminishes our understanding of his poem and its meaning. Dante is employing in this poem a way of disclosing truth through interpretation. The truth he proposes, if it is to be true for us, cannot simply be taken on his authority, the authority of one who has been there, to the other world, and has seen. This may after all, whether in the author's intention or in the reader's reception, turn out to be no more than a surface fiction. And at any rate it can distract attention from the truly extraordinary originality of Dante's poem as an interpretive act. The poem claims, as becomes explicit in direct addresses to the reader in the name of truth, to involve readers and their whole historical world in a journey of interpretation leading to a disclosure of their vital reality and final destiny. The present speculative reflection upon the *Commedia* contends that Dante has an understanding of truth and interpretation that can be appreciated more fully than ever today. He need be neither stigmatized nor patronized as a dogmatist with whom no dialogue is possible. He should rather be understood as engaged in an endeavor of interpretation that has a potentially universal message that would call all humankind to hear and heed.

2. TRUTH THROUGH INTERPRETATION AND THE HERMENEUTIC OF FAITH

> A guisa d'uom che 'n dubbio si raccerta,
>   e che muta in conforto sua paura,
>   poi che la verità li è discoverta,
> mi cambia' io . . .
>
> (*Purgatorio* IX. 64–67)

So far it has been argued that truth is revealed in the *Commedia* in and through history, where history involves immersion in the actual experience of existing individuals. Initially, however, the embrace of history creates problems for us in accepting or even in understanding the poem's claims to universal truth. The historicity of the *Commedia*'s characters and of Dante's encounters with them is all compounded by interpretation. The lives are recalled for us through the mediation of the characters' own memory and motivations; the encounters are mimetically reconstructed or invented by the interpretive art of poetry. Truth is purportedly revealed to us through a historicity that is itself the product of interpretation.

How can Dante pretend that his deeply personal convictions, not only about the providentiality of the Roman Empire but also about the individuals he knew or knew of are at the same time ultimate truths? Does not interpretation inevitably veer off into zones of opinion and personal belief remote from what can be established as "true" in the ordinary acceptation of something objectively so? It is not evident to us how truth and interpretation can live so comfortably together. Dante's *Commedia* makes extreme claims to truth of the most absolute kind; it claims to be representing some absolute—true and revealed—state of souls in an unchanging, transcendent realm. Yet at the same time, it goes to the other extreme of subjectivity in speaking the mind of Dante, replete with personal predilections and envenomed diatribes. This so-called true revelation patently consists of merely an interpretation (and a highly biased one at that) of this-worldly, historical being, which presumably can be known without revelation, but only as opinion or appearance, not as ultimate truth.

Why has it become so difficult for us today to understand how interpretation, permeated by prejudice and partiality, as it emphatically is in Dante, can lead to what may intelligibly be given the name of truth? Dante, evidently, could still take for granted that an absolute truth might very well be reached through interpretation. After all, the supreme method, the *via maestra,* for finding out truth in general in his day was through exegesis of the Divine Word, the source of all Truth, which could only be apprehended through a living and personally responsive interpretation. But this perspective has been forgotten due to a narrowing of the understanding of truth brought about through the hegemony of scientific paradigms of knowledge, in which truth tends to be opposed to "mere" interpretation. Can Dante, along with modern speculation in hermeneutic theory, help us recuperate an understanding of how interpretation can be a way of coming into the experience of truth?

Even before the Renaissance coined the term "Middle Ages" to designate somewhat contemptuously what stood between itself and the classical world, culture for the epoch consummated in Dante's poem was essentially just that, a middle, and as such a *traditio,* and inscribed within this, a *translatio.* This is one reason why the hermeneutic model is so germane to Dante's project. The Bible was held to contain the truth in its fullness for humankind, from their first beginning to their latter end; the function of knowledge and culture was principally to preserve and transmit this truth, to continue to live within its horizon and so participate in its ongoing event, rather than to discover new contents or continents. In this respect, the Middle Ages epitomizes a hermeneutic culture, in which knowledge is construed as the mediation of an experience rather than as the grasping of an object, or, in other words, as more like reading than like sense perception. It is not so surprising after all that copies and commentaries upon texts, to the exasperation of modern philologists, should have so freely altered and sometimes substantially augmented the texts even of highly revered works. For transmitting a text entailed reactualizing the whole experience sedimented within it, in such a way that the text became indistinguishable from its tradition.[28]

Dante simply brings to the fore the dynamic eventhood of this activity of mediation and transmission by his poetry articulated as personal address. Indeed, much of the burden of the ensuing chapters will be to sound the significance of Dante's employing a discourse of overt address to a reader. But this emphasis on receptivity and appropriation in the interpreter's act as intrinsic to the revelation of truth, swinging loose from strict enchainment to an objective reality to be known unaltered, which counts as the first imperative of science as classically construed, seems to us to throw the process open to individual caprice and *arbitrium*. We feel we must escape from the web of interpretation in order to attain the truth.

Yet interpretation understood hermeneutically and hence as a dynamic sort of knowing turns out to be a process of moving oneself into the event in which things are disclosed, that is, the event of truth.[29] Accordingly, the goal of Dante's whole interpretive journey is to move in perfect synchrony with the universe, in which his knowledge of ultimate being is made perfect by the conformity of his will to God's, symbolically his moving in step with the cosmos, moved concordantly by its final cause:

> ma già volgeva il mio disio e 'l velle,
> sí come rota ch' igualmente è mossa
> l'amor che move il sole e l' altre stelle.
>
> (*Paradiso* XXXIII. 143–45)

> (but already my will and desire were being revolved
> as a wheel which is moved uniformly
> by the love that moves the sun and the other stars.)

---

28. Rita Copeland, in *Rhetoric, Hermeneutics, and Translation in the Middle Ages: Academic and Vernacular Texts* (Cambridge: Cambridge University Press, 1991), develops the acknowledged fact that "Medieval arts commentary does not simply 'serve' its 'master' texts; it also rewrites and supplants them" (p. 3).

29. We have already noted in the previous section how truth in Dante's poetry is fundamentally conceived neither as accuracy of representation nor in the first instance as an entity to be grasped but rather as an event of disclosure. The conception of truth as disclosure, "alētheia," is treated by Heidegger in *Sein und Zeit*, sec. 44, and in "Vom Wesen der Wahrheit" (1930). Discussion of its applications in theology by Bultmann, Fuchs, and Ebeling can be found in Robert W. Funk, "Language as Event and Theology," pt. 1 of *Language, Hermeneutic, and the Word of God: The Problem of Language in the New Testament and Contemporary Theology*.

Interpretation as the transformation of the interpreter into conformity with truth, as a projective participating of the interpreter in the event in which truth is disclosed, returns to and specifies the characterization of interpretation as a form of involvement from which we began. It is a participation in the event of being in which things come to be *as* what they are, and so are revealed in their truth. Interpretation can be a way of entering into this event, a reorigination of one's own being and of all beings that has traditionally been figured as salvation, an event of dispossessing oneself of oneself in order to lend all one's being to the salvation event.[30]

The eventhood of truth and of being is presented in the *Commedia* through the eventhood of the author and also of that other author, the reader. Accordingly, the whole representation and disclosure of the poem is offered to readers in their own situated, historical particularity, and this includes Dante himself as first reader of his poem and journey, internally to its event. It is the very dynamism of Dante's own personal engagement with each person and idea along the way, the conditionedness by narrative circumstance of his responses, that makes the encounters revelatory. For only so, precisely in such narrative contexts, can they be truly apprehended as event. Dante must realize his own act of interpretation as event in order for it to be authentic participation in an event of truth that becomes intelligible in and through it. And, in turn, Dante must make this truth happen for his readers as an event in their own existence, if its character as event is not going to be betrayed. It is only through the event of the interpreter that being, or whatever is interpreted, can be grasped as event.[31]

The truth, then, apprehended and promulgated by the poem, for as much as its image is that of univocal verity, eventually realizes itself in the multiplicity and dispersion of the historical particularity and ineradicable difference of readers. Dante presents a total system of theology, but his specific contribution as poet is to concretely realize this monolith, to

30. This can be described in an idiom of the later Heidegger as "appropriation" ("Ereignis") of human being to Being, revealed in the event of unconcealment. Not by making Being its own, but rather by being appropriated to it, the human being who interprets comes into the truth. Of course, this may be characterized as an event of dissonance or "rift"—as in Heidegger's "Ursprung des Kunstwerkes"—as much as of concordance, and the range of Dante's images will embrace both possibilities.

31. This aspect of the work has been fathomed in numerous oblique ways by Dante criticism, perhaps nowhere more subtly than by Gianfranco Contini (who, however, credits Charles Singleton) in "Dante come personaggio-poeta della *Commedia*": "Ogni tappa e sosta del suo viaggio olreterreno è una modalità del suo 'io'" ("Every station and stay of his supraterrestrial journey is a modality of his 'io'"—p. 361). Contini teases out the implications of Dante's "doppio 'io,'" ("double 'I'"), both the *agens* and the *auctor* of the poem, a transcendental but nonetheless existential "I" (p. 336), and moreover an "'io' che è noi" ("I that is we"—p. 341).

make happen the event of its being experienced, in the actual historical existence of individuals. As an abstract symbolic system or book, the poem delineates a whole order of the cosmos enfolding within itself an ethical system. But for its truth to happen it has need of a reader; indeed, it is experienced in the first instance in correlation with Dante himself as reader, who in telling his story, and as an integral part of it, strives to understand its significance. For anything such as an event of truth can occur only in the existence of individuals and for them—whose being, moreover, comes into its own in and by this same event. This exigency is clearly recognized within the poem itself, in its addresses to the reader, which have been noticed as a peculiarly distinguishing feature of Dante's work, indeed a portentous novelty in the history of literature. Through its addresses to its reader, Dante's poem becomes veritably a divine co-mediation of truth and interpretation.

A Hermeneutic of Faith

We have dwelt on the extent to which Dante engages history, and we have seen how this has been widely acknowledged to be integral to his whole cultural project. But Dante's vision, as has already proved impossible to ignore, is equally a vision of transcendent truth. Not from history does Dante receive his assurances of imminent redress of the world's wrongs. Not from history can he acquire unshakable belief in God's providence. History seems to rudely contradict all his beliefs. His principle of interpretation is not any empirically historical principle but rather a hermeneutic of faith.[32] The interpretations he gives not only of the political past but also of the future destiny of humanity are based overtly on religious revelations and beliefs.

Conjoined, then, with his sense of the historicity of truth is Dante's vision and conviction of a transcendent revelation of truth. It is only this revelation by and from supernatural grace that makes history readable at all for him, since the truth Dante finds there is the opposite of what can be seen by an unadvised, unaided view. Does not such faith and the interpretive biases it entails prejudice any possibly historical understanding of truth? Does it not amount to a blanket acceptance of a metaphysical worldview and a dogmatic ethical-religious system as the basis for all one's subsequent interpretive endeavors, a refusal to submit to the test of history and let what happens pure and simple show the truth? Is it not to have decided what truth is in advance of all historical happenings on the basis of a message allegedly fallen out of the skies?

Such would be the case only for a shallow or at any rate intellectually

---

32. The notion of an "herméneutique de foi" is broached by Paul Ricoeur in "Existence et herméneutique," in *Le conflit des interprétations*.

unsophisticated understanding of faith. In actual fact, it is precisely the historicity of human existence and its full recognition that motivate the espousal of a hermeneutic of faith. The recognition of its historicity exposes the element of faith—of choosing to believe, for motives that may or may not be rational (and are not all reasons and motives compounded of both?)—that underlies all our "knowledge." For a historical being to judge that anything *is* thus and so is to overstep what can be strictly warranted on the basis of its own epistemic condition as constantly in flux; its historicity permits no simple unity and stability to human knowing.[33]

In the ground-breaking theological reflection of this century, precisely the recognition of the ineluctable historical conditionedness of the word of God in the text of Scripture, a result greatly encouraged by the generally acknowledged success of a historical-critical method of study, has led not only to the skepticism of some that there is any content to Scripture beyond that of human history abandoned to its own fate but also, paradoxically, to the sense of a new directness of encounter with the Word itself in faith. Precisely the recognition that all objective expressions and texts are only culturally relative manifestations of divinity frees faith to go beyond them—vehiculated all the same by those very words handed down through tradition—to a reality that directly illuminates the texts rather than being but a faint and dubious sort of inference from them. The directness of knowledge of God in faith thereby reached defines what is essentially a prophetic attitude that has enormous importance also for Dante.

This historic development in contemporary theology, pivoting on the step from recognition of the historical conditionedness of every actual word to the apprehension of a true Word that is not given as such, in the form of a cultural object, but may nevertheless give itself to be apprehended by apprehending the interpreter, has been concisely outlined by Robert Funk. Funk attributes especially to Rudolph Bultmann the break with the formidably empowering presupposition underlying the rise of modern biblical criticism that "when one does exegesis he is interpreting the text." It is reassuring to the scientifically-minded thus to be able to delimit the scope of inquiry even into religious matters in positive terms by reference to an objectively specifiable entity like "the text." Yet something is lost in this cleanly scientific treatment of what also has roots in

33. Cf. Nietzsche's account of the origin of knowledge ("Ursprung der Erkenntnis") out of "Glaubenssätze" (articles of faith)—such as "dass es dauernde Dinge gebe, dass es gleiche Dinge gebe, dass es Dinge, Stoffe, Körper gebe" ("that there are lasting things, that there are similar things, that there are things, materials, bodies")—which become part of the heritage and endowment of the species for their survival value. *Die fröhliche Wissenschaft ('La Gaya Scienza')*, pt. 3, secs. 110, 111 (Frankfurt Am Main: Insel, 1982), p. 127.

the experience of religious mystery. Divorced from the actual experience in which the religious text's meaning realizes itself as event, the text as such offers to investigation what is in effect a slough. Much can be learned about the supporting structures of a form of life from such a post mortem dissection, but it is deluded to expect that the whole truth about anything living and intelligent can be grasped in this way. What really needs to be interpreted, from a theological viewpoint, is not just a textual object produced by all the accidents of human history that can be so impressively documented, or at least suggestively inferred, by textual scholars. It is the word of God itself, after all, to which human text and tradition are but instrumental, that must be the primary concern. Otherwise theology simply reduces itself to documentary history.

Funk takes Bultmann to represent the culmination of the whole development of modern biblical criticism in its revelation that "the biblical text, like any other text, is composed of human language and is therefore culturally conditioned. It was but a short step to the conclusion that the New Testament is only a relative statement of the word of God" (Funk, *Language, Hermeneutic, and the Word of God*, p. 10). And yet this discovery harbors some extraordinary implications for faith that came to be felt particularly in Karl Barth's "Word of God" theology. Barth began from the divine Word rather than from human culture and its parameters in endeavoring to account for the possibility of revelation. As explained in the preface to the second edition of the *Römerbrief,* Barth's method is to live on intimate terms with the biblical text until it becomes so familiar that it is no longer seen as such and one is confronted with the divine Word itself. "One sees emerging here the view that it is not the text that is to be interpreted—the text is already interpretation—but the word of God itself, which, of course, cannot be equated with any human formulation" (Funk, p. 11).

Funk goes on to give special emphasis to the reversal of the direction of interpretation brought about by this newfound directness: the interpreter, the exegete, becomes the interpreted, and it is the Word that does the interpreting. His formulation is indebted to the contribution of the theologians of the so-called "New Hermeneutic":

> If it is God's word that is the object of exegetical endeavors, the process is at a dead end, for this word is not accessible to the exegete as an object for scrutiny. Yet this blind alley is precisely what led Gerhard Ebeling and Ernst Fuchs to the conclusion, remarkable as it may sound, that the word of God is not interpreted—it interprets! That is to say, it is indeed the word rather than the words with which exegetes have ultimately to do, but since they are in the embarrassing position of being unable to lay hold of that word, they can only permit it to lay hold of them. With this startling insight the direction of the flow between interpreter and text that has dominated modern biblical

criticism from its inception is reversed, and hermeneutics in its traditional sense becomes hermeneutic, now understood as the effort to allow God to address man through the medium of the text (p. 11).

A homologous sort of reversal is brought about in Dante's poem considered as an interpretation of the word of God. It is not the textual artifact that counts most in the end. This human work gives itself out to be merely a means of facilitating a more direct encounter with the divine Word. In effect, Dante employs poetry as a way of gaining a hearing for the Logos, a procedure he theorizes in De vulgari eloquentia.[34] In the Commedia, it is especially the addresses to the reader—but as an emblem of a much more general potential of poetry—that will effect this reversal, making the reader the one who is interpreted by the agency of the word of the text. In this way, interpretation is not an operation performed on a passive object but more essentially a rendering up, a restitution, of the interpreter's being to an event of truth in which the human interpreter is addressed by the Word speaking in the text. This inverted—or rather rectified—relation so fundamental to the Bible as word of God can be lost and/or regained in countless culturally specific ways in every age. This study proposes to render its discovery in Dante a little more evident through bringing the Commedia into relation with modes of understanding the happening of religious truth that are historically nearer to us.[35]

Of course, what is nearer may be more obscure depending on what

34. Cf. Roger Dragonetti, Aux frontières du langage poétique. Dante's invention by the art of poetry is brought out as a way of coming into ("invenire") the transcendent truth of the Logos. It is through vernacular language as a contingent human convention, and especially through poetic language as the invention of an individual's ingenio, that Dante, paradoxically, attempts to imitate the ordering principle at the origin of things themselves, the Logos, per quem omnia facta sunt. Dante seeks through the radically historically contingent and mutable language of the vernacular to recuperate an originary, absolute language of things themselves in the form of the "vulgare illustre." Through poetry, vernacular language, which is by definition agrammatical, can prove to be rule-governed in a higher sense by embodying universal harmonies and can, moreover, manifest an intrinsic order of things, all being in proportion to the One from which poetry and music alike devolve.

35. The contemporary search for religious understanding, so relevant to understanding Dante's search, beyond simply assessing this artifact as a historical and aesthetic monument, is provocatively explored by David Tracy in The Analogical Imagination: Christian Theology and the Culture of Pluralism (New York: Crossroad, 1981). Tracy proposes a phenomenology of "classic" expression in a sense that might help us to reinterpret the Divine Comedy's status as classic. The classic makes "a claim that transcends any context from my preunderstanding that I try to impose upon it, a claim that can shock me with the insight into my finitude as finitude, a claim that will interpret me even as I struggle to interpret it. I cannot control the experience, however practiced I am in techniques of manipulation. It happens, it demands, it provokes" (p. 119). Although the immediate inspiration here must be Gadamer, this construction of the classic also overlaps with Heidegger's theory of the work of art as an origin of truth. As Werner Jeanrond, Text and Interpretation as Categories of Theological Thinking, comments: "According to Tracy a classic expression discloses paradigmatic knowledge, even truth, even in fact transformative

conditions and affinities prevail in a culture. Today it seems especially difficult to understand how the postulate of providence, for example, operative a priori in interpretation, could possibly serve the ends of historical truth. Does it not rather foreclose real discovery and search by fixing a conclusion, and in fact presupposing a whole metaphysical teleology, in advance? This is how faith has often appeared to modern humanity's rationality. But that is because it has not really had a hermeneutic point of view on knowledge and understanding. And yet if modernity and its "enlightenment," radiated by such luminaries as Nietzsche, Freud, Marx, teaches us anything, it is that no knowledge is neutral, unbiased, purely objective. All our understanding and knowledge of the world take shape within our projections involving our own way of being, that is, within projections of possibilities that form the basic structure of a world as we can experience it.

It is precisely because of our historical predicament that we turn to faith, recognizing that all our "knowledge" is in any case of the nature of faith, that any stability or adequacy in representation that may be accepted as given, or necessary, is nevertheless predicated on that act of acceptance and consent in such a way that knowledge, however committed to being based simply on what is, can be claimed or asserted only as a mode of belief. This suggests how Dante's hermeneutic of faith can actually be continuous with his vision of historicity as constitutive of truth. The justification for faith, then, is that it is presupposed anyway. The question of *which* faith (and broadly considered this might include, for example, trust in technology) will be decided, as appropriate, by historical circumstances, those that present themselves once the openness to and disposition of faith, as no more than commensurate with the human epistemic condition, become active and conscious and ready to respond to possibilities and their occasions. To see this we need to turn to hermeneutic ontology and to Dante's investment in it. The ontological power of interpretation has been examined in an explicitly theoretical way especially in our own day,[36] though Dante already exploits it fully in practice.

The final form taken by the paradox, with which Dante presents us, of truth as belonging to interpretation rather than to "knowledge" is that of a revelation of truth of a transcendent, eternal order in the form of a historical event. Such a paradox is far from arbitrary, however, when we consider that it matches the founding paradox of Christian faith: namely,

---

truth, that is to say the kind of truth which changes the human being with whom it comes into contact" (p. 140).

36. For more on this, see the essays under the heading "Hermeneutic" in David Guerrière, ed., *Phenomenology and the Truth Proper to Religion* (Albany: State University of New York Press, 1990). Robert Scharlemann's *The Being of God: Theology and the Experience of Truth* (New York: Seabury Press, 1981) represents a major new contribution in a postmodern perspective.

the revelation of a transcendent God in the historical man Jesus of Naza-
reth. Above all, Dante's interpretive revelation of truth must gain its va-
lidity from participation in this master event.[37] Interpretation is thereby
revealed ultimately as an act of total existential conversion, of turning,
first of all upon oneself and one's past, in answer to a claim one recognizes
and the concomitant opening of a new horizon.

3. INTERPRETIVE ONTOLOGY:
DANTE AND HEIDEGGER

> Vie più che 'ndarno da riva si parte,
>   perché non torna tal qual e' si move,
>   chi pesca per lo vero e non ha l'arte."
> (*Paradiso* XIII. 121–23)

The claim that the realm of ontological truth, the other world of the
Christian afterlife, should be accessible to poetic interpretation marks an
extraordinary step of daring and confidence in the interpretive powers of
poiēsis. But not only does Dante's imaginative creation of the three
worlds beyond the grave claim to reveal something of what these pre-
sumed domains really are: his interpretations also are ontological in the
sense that they contribute to and are caught up in the realities they inter-
pret. The activity of interpretation locates itself on the inside of the un-
folding events and tale-telling beings it interprets. Hence, to mention
first only the most obvious and external form of this structure (besides
that of the explicit address to the reader), Dante writes a poem in which
he is commissioned to write a poem "in pro del mondo" ("for the
world's sake")—at several reprises, by Beatrice (*Purgatorio* XXXII. 103–
5; XXXIII. 51–57), by Cacciaguida (*Paradiso* XVII. 124–29), and by St.
Peter (*Paradiso* XXVII. 61–66)—situating the writing itself within the
event it is about. This integration of the making of the fiction into the
reality it represents is more indirectly indicated, furthermore, by the way
the journey of the poet-become-protagonist through the other world
actually catalyzes its events and affects its denizens.

In execution, Dante's work is remarkable for the freedom it exhibits

---

37. The incarnational thrust of Christian thought and sensibility, given a new impetus in
the Gothic age, registers in Dante in ways that have been masterfully delineated by Thomas
Altizer. In "Dante and the Gothic Revolution," Altizer shows how nothing short of a revolu-
tionary transformation of Western poetry and culture, expressed in a "new Gothic language,"
was brought about by Dante in the wake of Thomas Aquinas's speculative revolution in dis-
covering "the pure actuality of existence itself." This entailed the "discovery of a new glory
embodied in the very texture of the world . . . a glory that here and now is immanent and
transcendent at once." *History as Apocalypse* (Albany: State University of New York Press, 1985),
pp. 97–136.

in its interpretations. Dante does not scruple to step out in front of documentary evidence, settled traditions, or even historical fact in proffering his interpretations as more consequential than them all. He threatens Italy, for example, with the retribution of Henry VII of Luxembourg when this would-be Roman-revival emperor was already stiff in his grave.[38] Dante's prophetic stance, it would seem, can even stand against facts in dictating an ideal possibility, what *must happen* in history, which perhaps may be understood as having an ontologically higher status than any number of howsoever certain actualities.[39]

Many of the interpretations within the *Divine Comedy* have attracted attention principally for their arbitrariness. Interpretive acrobatics such as the saving of Rifeus Troianus, a relatively minor figure of a righteous pagan from the second book of the *Aeneid,* introduce elements from a highly personal reading of a classical poem interpreted in a Christian key into the realm of ontological truth that Dante claims to be adumbrating. Like Cato at the foot of the mountain of Purgatory, Rifeus in the heaven of Jupiter has provoked interminable scholarly efforts to justify his inclusion and collocation by Christian or any other plausible criteria. Such researches have mainly shown the scarcity of antecedent facts from which Dante's interpretations could be understood to be reasonable inferences.[40] The text itself, in the case of Rifeus, lays great stress on the surprise value of this discovery:

> chi crederebbe giù nel mondo errante
> che Rifeo Troiano in questo tondo
> fosse la quinta de le luci sante?
> (Paradiso XX. 67–69)

> (who down in the errant world would believe
> that Rifus Troianus in this orbit
> was the fifth of the holy lights?)

And yet Rifeus is presented as really there, believe it or not, among the souls of the just in the eye of the eagle. The very outrageousness, deliberately underlined, of such an interpretation by Dante, which nevertheless is presented as confirmed by how things really are in the end, revealed proleptically in his poem, amounts to an extraordinary claim for the role interpretation plays in constituting truth and in making things what they are. For it emphasizes that this was not necessarily so. In fact,

---

38. *Paradiso* XXX. 133–38. Henry's Italian campaign, spurred on by Dante's epistle (VIII) to him, ended in defeat and death in 1313, years prior to the completion of the *Paradiso.*

39. There is a tradition of "existentialist" thought, passing through Kierkegaard and Heidegger (see *Sein und Zeit,* sec. 6), that articulates the view that "possibility is higher than actuality."

40. Cf. Jeremy Tambling, *Dante and Difference,* chap. 2: "The eye of the eagle."

who would never have thought it? Yet Dante, having found a compelling motivation within the order of significances of his poem for interpreting things thus, can consider this an ontological ground for their actually being so. This suggests the ontological power at play in the work of interpretation.[41]

Relatively recently in the history of thought, new insights have opened up that enable us to come closer to Dante's sense of interpretation as ontologically consequential. Enlightenment paradigms had accustomed thinkers to think of interpretation in terms of a play of perspectives all at one remove from what things actually are. Still today we tend to oppose interpretations and facts. However, Martin Heidegger's existential hermeneutic, as worked out in *Being and Time*, argues compellingly for the role of interpretation in constituting the world in its very ontological foundations.[42] The fact that we have a world at all belongs to the constitution of "being-there" ("Dasein"), that is, to *our* constitution as the being who questions the meaning of Being, and whose mode of existence is intrinsically interpretive. It is fundamentally determined as affective state ("Befindlichkeit"), discourse ("Rede"), and understanding ("Verstehen"), and interpretation is always already at work in all these, most obviously in understanding, of which it is the working-out ("Ausarbeitung").

This means that beings in the world are not first given as what they are before being subjected to interpretation. They *are* at all only insofar as they belong to a world, a global order of significances, which itself

41. A heated discussion of the ontological implications of this episode has been joined by Mowbray Allan and Teodolinda Barolini in a critical exchange in the Italian issue of *Modern Language Notes* 105 (1990): 138–49. The ontological reading of Dante's text, taking the world it projects as real and consequential, is precisely what is under attack from Barolini. Although Allan gives no substantial theoretical defense in his "Reply to Teodolinda Barolini," his thoughtful and thought-provoking reading of Dante's Virgil in "Does Dante Hope for Virgil's Salvation?" *Modern Language Notes* 104 (1989): 193–205 admirably illustrates the rather exceptional sort of ontological questions that Dante's text has always raised and continues raising, Barolini's strictures, based on her own perhaps too narrow constructions as to what *is* the case with regard to textuality and truth, notwithstanding.

42. *Sein und Zeit,* especially sections 32 ("Verstehen und Auslegung") to 34. One might point out innumerable other researches that have revised the conventional opposition between fact and interpretation. Especially worthy of mention among the many recent contributions to the theory of history as interpretively constituted are Paul Ricoeur, *Histoire et vérité* (Paris: Seuil, 1964) and *Temps et récit* vol. 1 pt. 2 (Paris: Seuil, 1983–85); Michel de Certeau, *L'Écriture de l'histoire* (Paris: Gallimard, 1975); and Hayden White, *The Tropics of Discourse: Essays in Cultural Criticism* (Baltimore: Johns Hopkins University Press, 1978) and *The Content of the Form: Narrative Discourse and Historical Representation* (Baltimore: Johns Hopkins University Press, 1990). These works carry forward inquiries akin to those initiated earlier in the century and more contemporaneously with Heidegger's by Heinrich Rickert, *Die Grenzen der naturwissenschaftlichen Begriffsbildung: Eine logische Einleitung in die historischen Wissenschaften* (Tübingen: J. C. B. Mohr, 1929) and R. G. Collingwood, *The Idea of History* (London: Oxford University Press, 1946).

belongs to Dasein (the being that we are) and is determined by its modes of being, the fundamental structures of its existence ("Existentiales"), including understanding/interpretation. Thus, when a being within the world is presented to that other sort of being that *has* a world and is Dasein, the significance it may have as pleasing, repellent, frightening, useful, and so on, are not irrelevant to the determination of what it is. Significances, which, as a unified system, in the final analysis, do depend on significance *for* Dasein, are built into the world and the constitution of things, not superadded as pertaining to some extra sphere of interpretations based on reactions of a being extrinsic to them.[43] Indeed, as Heidegger expounds this conception in *Sein und Zeit,* intramundane beings simply *are* their significances: their being is to signify other beings within the total ambit of significances that is the world.[44] And so their being in the world is equivalent to their being part of a system of signs, or, in other words, to their being in language. Consequently, language is revealed as intrinsically constitutive of the world.[45]

Heidegger's interpretation of the existence of Dasein clearly shows how interpretation, and with it, inextricably, language, can be ontologically constitutive for the world and for all beings within it. On historically different bases, not, however, without terms of comparison, Dante too underscores the constitutive role of interpretation, especially of poetic interpretation in its intrinsic linguisticality, in making things what and as they are. The *Commedia*'s interpretations of classical myths, of Dante's own contemporaries, of the various spheres of medieval culture, and of

43. This modern phenomenological account strikingly overlaps on the essential point of the compenetration of being and significance with the outlook of "medieval symbolism" as described by Albert Béguin: "L'apparence des choses et leur signifiance sont tellement indissociables à ses yeux [aux yeux du moyen âge], qu'il lui est impossible de voir les formes concrètes du monde comme des réalités en elles-mêmes closes, complètes, ne portant pas d'autre sens que l'immédiat. Le moyen âge voit à la fois, d'un même regard, la chose et son sens" ("The appearance of things and their significance are to such an extent indissociable in its [the Middle Ages'] eyes, that it is impossible for it to see the concrete forms of the world as realities closed in upon themselves, complete, and bearing no other sense beyond the immediate. The Middle Ages sees at the same time, in one look, the thing and its sense"). Robert Guiette, "Symbolisme et 'senefiance' au moyen-âge," *Assoc. Internationale des Etudes Francaises-Cahier* 6 (July 1954): 107.

44. The idea that instrumentality, specifically in the form of significativity ("Bedeutsamkeit"), is the essence of the thing begins undergoing transformation in part 1 of Heidegger's essay on the origin of the work of art, which is dedicated to the thing and the work, especially when Heidegger concentrates his attention on the artwork—a thing defined precisely by its resistance to serving any practical function and by its creating a significance not assimilable within the systems of significances already in place, into which it does *not* fit. See Gianni Vattimo, *Arte e verità nel pensiero di Martin Heidegger,* p. 51.

45. This specifically linguistic dimension of our being in the world would be explored by Heidegger with increasing intensity in his later works. Dante concentrates on it especially in the *Paradiso.*

Christian revelation itself are wrought by Dante not merely as reflections on diverse orders of preconstituted facts. They rather participate ontologically in these facts in the forging. His *Commedia* is an awe-inspiring effort to exploit to the fullest all the resources of interpretation that poetic, linguistic art can furnish and that personal aplomb can authorize in mediating the reality of the ontologically true world by the disclosure of his poem and its event in history.

Heidegger's thought brought the ontological underpinnings of interpretive activity more clearly and explicitly into the open than philosophical speculation ever had. It stands within a tradition of existential and hermeneutic (and metaphysical!) philosophy that calls to mind the dependence of being on knowing, that is, the interpenetration of the two. Dante brings about an apotheosis of interpretation of a different but closely related sort. We can ascribe to him no theory of interpretation as ontologically consequential. Yet that is exactly what his practice of the art of poetry effectually demonstrates. Reduced to a visceral level, what Dante's poem with its prophetic pretensions stubbornly asserts is that interpreting—which involves one's whole way of being—makes it so. For the compelling nature of his interpretations empowers them to impose—and impose upon—the supporting structures within which what comes to be considered real comes to light. This must not be misunderstood, however, as an exaltation of the agency of the human subject, the author, since in interpretation the subject only lends itself to an event it does not control. In fact, when Dante stubbornly and willfully interprets, he is only trying to apprehend things as they really and truly are (in the sight of God), beyond the ineluctable distortions of whatever we are able to perceive as objectively real, that is, as already deformed by being figured into our framework or field of objectivity (the perspective of a finite creature). To reach this goal, interpretation must abandon subjectivity to its own fluidity so as to let it flow into the event of truth it does not comprehend, but is rather comprehended by.

Dante's method of interpretation is ontological in essence from start to finish. More than just autobiographical mania, there is a hermeneutic logic that dictates that Dante must actually *be* eschatological being in order to reveal anything about it.[46] Basically the same hermeneutic rationale becomes philosophically deliberate when Heidegger begins his quest

---

46. This has long been realized at some level by the poem's philosophically sensitive readers, for example De Sanctis: "Dante non è un viaggiatore che vaghi oziosamente per l'altro mondo e lo mescoli di sé e dei suoi tempi, ma è attore. . . . Egli è così la sintesi vivente dei due mondi, che hanno in lui la loro riflessione ed unità" ("Dante is not a traveler who wanders at leisure through the other world and mixes it with himself and his times, but an agent. . . . He is thus the living synthesis of the two worlds, which in him have their reflection and unity"— *Lezioni,* p. 17).

for the meaning of Being with an interpretation of the being who questions. The ontological inquiry into the meaning of Being must start from an existential analysis elucidating the mode of being of the being for whom the meaning of Being is a question. And the essential thing Heidegger shows about this mode of being of the being who questions is that it is always situated in a world: it is always a "being-there." This entails that the questioning human being is always a being "in relation to." A human being's being can be "there" only by virtue of being situated in relation to other beings.[47]

The philosophical breakthrough of Heidegger's *Sein und Zeit* was to show that we know the world not as an object but rather from a position within it and as already, always already, involved in it. There is not first a cognizance of self and then of something else at one remove, outside and around the self, which comes to be called "world." I do not first realize that I think and therefore am and then draw inferences from perceptions within me to what is in a world outside me. Consciousness of oneself comes primordially in the form of being-in-the-world. It follows that "truth," in the sense of the disclosedness of a world within and around me, belongs to the "basic state of Dasein's being": "Wahrheit, im ursprünglichsten Sinne verstanden, gehört zur Grundverfassung des Daseins" ("Truth understood in the most primordial sense belongs to the basic constitution of Dasein"—Heidegger, *Sein und Zeit,* p. 299).

Similarly, the world of the *Commedia,* presented as the true world, the "vera vita," where ultimately divinity itself is disclosed, appears filtered through the personal experience of Dante, protagonist and poet. The knowledge of things divine and of all else as it is ordered to divinity, which the poem, proposes to convey, thus comes to consciousness as inextricably situated within the experience of an individual. Abstract, universal, and doctrinal verities of Dante's Christian faith are affirmed within the poem as they occur in specific contexts, their realization conditioned by the circumstances of the pilgrim's existence and, by extension, of the author's and reader's, to the extent that their knowledge is mediated by the protagonist's. Heidegger showed how truth could be understood strictly in coordination with the openness of a region of disclosure that characterizes Dasein, the individuated being that we are. In Dante's poem, too, truth comes to pass, and even divinity or true being comes to be disclosed, in the opening of an individual's experience of existence, a sort of "being-there" as Heidegger develops this notion.

Dante thus makes theological truth attainable by treating it as not just dogma but as open to experience. This all could be interpreted as a fantasy of what it would be like to experience truth, which nevertheless in

---

47. On this last point, cf. Gianni Vattimo, *Arte e vertià nel pensiero di Martin Heidegger,* p.4.

truth remains what it is, beyond all human reach. But the poem's pro-phetic tone urges us not to settle complacently into this reductive view. We are made to face the other possibility that what the poem proposes as the experience of an individual is really theological truth, the true world, rather than (only) a fanciful fiction of it. One ground for this possibility is that truth itself may be something that consists and transpires precisely in the disclosedness of the experience of a protagonist's being-there. Dante gives no explicit philosophical formulation of this premise, but we have seen how he grasps the essential historicity of truth. In poetic-interpretive practice, he opens his whole revelation of theological truth within the experiential horizon of a protagonist situated in an indi-vidual life story and constituted as being-in-the-(other)-world. Dante-protagonist's knowledge is clearly shown as coming to him as a progres-sively augmenting awareness of his being in the world—from his first coming to consciousness in a dark forest where "mi ritrovai." The fact of his being represented as being in the other, that is, the true, world expresses the claim that this knowledge is true in some absolute sense.

Dante's poem brings the truth in the form of the disclosedness of be-ings to light in the horizon of a phenomenal world, the world of a pro-tagonist; furthermore, this world is constituted as a global order of sig-nificances having reference to the being of the protagonist. Perhaps the chief emblem of this is the vital role played by Beatrice, an individual of Dante's personal acquaintance, even as presented within the fiction. Recognized by some as Dante's supreme literary creation,[48] she signals the mediation of Christian theological revelation in an absolutely funda-mental way by the existential situation and irreducibly personal, intimate reality of an individual. His whole journey is accorded by grace that reaches him through the intercession of this person who had become for him "salute" (salvation), and in whom he seemed to see "tutti li termini de la beatitudine" ("the very limits of blessedness"—*Vita nuova* III).

It may seem out of the question that for Dante truth about the world, which God created, should be relative to human existence and historical experience. But we should not be so fast in dismissing the idea that on one side Dante might be very near to such a view. Indeed, persuasive arguments have suggested that reality and, in particular, its ordering prin-ciple of justice can have a kind of ambiguous relativity to human knowl-edge even for Dante.[49] The fact that God made the world on the basis of

48. For example, by Ernst Robert Curtius, "Myth and Prophecy," in *European Literature and the Latin Middle Ages*, pp. 372–78.

49. Mowbray Allan has linked this with Dante's "humanism," a term that perhaps needs some defense in the contemporary critical climate, though it is no more or less defensible per se than any of the other constructions or myths that come together with any language game. The question whether divine justice can or must be humanly intelligible is a very live issue in

his own, to us unfathomable, ideas might be metaphysically true even while human experience of the world might be conditioned by some necessary reference of all that is in it to the human being who experiences it, that is, to the being-there of a protagonist. Indeed, this is how all three worlds of the *Commedia* actually come into the horizon of experience—first Dante's experience, and through his ours. One could even speak in a Scholastic terminology that was second nature to Dante of a sort of *duplex causa* whereby God would be the absolute ground of the world, grounding a proximate cause that would be a humanly structured existence. So construed, Dante's very insistence on attempting to understand divine justice in human terms would recognize that its ultimate rationale is beyond his ken.

Dante's whole poem, patterned on the Christ event (which subsumes the Exodus), particularly as it is commemorated in the Easter liturgy, and leading up to a direct encounter with the being of the trinitarian God, is an attempt to think theology existentially, that is, from the basis of the being-there of an existing individual. It is precisely within this finite horizon that the mysteries with which theology is concerned reveal (and conceal) themselves in the poem. The form of first-person narration can, of course, be motivated literarily. One can credit it with dramatic effects of pathos and with effectively stimulating participation on the part of the reader. But the significance of Dante's first-person, experiential, and dramatic mode of presenting theological revelation in coordination with philosophical verity cannot be exhausted by considerations of literary technique. It constitutes rather a constatation that truth comes to pass, and that divinity or true being is disclosed, in the opening of an individual's experience of existence, or, in other words, in incarnate revelation.

Once the correlativity of truth and experience in the event of disclosedness has been affirmed, this does not void the heavens of anything real, making the immanent sphere of our experience the only reality. It rather entails that our "reality" always escapes us, and that our experience is hemmed with an otherness, a breaking in of truth that cannot be contained within experience or in any construction we may have of a metaphysical realm, but must rather continually revise the settled structures

---

the *Commedia*, as in medieval thought generally. The issue is brought to focus by Dante in his treatment of the salvation of righteous pagans in the heaven of Jupiter. See the discussion of this passage and of Dante's humanism by Robin Kirkpatrick in *Dante's* Paradiso *and the Limitations of Modern Criticism: A Study of Style and Poetic Theory* (Cambridge: Cambridge University Press 1978): "It is indeed one of the finest and most abiding characteristics of Dante's thought that he should acknowledge, as a force which men are bound to suffer, the reality of God in its most terrible aspect, and yet insist on the right of the human intellect to adjust itself towards this power in its own, albeit inadequate terms." Hence "the poet affirms the value of merely human sense, and announces without exaggeration a confidence in the conventions of the intellect" (p. 40).

of our world in self-transcendence.[50] This is perfectly compatible with the recognition of other, metaexperiential realms. It implies that experience is opened outward—an orientation toward what is as yet unexperienced. To represent this ecstatic character of experience by a metaphysical poetry, or a poetry of metaphysics, may be to find an appropriate expression for its self-transcending structure and, even more importantly, to find an appropriate response to what transcends it. We cannot say what is not experienced, but we can be open to it and can express this openness metaphorically even in an objective representational mode—as poetry. This is a significant way of relating to what is beyond our cognizance but which nevertheless can be intimated as an arbiter of our fate or as the meaning of our existence.

Although both Dante and Heidegger are radical and revolutionary in their conceptions of truth as dynamic and historical, for the former this can lead to the vindication of a metaphysical faith, while for the latter it supposedly means overcoming metaphysics. The modern, Heideggerian tendency is to say that the transcendence of the world just *is* the happening of the truth, which makes the world strange, wholly other than "this" world as we ordinarily know it. Not just strange things within the world but the whole order of the world per se becomes estranged by this advent of disclosedness that is truth.[51] Yet to say that the world is just *this* world, whether as familiar or as strange, is to pretend we can occupy a position outside it and say what the world is. Dante's poetic imagining of his world of truth revealed as a transcendent order of being concedes in advance that in saying what the world *is* we are inevitably imagining things or else proceeding on the basis of revelation, or both (the former being a possible means of participating in the latter), whether we imagine our constructions as ultimately referring to "this" or to the "other" world. A certain duality of worlds in the order of representation simply reflects the unobjectifiable aspect or residue of any consciousness of world. Ultimately, the world is other than all that enters into our field of objects, and it is no more accurate to construe that unattainable otherness as a structure belonging to "this" world than to figure it as pertaining to an "other" world; indeed, the latter may be preferred for more deliber-

50. So far, Heidegger could well agree. Christopher Fynsk, in *Heidegger: Thought and Historicity* (Ithaca: Cornell University Press, 1986), comments, "To the extent that a thinking opens to that which claims it and assumes the temporal structure of its activity—assumes its finitude—it carries itself into a movement that exceeds it and carries it beyond itself. . . . Heidegger suggests that, if thought cannot hold this movement in its grasp, it might hold itself in this movement in such a way as to find in it a certain measure. For the movement to which thought opens is understood by Heidegger to have a gathering and unifying character" (pp. 16–17).

51. This emphasis is brought out particularly by Gerald Bruns in *Heidegger's Estrangements: Language, Truth, and Poetry in the Later Writings* (New Haven: Yale University Press, 1989).

ately acknowledging and more generously leaving space for otherness. It would even allow that otherness to reveal its face and to make demands upon human individuals. But even on a strictly philosophical plane, the figuring of truth as antecedent and eternal can honestly express our discovering the disclosedness of beings as always already there in a way that transcends us utterly and unutterably.

For Heidegger, the retrieval of a more primordial notion of truth as event of disclosure replaces the metaphysical notion of truth as correspondence to a self-subsistent reality in some zone above and before history. Once we are able to give an account of truth as an occurrence of this world, who needs the other? Such an otherwordly hypothesis no longer seems necessary or justifiable.[52] But even from Heidegger's point of view, it is vital not to forget how the metaphysical illusion essentially belongs to the disclosure of truth.[53] The same goes for all the other non-metaphysical, antimetaphysical, empiricist, and deconstructionist illusions about what is or is not. Far from overcoming metaphysics, all are struggling to keep up with its creative power of disclosure. The real task for us is not to deconstruct metaphysics but to accept it, however critically, with all its limitations and all it has to contribute to configuring the unself-grounded character of human existence whereby it is structurally open to what transcends it. Only when we have accepted all that belongs to us will we be free; and it is Heidegger himself who reminds us that "the essence of truth is freedom."[54]

Hermeneutic theory has fostered a salutary awareness of the historical conditionedness of all forms of knowledge and culture. In this, Dante is a forebear whose grasp of the problem could hardly be stronger and would not be subsequently excelled. Yet what Dante also knew and what tends to be rejected in modern hermeneutic thought is that this very historicity of knowledge becomes the enabling condition for such a revelation of transcendence as is claimed in the Christian religion. Indeed, it is only the existential-historical nature of such belief that makes possible what from a Christian, incarnational perspective is genuine transcendence or revealed knowledge of God. Dante can help us see this continuity between historicity and transcendence—the central mystery of the

52. Thus Heidegger writes, "But truth does not exist in itself beforehand, somewhere among the stars, only to descend later among beings. This is impossible for the reason alone that it is after all only the openness of beings that first affords the possibility of a somewhere and of a place filled by present beings. Clearing of openness and establishment in the Open belong together. They are the same single nature of the happening of truth. This happening is historical in many ways." "The Origin of the Work of Art," p. 61.

53. See, e.g., "Überwindung der Metaphysik," in *Vorträge und Aufsätze*.

54. "Vom Wesen der Wahrheit," sec. 5.

Christian religion—which we tend not to able to fathom today, even while its effects spring up all around us in revivals of what seem irrational superstitions in this age of the technological domination of our material and mental lives.

Contemporary criticism, because of its too narrow and one-sided understanding of hermeneutics, has tended to see the radically historical character of Dante's poetic production, and particularly the exposure of how vulnerable and volatile his poem's meanings are, as *undermining* its claims to mediate an authentic revelation and a total vision. What remains to be seen, as we learn to read Dante ever anew, is the way historicity and its limits form precisely the ground for prophecy and its transcendence.[55]

The philosophical stake in this renewed look, from a less narrowly "medievalist" perspective, at Dante's poetic practice lies in its bearing on the question of the "onto-theo-logical" infrastructure of Western intellectual tradition and its viability or legitimacy, which has indeed been called into question.[56] While the questioning is certainly a vital part of the structure itself, its intrinsic vibrancy, so to speak, the conclusion that this tradition and everything built upon it is dead only falls into just the sort of unilateral, univocal entrapment it abhors.

There is, furthermore, a theological stake. Dante pleads for a religious revelation, and he strives textually toward a religious form of existence. Are we yet in a position to understand him and what is opened and offered through his poetic work? Are we yet free to choose whether to believe what poetry discloses in his poem? Or are our horizons obstructed in ways we might wish to overcome? *That* they are obstructed can be taken as a necessary condition of any determinate vision at all; but we may have more room to choose what to be blind to than we have yet discovered or accepted—especially if we have become comfortably used to being able to automatically write off anything having to do with metaphysics, transcendence, or truth, secure in our illusion that the refusal of all illusions and the agnostic state it in theory brings about are necessarily superior to any more risky form of cognitive or conative commitment. We drastically delude ourselves by pretending that our rational neutrality and diacritical sophistication do not also enfold enthymematical claims to what has traditionally been called moral wisdom—and which therefore ought to be examined critically. And for this purpose we might try measuring our intellectual framework and the possibilities it can accom-

---

55. The final section of the last chapter returns to the theoretical elucidation and defense of this proposal.

56. Heidegger himself, for example, in *Identity and Difference* (New York: Doubleday, 1961), has taken the lead in this, to be followed by Derrida et al.

modate against that worked out by Dante, before presuming that he can have nothing true to teach us after the apocalypse of Derrida.[57]

Note on Heideggerian Vocabulary

It is well known that various contingents of literary and philosophical scholars are uncomfortable with the language of Being that devolves from the writings of Martin Heidegger and forges the vocabulary of what may be termed "existential hermeneutics."[58] Some indications concerning the warrant for and intelligibility of this language are therefore in order.

When I use the word "Being" I am not referring to any thing in particular, but especially today, after the revolution of structural linguistics, we should no longer be beholden to the naive idea that it is necessary for a word to name a thing in order for it to be meaningful. We have learned (actually relearned) that such a simple one-to-one correspondence between word and thing is not the basis of language's meaningfulness. The word "Being" may still operate as a parameter of discourse, and in the present conjunction it is enough to know that it gestures toward language's (especially poetry's) promise of bringing us to experience or vision—even if never quite simultaneous or unified—of all that concerns our existence in its totality.

In attempting to articulate the at least virtual structural wholes that, however fragmentarily grasped, are operative as enabling conditions of our experience, we are always using terms that are not as yet defined, and those that are have been given definition in terms of other terms we have not yet defined. The fact that I employ the word "Being" is a reminder of this condition of assuming at any given point more than I have explicitly delineated or thematically understood. If I am saying anything about anything (i.e., if I am "interpreting" in Aristotle's sense), I am invoking, however implicitly or unconsciously, the undefined, "mysterious" notion of an "is."

In a hermeneutic perspective, everything is understood in terms of everything else, without isolatably self-intelligible, atomic principles.[59] Fullness of understanding is—which also means it is interpreted as being—always on loan from further relations and what can yet be gathered from them. Employment of a vague notion like "Being" signals the fact

57. The last phrase suggests what is an erroneous interpretation of the master (see his critique of rhetorical apocalypticism in *D'un ton apocalyptique adopté naguère en philosophie* [Paris: Galilée, 1982]), but not for that reason any less widespread and stultifying.

58. See especially Theodor Adorno's attack in *The Jargon of Authenticity* (Evanston: Northwestern University Press, 1973).

59. This is precisely expressed by Schleiermacher's dictum that "Language is infinite because every element is determinable in a special way by the other elements." *Hermeneutics: The Handwritten Manuscripts*, p. 100.

that we never get full command over all the contextual bearings upon sense. There is always an element of vagueness, of indeterminacy in meaning, in any discourse whatever. Even rigorously, mathematically defined languages suggest meanings, shading into significances, by virtue of philosophical penumbrae that prove ineliminable and are always yet to be pondered and further sounded. The vagueness in question is not exclusive of precision; it can often be even better evoked *by* precision, which sharply defines the limits of understanding.[60]

It is important to remember that no critical vocabulary should be taken as possessing exclusive rights to express the subject matter it is designed to interpret. The language of Being must not be confounded with the Being that the poem can make manifest. Other critical vocabularies, even antagonistic ones at the level of philosophical-ideological alignments, are powerful to the degree that they help make manifest what the poem is and what is at stake in it. My adoption of the language of Being is determined by an interest in rendering explicit the most general features of the disclosure that the poem makes. This particular language itself nevertheless remains merely one attempt to achieve this goal. It is not intrinsically the key to an otherwise inaccessible truth, even though language per se may be just such an indispensable key.

60. See Jack Kaminsky, *Language and Ontology* (Carbondale: Southern Illinois University Press, 1969) for discussion of Popper, Strawson, Sellars, Quine, Carnap et al. on Anglo-American attempts—and their failure—to liberate language from its ontological shadows. G. P. Baker and P. M. S. Hacker, in *Language, Sense & Nonsense* (Oxford: Blackwell, 1984), similarly critique the notion of a logically transparent language.

ONE

The Address to the Reader

Se tu sei or, lettore . . .
(Inferno XXV. 94)

1. THE ONTOLOGICAL IMPORT OF
THE ADDRESS TO THE READER

*T*he way he addresses his reader distinguishes Dante's style as a poet. Frequently recurring vocatives in the name of the "lettore" enframe the whole poem within the event of its being read. Some of these addresses are imperious directives claiming to guide the reader's understanding of, participation in, or judgment upon whatever is happening in the narrative, which they metanarratologically trump. Others are low-key asides that nevertheless serve as reminders of the situation vis-à-vis a reader that pragmatically contextualizes the "happening" of the poem.

Erich Auerbach maintains that the address to the reader is original with Dante, "a new creation, although some of its features appear in earlier texts." According to Auerbach, such a form of address is never used in classical epic poetry, and its occurrence in the broader literary tradition, in elegy, for example, shows it to be relegated consistently to the margins, to junctures where intensity and seriousness slacken, giving place to banter, so that, in other words, it constitutes an enframing designed to vary rather than to establish a normative structural framework. Although numerous addresses to the reader can be culled from the Latin and vernacular poetry of the Middle Ages, Auerbach inventories them to prove that none are "emphatic," which we can take to mean structuring, in anything like the way Dante's are. Hence Auerbach's claim that Dante's addresses "show a new relationship between reader and poet."[1]

---

1. Erich Auerbach, "Dante's Addresses to the Reader," *Romance Philology* 7 (1953–54): 268, 271. Auerbach is actually endorsing observations of Hermann Gmelin, "Die Anrede an den Leser in Dantes Göttlicher Komödie," *Deutsches Dante-Jahrbuch* 29–30 (1951): 130–40, to the effect that the addresses form a peculiarly distinguishing pattern of Dante's style. Gmelin observed that Dante not only adapted the address to the Muses from ancient epic, but also, for emotional heightening ("zur affektischen Steigerung"), employed "auch die Anrede an den Leser, die das antike Epos nicht kennt und die erst die mittelalterliche Dichtung als Ausdruck der Verbundenheit zwischen Dichter und Leser bzw. Hörer eingeführt hat" ("also the address

The twenty-odd overt apostrophes to a reader in the *Commedia* comprise only the most obvious showings of a structural openness to the reader that actually pervades Dante's poem in its entirety. An implicit address to the reader is written into the work from its very first verse: "nel mezzo del cammin di *nostra* vita" ("In the middle of the way of *our* life"). This same inflection occurs not infrequently, as again, near the opposite end of the journey, in *Paradiso* XXVII: "l'aiuola che *ci* fa tanto feroce" ("the threshing floor which makes *us* so ferocious"). And hortatory and exclamatory passages, such as

> Ahi giustizia di Dio! . . .
>   perché *nostra* colpa sì ne scipa?
>   (*Inferno* VII. 19–21; see also XII. 49–51)

> (Ah! justice of God . . .
>   why does our guilt so ruin us?)

or

> Or superb*ite*, e via col viso altero,
>   figliuoli d'Eva . . .
>   (*Purgatorio* XII. 70–72; see also X. 121–23)

> (Now wax proud and go on with haughty visage,
>   you children of Eve . . .)

or

> Ahi anime ingannate e fatture empie,
>   che di sì fatto ben torc*ete* i cuori,
>   drizzando in vanità le vostre tempie,
>   (*Paradiso* IX. 10–12)

> (O souls deceived and impious creatures,
>   who from such good turn away your hearts,
>   bending your sights on vanity,)

dispersed throughout the three *cantiche,* make the same dialogical assumption simply by virtue of their second-person grammar. Not only grammar but also content in such enunciations assumes and calls upon a reader: addressed to whomever it may concern, they claim to engage their recipient in an examination of conscience and in conversion of life. To this extent, they embody a diffused, continuous address to the one

---

to the reader, which is unknown to ancient epic and which medieval poetry first introduced, as an expression of the bond between poet and reader or hearer"—p. 130).

concerned by reading. In these as well as in other ways,[2] the phenomenon of presencing the reader subtends the whole poem, determining its every line.

We might even consider the fact of its being read alone to constitute a sense in which the poem is addressed to the reader de facto. Of course, this condition would no longer distinguish Dante's from any other poetry; it would rather belong to the essence of poetry as revealed by Dante's poem. The fact that a line of poetry exists for a reader belongs to its being as poetry, inasmuch as poetry is to-be-read. But if all poetry by its at least potentially readable nature is addressed to one who reads, and if Auerbach is right, then Dante's *Commedia* is peculiarly explicit and emphatic in this regard. It therefore solicits an interpretation of the phenomenon of the presencing of the reader, which is an inherent potentiality of poetry that becomes paramount in the *Commedia,* especially in the peculiar speech act of direct address to the reader.[3]

Auerbach notes that the ancient rhetoricians never catalogued the address to the reader along with the figures of speech. Only in the case of address to someone else, anyone besides the presumed audience of the discourse in question, was a rhetorical figure produced—namely, apostrophe. This exclusion of the voicing of the relation to the reader from the categories of rhetoric can be understood as stemming from its ontological character. The address to the reader is assumed to be constitutive of poetic discourse as such, rather than a technique or device that can be chosen ad hoc to produce a peculiar effect. Dante's seizing upon the address to the reader for special emphasis, previously unknown in the literary tradition he writes within, gives a hint of the ontological pretension and dimension that poetry assumes under his authorship. For such direct, dialogical engagement of the reader amounts to a calling to con-

2. Leo Spitzer, "The Addresses to the Reader in the *Commedia,*" *Italica* 32 (1955): 153, individuates another modality of implicit address in suggesting that Dante's evocations of familiar landscapes at the same time evoke an implied reader who would be familiar with them. Furthermore, we cannot deny the force for addressing readers of the exhortations, denunciations, admonitions, etc. voiced by various characters, but indirectly of course by the author, and directed to humanity or to specific groups and classes, but also to readers as potentially belonging to any of them, as, for example, St. Thomas's warning, "Non sian le genti, ancor, troppo sicura / a giudicar" (*Paradiso* XIII. 130–32), or Beatrice's, "Non prendan li mortali il voto a ciancia: / siate fedeli" (*Paradiso* V. 64), or Oderisi da Gubbio's exclamation, "Oh vana gloria delle umane posse!" (*Purgatorio* XI. 91).

3. It is possible to generalize further from poems to all texts and maintain with Paul Ricoeur that "the text, as writing, waits and calls for a reading." "What is a Text? Explanation and Interpretation," in David Rasmussen, *Mythic-Symbolic Language and Philosophical Anthropology: A Constructive Interpretation of the Thought of Paul Ricoeur* (The Hague: Martinus Nijhoff, 1971), p. 144. Within the character of all texts as "made" things (Greek: *poiēmata*), and as made specifically to be read, lies their potential to become interpellative in nature, as can be dramatically revealed by the poetic text and even more particularly by the prophetic poem.

sciousness the ontological status and basis of poetry in an event of understanding and appropriation.

The addresses manifest a presupposition that the poem, after all, takes on its meaning and achieves its significance in relation to a reader. They reveal the poem as having a specific kind of being, namely, that of being an event for a reader. But the poem's being an event for the reader does not exclude the reader's being an occasion for the poem to happen: the reader qua reader is *for* the event of the poem. The crucial importance of the addresses to the reader rests not in their shifting the focus of attention away from the text itself, which could be accused of being an inert, lifeless fossil, to the activity of the reader and so to reception as a life-giving principle. The point is *not* to replace a textual object with an anthropological object as the thing that the interpretation of poetry is really about.[4] Rather, an ontological perspective opens and originates with the addressing of a reader or readers in which the poem defines itself, by this ultrarhetorical gesture, as being-to-be-read. The addresses precipitate an engagement between text and reader that throws into relief the mode of existence of each as fed by and feeding on the other. The significance of Dante's writing expressly to the reader is of an ontological order and rests in its bringing the being of the poem as an event for, as well as of, the reader in general into view.

This ontological perspective on poetry and *of* poetry is highly ambiguous. The addresses present the text to the reader and offer advice on how to interpret it. At the same time they are with*in* the text, and to this extent it is the text that presents the addresses. What we have, then, is a text that announces itself as not just a text. Dante's text projects itself as a discursive event, as situated enunciation. The addresses speak up for the fact that poetic discourse exists as enunciation as well as in textual form.[5] They activate a pragmatics of poetic discourse that begins problematizing such assumptions as that the poem is an object, a thing contained within the covers of a book. More importantly still, by their enactment of the potential of the poetic work to become an event of

4. Thus the approach being proposed here must be sharply distinguished from reader-response theories, as well as from the "literary anthropology" they lead to, which in some forms attempts to assimilate literature to empirical, scientific forms of knowledge rather than to escape all positivist epistemologies in the search for a specifically poetic mode of comprehension. See Wolfgang Iser, *Prospecting: From Reader Response to Literary Anthropology* (Baltimore: Johns Hopkins University Press, 1989).

5. The terms "discourse" and "enunciation," which I do not intend to use in special technical senses, are nevertheless inevitably colored by the jargon of "discourse analysis" used by linguists and narrative theorists such as Teun van Dijk, *Some Aspects of Text Grammars: A Study in Theoretical Linguistics and Poetics* (The Hague: Mouton, 1972); see overview of the field by Joyce Tolliver, "Discourse Analysis and the Interpretation of Literary Narrative," *Style* 24 (1990): 266–84.

understanding, the addresses open the way for the poem to be realized as a happening of truth. That truth (*alētheia*) should consist in disclosure of phenomena in an event of understanding is no new idea, notwithstanding the new philosophical sophistication reached in expounding it in the present century. Not only pre-socratic philosophy, as Heidegger's interpretations have insisted,[6] but also the biblical representation of a truth which is to be 'done' (as, for example, in 1 John 1.6 and John 3.21: "*poiōn tēn alētheian*") and which is revealed by events, finally by apocalypse, presupposes such a conception of truth as a happening of understanding in an event of disclosure.

The fact that the two most incisive and decisive of the addresses to the reader in the *Divine Comedy* (*Inferno* IX. 61–63 and *Purgatorio* VIII. 19–21) are both explicitly concerned with the reader's grasping the poem's truth indicates what is at stake in the discursive event the text projects: it is figured as an event of truth (truth itself being figured as something perceptible). Hence in *Purgatorio* VIII, we read:

> Aguzza qui, lettor, ben gli occhi al vero,
>   ché il velo è ora ben tanto sottile,
>   certo che il trapassar dentro è leggiero.
>
> (19–21)

> (Here, reader, sharpen well your eyes to the true,
>   for now the veil is so thin,
>   certainly, that passing within is easy.)

This passage particularly articulates the situatedness of the event of the poem, including the interpretive act it enfolds and is at the same time contextualized by, through its specification in terms of the here ("qui") and now ("ora"). As such, it implements or invites a transition from the atemporality and atopicity of the text as a script for possible readings to a specific act of interpretation. The poem that is read takes on the specificity proper not to a text in the form of an ideal scenario existing nowhere and anywhere a copy or trace of the printed book may be found, or its informational contents accessed, but rather to a unique event of enunciation. In this respect, as a discursive event taking place in a definite time and space, the reading of the poem tends to recuperate characteristics of a speech event.[7] And, in fact, an oral mode of discourse is intimated

---

6. Heidegger, *Early Greek Thinking*.

7. Cf. Ricoeur, "What is a Text?" pp. 145–46: "[T]his character of actualization reveals the decisive function of reading, namely that it achieves the discourse of the text in a dimension similar to speech. . . . In interpretation, we shall say, reading becomes like speech." Or in other words, "Avec les textes écrits, le discours doit parler par lui-même" ("with written texts, discourse must speak by itself"). Ricoeur, "La métaphore et le problème central de l'herméneutique," *Revu philosophique de Louvain* 70 (1972); 93.

in the syntactical dislocation of "certo che," which grammatically does not fit into the explanatory clause, for the "certo" should, strictly writing, operate within, not upon, the "that" ("che") clause. Yet this "certainly!" is quite normal as the sort of metasyntactical interjection that is common in actual speech. Hence the solecism marks a vestigial orality that serves as a reminder that the poem has its being in a situated event of reading or interpretation approximating a speech act.[8]

Dante uses speech and writing terms flexibly, as in "O tu che *leggi, udirai* nuovo ludo" ("O you who *read,* you will *hear* new sport"—*Inferno* XXII. 118), in what Paul Zumthor might describe as "oralité mixte" or "oralité seconde."[9] The moment a recipient is addressed, the text defines itself as situated discourse, whether this phenomenon is described in terms of an oral or written convention. For Dante, the written word itself has become an event, specifically an event of interpellation of the reader, rather than remaining merely a mimesis of spoken address. This may be motivated by the endeavor to emulate biblical truth, decidedly a truth of the written word, especially for a believer whose Bible is the Vulgate.

That precisely truth may happen in this language event, then, makes for a certain oscillation between the imagery of a speech event and that of a writing/reading event. For the text has an openness or repeatability in that it can always be entered into and activated anew; the text is never "over." Yet the utterance has a uniqueness and an actuality that is equally necessary to an event of truth as disclosure. Only thus could Dante imitate the true Word that is actually uttered and yet remains integrally intact and itself, according to the Augustinian paradigm of the Logos.[10] By maintaining its speech/writing ambiguity, Dante's poem, like the Logos, might retain both its transtemporality as a textual work and the singular actuality of an enunciatory event. By standing out from these two alternatives, avoiding reduction to the status of an object in either order, that is, to the positive material existence of either physical voice or script, the being of the poem as originary address shows up in relief.

8. For the transposition from orality into grammar and the general thesis that "la langue littéraire médiévale dans son ensemble est une mise en forme de l'idiome vernaculaire" ("medieval literary language on the whole is a formal setting down of the vernacular tongue"), see Bernard Cerquiglini, *La parole médiévale: Discours, syntaxe, texte* (Paris: Minuit, 1981). On the transition to literary models and its hermeneutic implications, see also Brian Stock, *The Implications of Literacy: Written Language and Models of Interpretation in the Eleventh and Twelfth Centuries* (Princeton: Princeton University Press, 1983).

9. Paul Zumthor, *La lettre et la voix: De la 'littérature' médiévale* (Paris: Seuil, 1987), pp. 18–19. Cf. also *Inferno* XXXIV. 23–24.

10. Augustine, *Confessions* 11, vii, 7. See discussion of Eugene Vance, "Saint Augustine: Language as Temporality," in *Mimesis from Mirror to Method, Augustine to Descartes,* ed. J. Lyons and S. Nichols Jr. (Hanover, N.H.: Dartmouth University Press, 1982).

From this point of view, perhaps more important than the hidden senses of any particular narrative events that need to be searched out, and more important than stabilizing the poem's status either as oral or as written discourse, what the apostrophes to the reader openly thematize is precisely the event of the poem as a happening that involves human existence in the instance of the reader as a site where meaning is to be realized and a revelation of truth to take place. What the poem *is,* brought in this way by Dante into view, cannot be directly described or analyzed any more than we can say what Being is. But we can remark ways in which the ontological perspective opened in and by the addresses renders perceptible presuppositions of poetic discourse commonly taken for granted and not thematically focused.

The inscription, by means of the address, of the reader's interpretive activity into the text, that is to say, the textualizing of the situational context of interpretation, means that rather than the text's being reduced to whatever the reader can get out of it, and so being qualified as a kind of appearance to the interpreter taken as reality, the reader qua reader gains self-awareness of her own reality only insofar as this is disclosed in, and in responding to, the text. In other words, the text is not just a sort of object appearing within the sphere of awareness of a reader who is taken as the bottom line, the reality in which textual fiction is finally cashed out; rather, the interpreter too becomes a signifier to be negotiated, a text to be determined as to its meaning in the event of interpretation. Thus is achieved, in the case of a fictional text (which may include all texts as woven, fabricated), a correlativity of fiction and reality. This is intimated by the specific terms of the text—beyond belonging to its textuality as such—of the address to the reader in *Purgatorio* VIII. A subtle play of sequentiality and phonetic similitude between "vero" and "velo" in "Aguzza qui, lettor, ben gli occhi al *vero* / ché il *velo* è ora" suggests how truth is intertwined with the concealment wrought by narrative or fiction, that is, the textual weaving of a veil.[11]

The reader, by becoming an instance within the poem, moves from the position of epistemological subject, a contextual reality outside the fiction, a fixed framework in conformity with which the fiction unfolds, to a position within an interpretive ontology set up by the poem. The reader becomes part of what is sometimes called "the world of the text."[12] Both the fictional world projected by the text and the "real"

11. These verses, as interpreted here, illustrate Roman Jakobson's dictum that in poetry "anything sequent is a simile." "Closing Statement: Linguistics and Poetics," in *Style in Language,* ed. T. Sebeok (Cambridge, Mass.: MIT Press, 1960), p. 370.

12. Such a notion is used in somewhat different ways by both Gadamer, *Truth and Method* (e.g., p. 428), and Ricoeur, *Interpretation Theory: Discourse and the Surplus of Meaning* (Fort Worth: Texas Christian University Press, 1976): "What has to be understood is not the initial situation

world of the reader, in which text and reader alike ordinarily figure as objects, are included as correlative participants in the interpretive ontology of the poem happening as an event of address by being interpreted as such.

Recognizing the discourse of the poem as direct address of a reader, then, allows not only the poem but also the reader to occur as an event. The reader, the author of interpretations of the poem, cannot stand or speak for a final ground of meaning of the poem, for the reader is rather one spoken to, the object of the action in speech of the address. Indeed, all such positive entities as text, reader, and similarly author can be articulated by the poem's discourse, but they cannot be any antecedent grounds for it in reality, if the address is to be hearkened to and so be taken seriously as an origin for the poem's meaning. Hence Ricoeur rightly takes the "injunction" inherent within the text as irreducible, as not just a function of any other known quantity like author or reader.[13] What speaks in the addresses escapes any pre-established definition from outside the action of address, which is a happening, a revealing, relative to which no extrapoetic identity, whether that of the individual poet or reader or even of the poem itself as textual artifact, retains its stability and simply is what it is.

As enunciatory event, the address to the reader places the poem within and in command of a general event of beings that has unbounded repercussions within and beyond the poem, and that is bound up with what is sensed to be characteristic and extraordinary about the *Commedia*. In the addresses is manifest an event not merely of the reader or of the author or of the text, but also more broadly of history, world, Being . . . occurring, we can only say, in the language of the address. The address to the reader enables, and in a freeing way constrains, us to understand poetry as an event of Being, and moreover to understand Being as event, for it shows how everything that has being, which is to say all beings, including such ordinarily privileged beings as subjects, appearing as reader and author in poetry and expressly in the address, are themselves made by the poetic event to which they belong, rather than standing outside it as its transcendental conditions.

What the addresses bespeak, beyond the reader, beyond the author, is

---

of discourse, but what points towards a possible world, thanks to the non-ostensive reference of the text. Understanding has less than ever to do with the author and his situation. It seems to grasp the world-proposition opened up by the reference of the text. To understand a text is to follow its movements from sense to reference: from what it says, to what it talks about" (p. 92).

13. Ricoeur, "What is a Text?": "[T]he intended meaning is not the supposed intention of the author, the vivid experience of *the writer,* into which we should have to transport ourselves, but rather that which *the text* wants to say. Not the psychological intention of the author, but the *injunction* of the text. What the text wants, is to orient our thought according to it. The sense of the text is the direction which it opens up for our thought" (p. 148).

the peculiar, ontological power of the poetic word to address, command, provoke, engage, and totally redefine a given situation or historical moment. The autonomy that belongs to discourse as such, as Ricoeur brings this out, or to language, as Heidegger pursues it on the way,[14] enables the poem as Dante creates it to assume (or at least simulate) characteristics of a free and personal agency, that is, to become, in a quasitheological sense, Word.[15] The address to the reader, as an instance of writing, invoking, and necessitating interpretation, triggers a dynamics of discourse in which the speaking agency cannot be reductively construed as an empirical individual or even in terms of finite constructions like "reader" or "Dante-author," because it is essentially characterized, rather, by the openness of the text and the infinity of language.[16]

Of course, the openness of the text is itself a mirror image of the open structure of readerly, interpretive existence (what in *Being and Time* figures as "futurity"). Even apart from the justification of Auerbach's proposition as correct concerning the history of rhetoric, an indisputable newness inhabits Dante's addresses, the newness belonging to the existence of the reader, an existence the reader is always endeavoring to possess anew no matter how old it is. For human existence, being temporal in nature, constitutes itself out of the not-yet as an anticipated retrieval of the already.[17] Whether or not the address to the reader, and in exactly what specificity, originates with Dante, or rather repeats some aspect of the perennial essence of poetry as something to-be-read, the addressing of the reader in the *Commedia* opens an origin for meaning in the reading of the reader, that is, it opens this origin of meaning to view by explicitly thematizing it. Even apart from its content as figuring the locale and

14. See essays in Martin Heidegger, *On the Way to Language,* trans. P. Hertz; originally published as *Unterwegs zur Sprache.* Ricoeur's thought on this matter is developed in the essays in *Du text à l'action: Essais d'herméneutique II.* See especially "La fonction herméneutique de la distanciation."

15. In this respect, by imitating the divine speech act in which the world is originated by the Word, Dante is in line with the Logos tradition of Christian theology finding its source text in the Gospel of John 1.3: "[A]ll things were made by him [the Word—*ho logos*], and without him was not anything made that was made." Implicitly—and apart from how he would have understood the act of address in his own theoretical terms—Dante appropriates this theological paradigm in an application of it to the poetic word.

16. Cf. Schleiermacher's previously quoted dictum: "Language is infinite because every element is determinable in a special way by the other elements."

17. *Being and Time* remains for this discussion the most detailed philosophical probing of an insight that actually animates the whole tradition of Western humanities and is massively incorporated, for example, into Virgil's *Aeneid.* In this work, a Trojan past is retrieved by the epic, empire-translating action of Aeneas and projected into an ideal Roman future also made to happen in the present through the hero's resoluteness, which anticipates, and thereby begins to enact, the future glory of the empire. This "historical" past of Aeneas in turn projects a heroic ideal and future possibility both anticipated and imperative in Virgil's own time, the Augustan Age.

occasion of an interpretive event, any appeal to or mention of someone who reads it conspicuously situates the text self-reflexively within an interpretive process being carried out by an historically existing individual whose mode of being may be modified by the text at hand and in act as structuring, occasioning, guiding, informing this existence.

The address to the reader is not new in any absolute sense even relative to the traditions Auerbach himself examines. He recognizes Dante's addresses' particular affinity with "religious apostrophe," for example in exegetical or apologetic Christian literature. But a crucial feature that is new about it is that Dante uses such a form of address in poetry as internal to its event, rather than only as a decorative trimming, such as one finds, for example, in Chrétien de Troyes, a sort of conventional statement by way of introduction to the poem, typically in order to solicit the attention and good graces of its audience.[18] Rather than deferentially apostrophizing an audience, Dante specifically draws a reader into his poem to participate as interpreter: reading becomes for Dante a dimension of interpretation in which the poem can happen as an event of truth. This event is projected from within the poem itself by its addresses, but it is not thereby confined to any framework of fiction or subordinated to the surrounding social ambience in which it would be digested along with other entertainments, for it potentially encompasses all realities, interpreting them and revealing their final truth by its own event as truth. Dante often chooses a dramatic climax of poetic representation, writing the reader right into it, while at the same time relating what is represented therein to the reader's extratextual reality. By this means, Dante opens up a dimension of interpretation in which poetic fiction becomes integrated into real existence and vice versa.

The universally acclaimed originality of Dante's poem, "unica nella storia della cultura occidentale,"[19] becomes a source of embarrassment as soon as anyone tries to show in what exactly it consists. There are virtually no elements in Dante's poem not to be found elsewhere in the ancient and medieval cultural repertoire, Auerbach's accent on the newness of the address to the reader notwithstanding. And yet, most every ap-

18. Gmelin, p. 130, gives examples of how "Chrestien von Troyes wendet sich in einigen Werken mehr oder weniger konventionell an den Zuhörer" (Chrétien de Troyes in some works addresses himself more or less conventionally to the hearer"). Another foil showing how in addresses antecedent to those of the *Commedia* an audience may be causally apostrophized is drawn by Gmelin from the *Chanson d'Aspramont:* "Plaist vos oïr bone cançon vallant / De Carlemainne . . . / Or vos dirai d'Aumont et d'Agolant" ("May it please you to hear good song and worthy / Of Charlemagne . . . / Now I will tell you of Aumont and of Agolant").

19. This phrase—"unique in the history of Western culture"—epitomizing a general consensus among specialists and an *idée reçue* among the literarily literate in general, is borrowed from Zygmunt G. Barański, "La lezione esegetica di *Inferno* I: Allegoria, storia e letteratura nella *Commedia*," p. 97.

proach to Dante is predicated on his presumed, almost peerless, originality and the need to define and account for it. The fact that nothing very definite that is adequate for this purpose can ever be produced may, after all, be the most suggestive sign that Dante's poem *is* indeed tremendously original, and in no trivializable sense—a sense, however, that makes it essentially *like* other poetry. Perhaps nothing explains it and its power, no technical innovation or audacity, because it is itself an origin, a "poiēsis" or making, and has succeeded historically in imposing itself as such on generations of readers.

The addresses to the reader, then, enable to the poem to be seen in its being, from the standpoint of its origination of a world. To the extent that a whole new ontological order is made possible in this event, it may be called, following Heidegger, an event of Being. Being happens in being understood, and perhaps equally in baffling understanding, and the address with its call to the struggle of interpretation signals this. By thematizing the kind of being the poem has, the way it is and, along with this, *that* it is, what the addresses ultimately bring into view is Being itself. For the focus on the question of what it means for this "made" thing, the poem, to be raises in exemplary fashion the question, What does it mean to be? It is especially the made thing, the thing that does not have to be but nevertheless is, gratuitously, that raises the question of Being through the fact that, after all, it *is*.[20]

Dante's ambition to see Being through poetry culminates in the visions of divinity, the supreme being, at the end of the *Paradiso*. Being, as revealed in the poem, has a totally theologized character including a universally embracing structure of providence. The epochal specificity of Being as disclosed by the *Commedia* will need to be delineated in order that the truth of Being the poem strives to reveal may shine out. But even apart from these specifics of content, what counts most for the Western speculative tradition running through Dante, as well as through Augustine and Heidegger, is the ontological perspective itself that the poem opens through its addresses.

Dante's Address to the Reader and Apostrophe in General

Dante's address to the reader achieves in a hermeneutically (and, in the final analysis, theologically) self-conscious way what poetry since Homer has achieved essentially through the use of apostrophe. The stock-in-trade of poetry generally, apostrophe or invocation enables poetry to pretend that everything and everyone is at the beck and call of poetic language. Such language thereby becomes in a broad sense prophetic,

---

20. See crucial development of this point by Heidegger, "Die Wahrheit und die Kunst," in *Der Ursprung des Kunstwerkes.*

revealing a world where language dictates life, where all are responsive to the poet's call, and in which the poet is figured as capable of communicating with every sort of being: "dead things with inbreathed sense able to pierce," as Milton puts it in *At a Solemn Music*.

The poetic afflatus exhaled in the act of apostrophizing permits the poet to address an animate, sentient nature and carry on a spiritual conversation with all creation—or at least claim to do so. Prima facie apostrophe is animistic, speaking to natural things, artifacts, and abstractions as though they could listen and respond. But what has been realized, especially by critics of romantic poetry like Harold Bloom and Jonathan Culler, is that the apostrophe always at the same time evokes the power of speech to animate, in particular the capability of the poetic word to create a linguistic universe where language is omnipotent. There is a recursive feature built into the apostrophe such that in exalting its addressee to animate status it also exalts itself and its own life-bestowing power.[21] This creative power—not specifically to animate but nonetheless interpretively to make things real—becomes the focus, rather than just an epiphenomenon, of apostrophe as Dante foregrounds it in his prophetic address directly to a reader. Of course, in bringing the quintessentially poetic act of apostrophe to consciousness of itself, Dante transforms its character, at once bringing it down to earth, down to such mundane realities as author and reader, and yet finding revealed precisely there, in the event of poetic art by and for human individuals, the spiritual work of a transcendent power.

Dante's I-Thou relation to a reader at first seems a much more prosaic instance of apostrophe than the "pantheism of apostrophic poems" evoked by Culler. There is no animistic magic involved in addressing speech to other ordinarily sentient, speaking beings like humans. And yet Dante's address to the reader reflects precisely on the way in which reality is made poetically in an event of interpretation where the "real" situation of a poem's event for actual readers is seriously taken into account. In an important way, this moves beyond the unmediated license to invoke anything and anyone in the free speech of apostrophic fiction. The address to the reader bespeaks poetry's use of its invocational prerogatives together with a further self-consciousness of how this power of invoking all manner of things that are not really present, and thereby apparently achieving a kind of magical transcendence over the constraints of time and place, is itself grounded in the relation to a reader who is really present at the event of reading the text. This grounds invocation in an event of interpretation that can reopen and redefine the boundaries of the real.

21. See Jonathan Culler, "Apostrophe," *diacritics* 7 (1977): 59–69.

The power of presencing that belongs to poetry and its magic, spe-
cifically to the spell of the apostrophe, is interpreted by Dante as funda-
mentally a function of an event of reading. This is the event that is
at once real and miraculous. Dante's invoking the reader does not make
the reader exist as interlocutor, as does the invoking of the West Wind.
Dante's apostrophizing a real person in the act of reading his poem maps
this key device of lyric and prophetic-poetic utterance onto the contex-
tual reality that is supposedly a given outside the bounds of his text. But
in so doing he inscribes, reciprocally, this extratextual reality into his
poetry and its event. The correlativity of reality and fiction, which is
latent within all apostrophe, thus comes to be thematically expressed in
the address to the reader. By this means, the transcendence that was fic-
tion or myth as pure apostrophe, in Dante's address, with its engagement
of the historical, existential reality of the reader, attains a dimension of
interpretation that can appropriately be called "prophecy."

With Dante's address to the reader, the mode of apostrophe, through
which poetry is capable of calling into presence and engaging in speech
in ways transcending normal powers, no longer articulates itself simply
as a transaction between the poet and his imagined world. Now, rather,
the presencing power of poetry expressly involves the reader as well. This
is a step from the imaginary to the real, from apostrophizing the beings
conjured up by poetic invention to addressing the empirical individual
who is reading. Thus Dante's forging of the device of the address to the
reader takes a step in the direction of demystification. It coincides with
Christian readings of pagan religion as myth reflecting psychological or
existential realities and even adumbrating the transcendent order that had
been prophetically revealed in biblical tradition.

What could be more straightforward, prosaic, and mundane than a
writer using forms of address to a reader, just as in letters and advertise-
ments? And yet the poetic afflatus is not in the least renounced by Dante's
address. Quite to the contrary, it is raised to a new level. The inspiration
of the muse is no longer construed, as in Homer, simply as the power to
be present to all that happened in the past.[22] This level of knowledge
now constitutes merely the historical sense of poetic narration. The pow-
ers invoked through the apostrophe to the reader concern sight or rather
insight into the truth of, in, and behind the presences of the literal level
of the narrative. What happens in the poem that happens within the
understanding of a reader is not just a sequence of ordinary or extraordi-
nary happenings, but rather the disclosure of truth. The poem, through
its addresses, shows how truth as disclosure is the general form of any

22. See the excellent discussion of George Dimock in *The Unity of the Odyssey* (Amherst:
University of Massachusetts Press, 1989), p. 8.

happening whatsoever considered hermeneutically, that is, as happening in the experience and understanding of some specifically situated individual.

Dante commonly uses apostrophe to invoke inanimate beings (like the river Po) and abstract entities ("Ahi Italia"), as well as persons dead and gone ("Da poi che Carlo tuo, bella Clemenza"), as if they were present and listening to his poem. But Dante's concentration on the address to the reader opens up a special dimension of all such apostrophes as they function in poetic discourse, a specifically interpretive dimension. In the apostrophe directly to the reader, the condition of pure pretense or fiction is transcended. The reader really can be called upon and can respond to the directives for interpretation articulated in the addresses. Indeed, upon just this response (or at least its possibility) depends the whole power of poetry to originate a world. With Dante, poetry is no longer content simply to pretend to call worlds into existence, nor even just to call attention to its own prophetic power presupposed for doing this, but goes a step further in calling attention to the real hermeneutic conditions that make possible this creative, seemingly magical working of poetry. Truly, it is as interpretation that poetry in all ages is able to effect its world-renewing miracle. This is implicit even in lyric apostrophe, designed, as Culler (and Frye before him) argues, to be overheard by a listener who will interpret the voice speaking with inanimate or immortal beings as inspired. Dante's poetry probes just this character of poetry as interpretation, from which all its peculiar powers derive.

Culler points out how often apostrophes in romantic poetry doubt their own power to effect the reality they project and so overcome the alienation of subject and object, man and matter, prevailing in the world as seen unpoetically: they may even parody their own apostrophizing. Typically, Keats's and Coleridge's lyrics end with a question whether the vision vouchsafed may have been no more than a figment of fantasy or a dream (Culler, "Apostrophe," p. 64). It seems that poetic apostrophe can actually work, without reservations, only for sincerely naive animism— or else, in Dante's way, for a faith like Christianity. The prophetic address by the author, in the name of a higher author, calling upon the reader to interpret, locates the animating principle in an event of human, meaning-seeking being in which may transpire a work of divine grace. In either case, what is ultimately at stake in the poetics of the apostrophe is the possibility (or necessity) of real religious experience.

Culler remarks that in general, apostrophe, in contract to other tropes, "makes its point by troping not on the meaning of a word but on the circuit or situation of communication itself" ("Apostrophe," p. 59). It exposes the presumed situational context, the ontological infrastructure, undergirding poetic enunciation. By dealing not only with a pretended but with a real situational context, and by dealing with it as such, Dante's address to the reader takes the prophetic powers of the poetic word a little more seriously than does the classical topos of the invocation of the Muses or of "buon Apollo" (*Paradiso* I), and reflects more deeply upon their ontological grounds. Dante's apostrophes in no way curtail poetry's claim that it transcends all empirical limits of time and place in its penetration of the inner life and reality of things, yet they reflect upon the natural conditions of communication between writer and reader as channeling this extraordinary event of supernatural grace. The miracle of Dante addressing us, his readers, today across the abyss of elapsed centuries—itself a specific heightening of the miracle of communication in absentia enshrined in any poem—accentuates what finally may be admitted to be a mystical sense present and speaking in the address. In the final analysis, the address to the reader, for those willing to believe, brings out the implicitly apostrophic character of poetry and language in general as harboring and intimating a revelation of a noncircumscribable transcendent reality of speech.

2. READER'S ADDRESS AS SCENE OF THE PRODUCTION OF SENSE

What the addresses to the reader disclose about the ontology of Dante's poem can be placed in perspective by considering the traditional way in which the question of the poem's relation to reality has been posed, together with the antinomies arising therefrom. Typically, the three-fold medieval classification of narrative into *historia, argumentum,* and *fabula* has served as the obligatory point of departure for determining the ontological status and claims, the *modus tractandi,* of the *Commedia.*[23] A determined effort to establish that its literal sense is presented as historical, or, in other words, that as narrative it falls under "historia," has been sustained by Singleton, Hollander, and others who, following a cue in Dante's (?) Letter to Can Grande together with the terminology of his *Convivio* (II, i), read the *Commedia* as an "allegory of the theologians,"

---

23. This classification finds a locus classicus in the *Etymologiae* (1 and 44) of Isidor of Seville. It was widely used in critical and theoretical literary discourse throughout the Middle Ages. It has been applied to Dante's *Commedia* by countless critics, influentially by Ernst Robert Curtius in *European Literature and the Latin Middle Ages,* p. 355 ff. The ontological bearing of these categories upon the poem is expressly stressed in Barański, "La lezione esegetica di *Inferno* I: Allegoria, storia e letteratura nella *Commedia*," p. 86: "Stabilita la narratività della *Commedia,* sorge la questione dello statuto ontologico di questo racconto. Benché al medievo mancasse una terminologia retorica costante, la divisione della forma narrativa in *historia, argumentum,* e *fabula* ebbe una diffusione pressappoco universale."

modeled on scriptural allegory, as this was understood in medieval exegetical tradition.[24]

As constantly reaffirmed throughout this tradition, not only is the literal sense of Scripture true in that it signifies historical facts. This would be the case for any true history or narrative. In Scripture, uniquely, the facts signified by the literal sense themselves signify other facts, and these other facts are the bases for the other, that is, the allegorical (or spiritual), meanings also intrinsic to Scripture's truth. That Scripture's allegorical meanings be signified by facts or things not just by words was made into an interpretive canon by St. Augustine's exegesis of Paul's use of the term "allegoria" in Galations 4. 24: "But where the Apostle says 'allegory,' he finds it not in words (non in verbis), but in things (sed in facto), since he shows that two testaments are meant by Abraham's two sons, one from a servant and one from a freewoman, which were not merely told of but in fact were."[25]

Following Augustine's massively influential distinction, this was, by common consent of exegetes, how allegory worked in Scripture, where real personages and events signified other historical realities. Normally, this form of allegory, which would also be called *allegoria in factis,* was recognized as uniquely the prerogative of the divine creator and author of all things. Just such a restriction is clearly stipulated by Thomas Aquinas:

> The author of the Holy Scriptures is God, in whose power it lies that not only words be ordered to a meaning (voces ad significandum accommodet), which man too can do, but also things themselves (sed etiam res ipsas). And therefore while in all branches of knowledge words signify, this science [theology] is unique in that the very things that are signified by words themselves also signify something. That first meaning, therefore, by which words signify things, belongs to the first sense, which is historical or literal. But that meaning by which things signified by words further signify other things is called the spiritual sense, which is founded upon the literal one and presupposes it.[26]

24. Charles S. Singleton, *Dante Studies I: Elements of Structure,* p. 88 and passim; Robert Hollander, "Dante *Theologus-Poeta,"* *Studies in Dante.*

25. *De Trinitate* 15, ix, 15, Patrologia Latina, vol. 42, p. 1069. Latin text: "Sed ubi allegoriam nominavit Apostolus, *non in verbis* eam reperit, *sed in facto,* cum e duobus filliis Abrahae, uno de ancilla, altero de libera, *quod non dictum, sed etiam factum fuit,* duo Testamenta intelligenda mostraret" (emphasis mine).

26. *Summa theologiae* 1, q. 1, art. 10, *Resp.* Thomas's denial that anyone besides God Himself can author allegory of the scriptural type follows also from the view that Scripture alone can have more than a literal sense: "Unde in nulla scientia, humana industria inventa, proprie loquendo, potest inveniri nisi litteralis sensus; sed solum in ista Scriptura, cuius Spiritus sanctus est auctor, homo vero instrumentum" (*Quaestiones quodlibetales* 7, q. 6, art. 3, *Resp.*). Precedents for Thomas's statement by Hugh of St. Victor and John of Salisbury are cited in Jean Pépin, *Dante et la tradition de l'allégorie,* p. 72.

Just this sort of writing with things rather than only with words is precisely what Dante, in the view of Singleton and company, would have undertaken to achieve in his theological allegory, his "poema sacro" imitating God's own way of writing, embarking on never-before-navigated poetic seas ("L'acqua ch'io prendo già mai non si corse"—*Paradiso* II. 7). And the defining characteristic of this way of writing, which perhaps in reality could be practiced only by God but which Dante could at least pretend to imitate, is that the things signified by the words themselves signify other things ("res significatae per voces, iterum res alias significant").

But is it not obvious, after all, that the things poets, or any speakers for that matter, designate with their words can themselves signify other things? Such further significances can be considered either to be merely conventional (for example, the patriotic things symbolized by the thing named "flag") or to belong to the things themselves by virtue of relations inherent in their natures (smoke signifies fire) quite independently of their occurrence in a poem or any other given communication. Indeed, the things designated by human discourse are necessarily significant of other things or beings, if for no other reason than that all beings in the world we know and refer to are signs of God their maker, as is affirmed by another familiar principle of Augustine's theory of signs.[27]

What usually seems to be overlooked in the discussion of *allegoria in factis* (and hence, equivalently, of scriptural and theological allegory) is that it is distinguished not simply by the *facta* verbally designated signifying other *facta;* this happens in any case, whether the writer intends it or not. What truly distinguishes an exceptional sort of writing is that this relation of significance between things itself be produced by, or even coincide with, the writing or verbal action of the allegory. Not that the things signified in turn signify other things, but that they be made to signify those things by the writing, or, in other words, that the writing be ontologically productive of the intrinsic significances of things, of meanings belonging to their very being—*this* is the veritably special sort of writing that there were grounds for believing was the exclusive privilege of the Almighty.

27. *De Trinitate* 6, x, 12. Augustine remarks that all things in virtue of possessing unity, kind, and order bear the *vestigia trinitatis.* This assertion of the universal symbolism of all creation of its Creator, of all beings of Being, is offered as a gloss on Romans 1.20: "Invisibilia Dei per ea quae facta sunt, intellecta conspiciuntur." This view of the universal allegory of creation is confirmed by Bonaventure in the prologue to his *Breviloquium,* which concisely states the basic metaphysical assumptions of *allegoria in factis* as we have been delineating it: "Quoniam autem Deus non tantum loquitur per verba, verum etiam per facta, *quia ipsius dicere facere est, et ipsius facere dicere;* et omnia creata tanquam Dei effectus innuunt suam causam: ideo in Scriptura divinitus tradita non tantum debent significare, verum etiam facta" (emphasis mine here and throughout in citations from medieval, originally manuscript works). *Opera omnia,* vol. 5 (Ad Claras Aquas [Florence]: Quaracchi, 1916).

What has not generally been emphasized, either in the exegetical tradition or in modern scholarship, is the necessary connection between the significant relations among real entities that are the ground of any *allegoria in factis* and the signifying procedures of allegory itself. The assumption about how the relations of significance in question are produced has been quite simply that God creates them by his absolute powers of disposing nature and history in accordance with his divine will. Does writing allegorically then supervene upon a fait accompli without impinging in any way on its constitution, without affecting 'what it is'? There is perhaps no urgent need to pose this question so long as God is considered to be the only maker of *allegoriae in factis*. To distinguish God's creative and providential activity (themselves only relatively distinguishable in orthodox Christian theology) from his activity as author of Scripture would be arduous and theologically bootless. His power and activity are in essence one; they are articulated in diversity only according to the economy of salvation, that is, relative to human beings. But when a human activity of writing is also in question, we need to carefully consider *why* it is consistently affirmed in the exegetical tradition that only God's word, Scripture, can signify things that then signify other things ("quod ipsae res significatae per voces etiam significant aliquid"). The proposition harbors a metaphysics of signification that is glossed over with the simple but hardly equivalent thought that God alone is omnipotent.

Indeed, the proposition concerning God's unique privilege to employ *allegoria in factis* rests on an unspecific subtlety. We accept it because we understand that to God is attributed an absolute sovereignty to make whatever he wills come about, to compose history as an author writes a book. We understand that this makes the crucial difference between his writing of allegory in the Scriptures and any human poet's efforts. Yet it is not quite enough to say that the things designated by scriptural allegory, and they alone, "signify" other things, if something distinctive or even unique to scriptural allegory is supposed to be indicated by this. What must be surreptitiously implied in this "signify" is that the signifying not only refers to events but actually, in a sense (precisely!), makes them. Abraham's son Israel by the freewoman Sarah can signify the New Covenant because God actually brings it about in the fullness of time that Christ is born free from sin and the first of many brethren. The signifying in scriptural allegory is continuous with the authoring of events in history. A human author might very well refer to Israel and even employ him as a figure of redemption in Christ. But the signifying relation in this case depends on what sacred history, itself a historiography in the Bible, establishes independently of this human signifying act.

Strictly speaking, *allegoria in factis* not only signifies other things through the things it directly refers to but actually enables those further

things to come to pass *as* the consequence and culmination of a signifi-
cant historical development. This is what human allegorical writing, sup-
posedly, cannot ordinarily do, but what Dante, exceptionally, would have
undertaken to achieve in the *Commedia*. His allegory emulates the divine
one in claiming to be ontologically efficacious. His allegory strives by its
interpretive powers to make things really so.

Sensing itself to be in the presence of a religious mystery, scholarship
tended to pass along the notion of theological allegory on the testimony
of tradition without actually trying to understand or directly experience
the possibility of its truth. Only so was it possible to blur together the
phenomenon of things signifying other things in general and the suppos-
edly supernatural power of immediately effecting things through words,
as in "Let there be light, and there was light." This result betrays an as-
sumption that the religious is totally alien from theoretical understand-
ing; where religious experience begins, thought ceases. But Dante's
poem, like Augustine's *Confessions,* struggles toward thoughtful, specula-
tive understanding of just such religious mysteries.

Not only modern scholarship but also the exegetical tradition itself
generally failed to interrogate the relation between the *allegoria in factis*
that God employs in Scripture as a signifying procedure and the real
relations among events or persons that it signifies. Its metaphysical pre-
suppositions allowed it to assume that the two spheres, the real and the
semiological, were completely independent. But when a human au-
thor—Dante—attempts to produce *allegoria in factis,* he can do so only
by employing instruments of signifying available to him through his po-
etic art. At this point it becomes crucial to consider the disposing of
reality and the signifying of *facta* in their interrelatedness. Such a connec-
tion is certainly not excluded or denied by the exegetical tradition: it is
fundamentally implied in the biblical doctrine of creation by the Word.
But there had been no need to distinguish moments of signifying and
of disposing the *facta* presupposed by the *allegoria in factis* until the author
in question no longer seemed to have unlimited and, finally, equivalent
powers to perform both. It was simpler and easier to rest content with
the unreflectively metaphysical conception of a God who can do all
things, writing and history making alike, without attempting to clearly
conceive the relation between the two, between signifying and effect-
ing reality.[28]

---

28. The assumption in discussions of allegory—including perhaps Dante's own—has tradi-
tionally been that there is a neat separation between things and language. This is reflected, for
example, in Maria Corti's discussion of Dante's "personale applicazione laica della *allegoria in
factis*," where this last term is understood as referring to something extralinguistic and "avantes-
tuale," in "Dante e la Torre di Babele: Una nuova 'allegoria in factis,'" in *Retorica e critica letteraria*,
ed. Lea Ritter Santini and Egio Raimondi (Bologna: Mulino, 1978), pp. 25, 31.

Now Dante, without denying or ever attempting to disguise the fact that the world he produces as poet is constructed by interpretation, nevertheless maintains (in effect, if not in intent) that his creations are themselves things (or at least ontologically bound up with things) that can signify other real things. God can do this because his creations are not just words, like those of ordinary poets; they are things or events (*res*), and they may signify other things by virtue of meanings written into them intrinsically by their creator and his intentions. Of course, Dante's poetic creations are in an immediate sense just words, but Dante grasps— at least qua poet—that as verbal signifying structures they can also have an ontological power. To be significant is to really be and effect something, and vice versa.

The poet can create significances by his interpretive art. And if these have the force of realities, being able to condition and shape what things are, then the poet uses words not simply to signify, that is, to denote things, but to signify further things that become what they are in and through the way they are signified. Dante, in imitation of and dependence upon the divine author, calls or mediates into being himself and his reader and a whole history of salvation by means of his poetic art of interpretation. But this art has a focal point in the event of reading, which is really an origin of meaning and of being. The significances that determine what things are in their being are open to being determined in this opening that is reading. The event of interpretation that Dante's addresses to the reader bring into focus is just such an ontologically real *factum* as can really signify other things, not just by conventional association but by effectively making them, or contributing to making them, what they are.[29] To the extent that the realities Dante's theological allegory designates are real in correlation with the reality of a reader—as is the case generally with human, historical realities—they can actually be forged by the signifying process under way in the interpretive event of the poem.

Thus the capital importance of the addresses to the reader is that they suggest that relations of significance such as make up the realities of history and world in the *Commedia* are actually forged on the basis of occurrences of interpretation involving a reader. The "historical sense" that gives Dante's narrative its ontological grounding ultimately rests not on past facts over and done with but on an event of sense making that hap-

---

29. That history, in Dante's vision, is made by acts of reading has already been persuasively argued in Dante criticism, in particular by Giuseppe Mazzotta. Through detailed examination of, for example, Dante's interpretations of Virgil and Augustine, with their subjections, appropriations, and misprisions, Mazzotta is led to conclude that "the act of reading emerges as the fundamental metaphor upon which Dante's view of history depends" (*Dante. Poet of the Desert,* p. 171).

pens in the historical existence of the reader invoked in the addresses. It is in the historical existence of the reader that the significances that define what things are can be effectually realized. And in the address to the reader we have something real, a discursive event, which actually contributes to creating the significances of other realities, the "facts" of history, such as they come to be meaningfully understood.

Dante's poetic adaptation of theological allegory in this way opens up insight into how things can signify things in the quite extraordinary sense in which they are considered to do so in biblical typology, namely, by being their historical fulfillment. That Christ is the fulfillment, in a typological sense, of all history—as good as the central claim of the Christian Bible—depends on establishing an order of significances that coincides with the very structure of historical reality. In biblical typology the significances of personages or events of Old Testament history are established by God in the form of real relations with personages and/or events in New Testament history. These significances are not merely conventional or invented correspondences, but are built into the reality of history itself, so as to be significances that are ontologically constitutive of the beings in question.

A likewise ontologically constitutive function is performed, at least arguably, by Dante's allegory in the *Commedia*. The significances revealed by the protagonist's journey and, through it, in the situated existence of the reader not only point or refer to allegorical, moral, and eschatological realities in the reader's life and field of possibilities; they actually bring these realities as possibilities for the reader into existence through their action of signifying them. This is truly to create an allegory *in res* or *in facto,* and thus Dante's claim of imitating the allegorical mode of God rests not only on arguments from the Letter to Can Grande and inferences from the poem's diction or other supposed hints about Dante's intentions. It has a further compelling rationale following from the way the poem effects its significances, rendering them active, in the appeal to a reader.

This can give some insight into why Dante tended to allegorize in the theological mode, whether or not he consciously intended to make the attendant theoretical claims—about which, in any case, considerable confusion was left in his wake.[30] It could be that his intention was neither

30. Opposition to Singleton's view by those who read the *Commedia* as an "allegory of the poets," maintaining the equally ancient position that its narrative is unequivocally a "fabula," begins with Richard Hamilton Green, "Dante's 'Allegory of the Poets' and the Medieval Theory of Poetic Fiction," *Comparative Literature* 9 (1957): 118–28. David Thompson, in *Dante's Epic Journey,* attacks the theological approach to the *Commedia* in modern, especially Singletonian, scholarship and endeavors to supplant the scriptural model for allegory with a literary one,

to make such claims nor to disclaim them, but rather to let the allegory perform its work of interrogating its readers and so of reoriginating their world and its possibilities (hopefully in the direction of regenerating them). In any case, he gave the allegory of his poem such a function by accentuating its address to the reader.

Rediscovery of the Ontological Significance of the Sign

Thomas Aquinas had attempted to deny all ontological efficacy and depth to poetic language. The poetic image was for him of no importance for what it intrinsically is, but only for its referent. In Augustine's terms, it was *signum tantum* (only sign) and not *res et signum* (thing and sign). Thus poetry could never be used to produce anything like an *allegoria in factis*. Thomas is very explicit and aggressive on this point. He denies poetic fiction every possibility of truth, for it can have only a literal/historical sense, no spiritual senses,[31] and if it is fiction, we can infer that even this first and only sense is in principle false. Language and poetry can at best be a sheer transparency to beings and their truth, without any intrinsic ontological density and dynamism. And here Dante would have to prove him wrong,[32] not by theoretical argument, but by originating a world in his poetry, that is, letting what he took to be *the* world, and what's more, the true world, find the site of an original self-disclosure in the interpretive and imaginative event of reading.

This rehabilitation of the ontological significance and efficacy of

---

specifically epic. His "argument" is that "Dante instead wrote allegory in the epic tradition, as it was conceived of in antiquity, in the Middle Ages, and in the Renaissance; and more specifically, that the *Aeneid*, as allegorized by Bernard Silvestris, afforded Dante a significant precedent for his two-fold physical/spiritual journey" (p. 11). Cf. also Thompson's "Figure and Allegory in the *Commedia*," *Dante Studies* 90 (1972). A discussion that succeeds amazingly well in doing justice to and in integrating the opposed views of Dante's allegory is Peter Armour's "The Theme of Exodus in the First Two Cantos of the Purgatorio," in *Dante Soundings,* ed. D. Nolan (Dublin: Irish Academic Press, 1981).

31. *Quaestiones quodlibetales,* 7, q. 6, art. 16, ad 3: "Significare autem aliquid per verba vel per similitudines fictas ad significandum tantum ordinatas, non facit nisi sensum litteralem, ut ex dictis patet. Unde in nulla scientia, humana industria inventa, proprie loquendo, potest inveniri nisi litteralis sensus; sed solum in ista Scriptura, cujus Spiritus sanctus est auctor, homo vero instrumentum; secundum illud Psalm. 44, 2: *Lingua mea calamus scribae velociter scribentis.*" Cited in part in Armand Strubel, "'Allegoria in factis' et 'allegoria in verbis,'" *Poétique* 6 (1975): 355. For example, the image of the goat in Dan. 8.21 signifies the "king of Greece" in such a way that the literal sense of the word and image of goat is this king. The literal sense identifies itself with the metaphorical sense, what the author intended to denote, eliding any other putatively immediate sense attaching to the signifier. The goat itself does not in any way (i.e., figuratively) embody the king of Greece. It is simply used metaphorically in this sense, and any other image would be fully equivalent for this purpose. *Quodl.* 7, q. 6, art. 3, ad 2. See Johan Chydenius, "La théorie du symbolisme médiéval," *Poétique* 6 (1975): 339.

32. Cf., however, Hollander, "Dante *Theologus-Poeta,*" p. 84, reading Dante as taking sides *with* St. Thomas in the polemic against poetry.

poetic language has carried on into modern times, for example in the symbolist poets, and has sparked interest as a vital issue especially in contemporary thought. Dante's extreme sensitivity to the problem of signification as properly linguistic in nature, his poetic awareness of language and of its event as address, can be helped to stand out in relief by the perspective of some forms of modern linguistic theory.[33] Structuralist linguistics, as reflected, for example, in the work of Émile Benveniste, has been especially important in reversing the priority of signified over signifier that has been considered typical of the medieval period[34] and in the discovery of language as an origin of world and being. Tzvetan Todorov has specifically studied the Christian exegetical tradition, deploying a modern structuralist apparatus to reformulate its distinction between factual and verbal allegory.[35] He attends to the linguistic considerations that were elided in the thought of the exegetes who gave precedence to metaphysics over language and finds that the dichotomy *in factis/in verbis* collapses into a "symbolisme des faits." It is this collapse that Dante anticipates by refusing to abide within the terms of the dichotomy, realizing that his verbal work as poet could effectively work upon things and their intrinsic significance.

For the exegetes, at least theoretically, language supervened upon a universal order already perfectly constituted as to what it was as well as what it signified. All was ultimately a sign of God. But the significances that Dante's poem discloses emerge in and through the dynamisms of language.[36] Though he may have shared the same metaphysical outlook as contemporary exegetes, he also envisaged something else besides. He manifests a sense of how things in their significance come to experience as real through the handling of language and through an interpreter's existential engagement in its event in poetry. The language-event becomes for him the site of an original production of sense—which does not exclude that this might be caused antecedently at a superior ontological level by a primary cause, namely, God.

In fact, medieval metaphysics and ontology tended to presuppose a

33. At the same time we are reminded that "the 'modernist' bias given to [Dante's] linguistic thought has potentially distorting implications" by Zygmunt Barański, "Dante's Biblical Linguistics," *Lectura Dantis* 5 (1989): 105.

34. See, e.g., Ruth Morse, *Truth and Convention in the Middle Ages: Rhetoric, Representation and Reality* (Cambridge: Cambridge University Press, 1991): "[M]edieval (and many renaissance) readers and writers seem to have thought they could read through or across conventional styles, narrative types, and languages to a kind of prelinguistic core of truth that lay underneath" (p. 3). The "main point" is that for medievals, through howsoever various expressions, "there was *a* reality to be expressed" (p. 20).

35. Tzvetan Todorov, "On Linguistic Symbolism," *New Literary History* 6 (1974): 111–34.

36. The full appreciation of this point depends on some acquaintance with the sorts of interdependencies of language and the significance of things in Dante's poem that have been

world conceived as intrinsically linguistic in nature.[37] The priority of be-
ing to knowing assumed by the medievals on the basis of Aristotelian
philosophy was fundamentally complicated through the influence of bib-
lical Logos theology harboring the sorts of realizations concerning the
linguisticality of being as it is known humanly that reach maturity in
modern hermeneutic thought but can be found to be embodied prolepti-
cally in Dante's poem as an experiment in signification.

Admittedly, such suppositions as that the nature of things should be
revealed to humans precisely through language and in correspondence
with their linguistic structurations of a world, and that the way of draw-
ing humanly nearer to a knowledge of things even in their absoluteness
should pass only by way of a reflective consciousness trained on its own
activity of signifying, may run counter to certain ingrained habits of
thinking that Dante may very well be expected to have shared. And yet
that hardly kept him from forging ahead on his journey of discovery of
all that was latent within the linguistic medium of his art. Religious rea-
sons and orthodox justifications could always be found for the explora-
tion of the new seas of culture and speculation that his project propelled
him toward. Whenever he risked curtailing certain of its precepts, he was
at the same time always in line with fundamental impulses of the faith in
its catholic embrace of the full range of human experiences and signifi-
cances all the way down to their existential grounds.

Julia Kristeva views the period in which Dante lives, especially in so
far as it saw the antefacts and the rise of nominalism in philosophy, as a
phase of historic change that would restore to the signifier its dynamism
by releasing it from a position of total subservience to the signified and
to things. "The second half of the middle ages (13th–15th Centuries) is
a period of transition for European culture: the thought of the sign sup-
plants that of the symbol."[38] Kristeva understands the symbol in terms of
the function of referentiality, and hence of external relation to a being
constituted independently of the signifying process. The new situation
that arises with the ascendency of the sign is one in which signifiers, in
their autonomy purely as language, are no longer strictly constrained by
their extralinguistic object but can be recognized as being themselves
productive of significances. Kristeva particularly stresses the multiple gen-
erative and transformational capacities of the sign, its infinite metonymic

---

prodigiously brought forth by the painstaking work of innumerable critics, and particularly
by Mazzotta.

37. See Marcia Colish, *The Mirror of Language: A Study in the Medieval Theory of Knowledge*,
rev. ed. (Lincoln: University of Nebraska Press, 1983), p. 1 ff.

38. Julia Kristeva, "Du symbole au signe," *Tel quel* 34 (1968): 35. Cf. also Umberto Eco,
"L'epistola XIII, l'allegorismo medievale, il simbolismo moderno," in *Sugli specchi e altri saggi*
(Milan: Bompiani, 1985).

combinatory potential, as it comes to be newly discovered in this epochal transition. We might add that this production of significance is tantamount to ontological productivity, once the categories of meaning and being are no longer held rigidly apart as mutually impermeable. It becomes all the more conceivable, in light of Kristeva's thesis concerning the newfound productivity of the sign in his time, that Dante should have found in his address to the reader a locus for bringing into focus the ontological import of the signifying act.

A Word about Metaphysics

If I point out the metaphysical character of the doctrine of allegory *in factis,* it is not to imply that there is something illegitimate in this, but only to indicate that it leaves the connection between signifying reality and its making or effecting unilluminated and mysterious. Thought, especially as hermeneutically understood, inevitably and properly opens in the end upon mystery. Nevertheless, it remains possible to think through the relation to and experience of mystery. This is something poetry can help to achieve.

As an integral part of itself, the present project enfolds a defense of the possibility of metaphysical knowledge such as we find it represented in the *Divine Comedy.* Of course, this is no purely rational or philosophical knowledge; it is rather a poetic knowing and thinking. Yet, I would maintain, so was the great metaphysical thinking of the past, even that of those known to tradition as philosophers and theologians.[39] At least since the Enlightenment—and so with the hegemony of a scientific paradigm for measuring all claims to truth—metaphysics has been held in deep suspicion. In systematic ways since Kant, philosophy has continually endeavored to draw the bounds of the knowable so as to expose the illegitimacy of claims to rational knowledge that reaches beyond what have been determined as the conditions of the possibility of knowing for human beings. But blanket legislation against metaphysics not only fails to understand the poeticality, the creative making, inherent in the Logos and expressed in genuinely speculative metaphysics; it also makes a categorical, absolute claim about the limits of knowing that cannot be justified by its own criteria, for the totality it circumscribes is not itself given empirically, like all the items within it.[40] To know the bounds of knowing

---

39. Cf. Mircea Eliade, *The Sacred and the Profane: The Nature of Religion,* trans. W. Trask (New York: Harper & Row, 1967), p. 95, and B. Madison, "Metaphysics as Myth," in *The Hermeneutics of Postmodernity: Figures and Themes* (Bloomington: Indiana University Press, 1988).

40. Hence the paradoxes of set theory that show the incapacity of mathematical reasoning to be a self-contained system of truth. The issue reaches a high degree of sophistication in Gödel's Incompleteness Theorem.

in some unbounded way, ruling out anything "meta," is as unwarrantable
a pretension as metaphysics ever concocted.[41]

3. TRUTH, SENDINGS, BEING ADDRESSED: DECONSTRUCTION VERSUS HERMENEUTICS OR DIALOGUE WITH DERRIDA?

"Hermeneutics" has become a frequent target of attack today from those
who have closed ranks under the banner of "deconstruction." In recent
years, a call to arms, "beyond hermeneutics," has often been heard in
various subtitular forms summoning this particular faction of the literary-
theoretical avant-garde to conferences.[42] Such musters have even been
known on occasion to turn into virtual pogroms where hermeneutics
serves as a scapegoat whose condign chastisement and ritual banishment
are carried out presumably to permit criticism, or better "writing" (écri-
ture, Schrift), to enter into some Dionysiac festival of free play of the sig-
nifier, liberated from bondage to any transcendental signified.

This, of course, represents a travesty of deconstruction's subtle and
complex insights. My staging its latent violence in this way is meant
to suggest how the very power of these insights risks betraying them
into the hands of just the sort of self-affirmation through negation of
the other, the very logic of opposition and repression, that deconstruc-
tion is in fact conceived to dismantle. Admittedly, Derrida's pronounce-
ments on deconstructive strategy have sanctioned an initial "phase" of
reversal consisting in the inversion of hierarchical structures (and their
violence), whose oppositional terms in a second phase must be reinscri-
bed in a new, nonoppositional conceptual space.[43] Nevertheless, it is im-

41. Panajotis Kondylis, *Die neuezeitliche Metaphysikkritik* (Stuttgart: Klett-Cotta, 1990),
brings out the interdependence of metaphysics and its critique, from medieval nominalism to
the purportedly definitive rejections of modern times. A nuanced understanding of how the
critique of metaphysics also always lies within it can be found in Heidegger's "Uberwindung
der Metaphysik," in *Vorträge und Aufsätze.*

42. The conflict between the French deconstructive and the German hermeneutic currents
in contemporary theory was brought to a forum in April 1981 in the historic debate beween
Derrida and Gadamer sponsored by the Goethe Institute in Paris. Gadamer's opening address,
"Text and Interpretation," together with Derrida's answer in the form of three questions, plus
further materials by each, can be found in *Dialogue and Deconstruction: The Gadamer-Derrida
Encounter* (Albany: State University of New York Press, 1989). Some of the same materials are
also available, with illuminating comments by Maurizio Ferraris and Gianni Vattimo, in *aut aut*
217–18 (January–April 1987).

43. For example, in *Positions* (Paris: Minuit, 1972): "Il faut donc avancer un double geste
. . . d'une part, traverser une phase de *renversement*" (It is therefore necessary to advance a double
gesture . . . on the one hand, to traverse a phase of reversal"—p. 56). Mark C. Taylor, in
Erring: A Postmodern A/theology (Chicago: University of Chicago Press, 1984), explains that "If

portant to distinguish Derrida's writing from what Rodolphe Gasché calls "deconstructive criticism," which "obeys laws and follows intentions that are not at all those that underlie Derrida's philosophical enterprise."[44] My immediate concern is to dispel the presumption that hermeneutic projects such as Dante's and my own are impossible or illegitimate (except in so far as being impossible may be necessary and being illegitimate appropriate). This is only a first layer of response to generalized attacks on hermeneutics. It has to do with what can be an antagonistic aspect of deconstruction when distorted into a general paradigm rather than with Derrida's seminal thinking on the address, which, with its opportunities and challenges for interpretation, calls to be dealt with in detail in another context—to come.[45]

Whatever disentanglement or "twisting free" of the metaphysics of representation may be attained by deconstruction cannot be the recuperation of an original state before hermeneutics, any more than it can be an eschatological state after hermeneutics: only reactively or interactively, in its relation to hermeneutics and interpretation as traditionally understood, can deconstruction operate freely or at all, precisely in its differential relation to what it confronts as its other and calls "hermeneutics." The questionableness of every hermeneutic venture is the element within which deconstructive criticism makes its way, thriving on the inherent weaknesses of its host.[46] But the generic rejection of hermeneutics, treated as an impediment to be removed, goes against the grain of its own differential logic.

Deconstruction has without doubt prodigiously sharpened critical insight into the inescapable rhetoricity and textuality of our communicative practices. Nevertheless, its insight remains parasitic upon creative projects of synthetic thinking, with their inevitable, constitutive gaps and glitches. Deconstruction is not radical and skeptical enough if it succumbs to the delusion of having found, or of ever finding, a new dis-

---

hierarchical oppression and repression are to be overcome, it is necessary to *pass through* a phase of inversion. But reversal can remain caught within a dyadic economy of conflictual opposition. . . . In place of simple reversal, it is necessary to effect a dialectical inversion that does not leave contrasting opposites unmarked but dissolves their original identities" (p. 10).

44. Gasché, *The Tain of the Mirror: Derrida and the Philosophy of Reflection* (Cambridge: Harvard Univesity Press, 1986), p. 3.

45. Derrida has meditated extensively on the address in "Pas," in *Parages* (Paris: Galilée, 1986); "Comment ne pas parler: Dénégations," in *Psyché: Inventions de l'autre* (Paris: Galilée, 1987); *La carte postale* (Paris: Flammarion, 1980); and elsewhere. Detailed discussion of this material is at the fore of the agenda for the sequel broached at the end of this book.

46. The paradoxical relation of host and parasite in deconstruction is taken up by J. Hillis Miller, "The Critic as Host," in *Deconstruction and Criticism* (New York: Seabury, 1979); first published in *Critical Inquiry* 3 (1977): 439–47.

course, free from ontological shadows and hermeneutics, to replace an old, invalidated, "metaphysical" discourse.[47] The idea of purging language of erroneous assumptions and metaphysical underpinnings, of defining some sort of philosophically correct or clean form of discourse, is in fact absurd on deconstruction's own contamination-conscious premises, and could only result in radically impoverishing and constraining discourse, which might better be left free to express ontological prejudices—that is, reference to "what is"—perhaps even as belonging to the inherent poeticality of language and its constitutive tendency to express and objectify.

Dante's address to the reader, with its orientation to "truth," epitomizes the structures of authorial intentionality and a transcendental signified that have been impugned by deconstructionist writers, among other sorts of "postmoderns." Moreover, the present "hermeneutic" treatment deliberately underscores the "ontological" character of Dante's language of address, the grounding of language in being or existence and vice versa, which has become anathema to this influential current in contemporary theory. The critique, spurred by Derrida's playing upon Heideggerian metaphors of a sending ("Schicken") and destiny ("Schicksal") of Being,[48] has even modulated into a parodic mode, caricaturing the traditional interpretive apparatus of communication as a transcendental postal system.[49] A postal metaphorics has been played with and exploited in an attempt to wreak havoc on the hermeneutic paradigm established on just

47. This is in fact emphatically stated by Derrida: "*[I]l n'y a aucun sens* à se passer des concepts de la métaphysique; nous ne disposons d'aucun langage—d'aucune syntaxe et d'aucun lexique—qui soit étranger à cette histoire [de la métaphysique]; nous ne pouvons énoncer aucune proposition destructrice qui n'ait déjà dû se glisser dans la forme, dans la logique et les postulations implicites de cela même qu'elle voudrait contester" ("*It makes no sense* to forego the concepts of metaphysics; we do not possess any language—any syntax or vocabularly—which is foreign to this history [that of metaphysics]; we are incapable of enunciating any deconstructive proposition that has not already had to slip into the form, logic and implicit premises of the very discourse it wishes to contest"). "La structure, le signe, et le jeu dans le discours des sciences humaines," in *L'écriture et la différence* (Paris: Seuil, 1967), p. 412.

48. See especially Derrida's address to French-speaking philosophical societies at Strasbourg, "Sending: On Representation," in G. Ormiston and A. Schrift, eds., *Transforming the Hermeneutic Context;* first published in English in *Social Research* 49 (1982): 294–326; originally published as "Envoi," in *Acts du congrès des societés de philosophie de langue francaise* (Neuchâtel: Édition de la baconnière, 1981). Derrida's questioning of hermeneutics and its metaphysical underpinnings, with frequent attention to Heideggerian versions of destiny and "destinerrance," is pursued passim in a wide spectrum of his works, including *Éperons: Les styles de Nietzsche* (Chicago: University of Chicago Press, 1978) and *Otobiographies: L'enseignement de Nietzsche et la politique du nom propre* (Paris: Galilée, 1984).

49. This picture is elaborated by John Caputo in *Radical Hermeneutics: Repetition, Deconstruction, and the Hermeneutic Project.* Despite its aim to salvage some form of hermeneutics by reconciling Derrida to a "demythologized Heidegger," this work tends to exemplify the sort of reversal of hermeneutics by deconstruction that, from my perspective, risks misconstruing both.

such pillars of the philosophical or literary canon as the *Divine Comedy*.

Postal images, as a matter of fact, seem rather apt for the communication system enacted by Dante's addresses. The "vero" which the "lettore" is supposed to see, the message he is supposed to receive, is given the character of a "sending" by the instance of the address. Since the meaning, the truth and teaching, of the poem is addressed expressly to the reader, the scene of reading evoked in the apostrophes to the reader may be construed as the "address" at which the sending of significance is supposed to arrive. As has already been stressed, not just the *locus* nor even just the moral self-consciousness, but the very being of the reader may be said to be "called on" in the address. Dante's address in these respects represents the archetypal hermeneutic situation that has come under suspicion in a self-styled "posthermeneutic" age of culture.[50]

A question often presumed to be fundamental to, and unequivocal in, this problematic of missive and address, though not necessarily by Dante, is "Do these sendings arrive?" Believers in the communication system are culpably naive if they suppose that its messages arrive in some straightforward fashion, "special delivery."[51] Sophisticated analysis of the signifying process can be deployed to show that the messages sent by the "onto-hermeneutic" postal system to the reader's address, and even to the reader's being, having been sent by the author or even from Being, can never actually arrive. For structural, or, more exactly, poststructural, reasons, Derrida would seem to have shown that the system cannot work, but rather is conditioned by failure in its very possibility of generating significance. Significance arises precisely from the difference and the deferral of the message received with respect to the one that was supposedly sent but, as a matter of fact, is never ascertainable at all in its original integrity. Indeed, given the differential structure of signification, there is really no original message at all, no self-identical meaning that could even in principle be transmitted from sender to receiver.

But Dante does not say what the truth or message or meaning is outside of the situation that is set up by the address. The allegory of the poem is never disclosed except in and by the action of the address. That is why the reader, even within the figurative rhetoric of the poem itself,

50. A relatively early sally was made by Susan Sontag's *Against Interpretation* (London: André Deutsch, 1962), arguing that criticism should concern itself with sharpening and intensifying the sensory experience of art, hence with the vocabulary of form rather than with content and consequently with substituting meanings for the work of art itself. "In place of a heremeneutics we need an erotics of art" (sec. 10). In other words, it seems criticism is to guide response to something more like a sex object than a personal address.

51. Caputo, *Radical Hermeneutics,* p. 170: "Getting over the postal principle means that we stop waiting for the mail as if it contained a private message coming special delivery." "[A]ll there is (il y a) is the plurality and plurivocity of dispatches flying in every different direction."

must look to find the meaning hidden beneath the allegorical veil of the strange verses. The poem and the truth of the poem are actually addressed to the reader, and all that the poem says is said in this form of address. Should we conclude, then, in typically modern fashion, that the meaning just *is* what the reader in the event of being addressed determines it to be? Have we not then found out the real meaning behind all the transcendental imagery? Or is Dante perhaps more open-minded and rigorous, less grasping after certitudes, in leaving open the possibility that even this meaning, one to be grasped only by the reader, may neverthe-less have some antecedence in an event by which the readers and their reading and perhaps whole existence are in turn grasped?

The address, because of its being both within and outside the poem's rhetoric of fiction, maintains an ambiguity about the message's possibly being sent from or "representing" a *signifié* beyond the whole signifying system, which too one-sided and self-confident a deconstruction does away with, short-circuiting the structure of deferral of the signified by finally closing the latter out altogether, completely erasing the difference between signifier and signified. The question whether a message can be heard, or whether an authority can be heeded, might best be left open to determination by the one who is being addressed, instead of being foreclosed at a systemic, structural level by an appeal to philosophical rigor. The certainty that no post will arrive, no claim be made, no address demand a response, no responsibility become personal, and so on seri-ously risks reducing risk, making things easier, rather than "restoring life to its original difficulty," as Caputo indicates he means (nota bene) to do.

Dante's poem transpires within the discourse of the address. This maybe goes for any poem as "made" by someone, which is as good as to say *for* someone.[52] Letting this discursive event occur is less dogmatic and "essentializing" than saying what it cannot be—legislating against its possibly being an event of truth or meaning, when the very meaning of truth and meaning is opened to interrogation and to receiving new, other sense in the address. Are we supposed to *believe* the denials stating that there are no origins, no identities, no truth, and so concede that these denials are true? They can point out some of the complications and con-structedness involved case by case very time "truth" is disclosed. Admit-tedly, any origin or coming to be of truth, at least by the time it is appre-hended by us, can always be shown to entail the work of artifice, that is, of *poiēsis*. But does this insight ever give us exhaustive knowledge of what may be in it or behind it, that is, of how the constructedness itself may

---

52. Compare Derrida: "[A]ll language, all writing, every poetico-performative or theoretico-informative text dispatches, sends itself, allows itself to be sent." "No Apocalypse, Not Now! (Full Speed Ahead, Seven Missiles, Seven Missives)," *diacritics* 14 (summer 1984): 29.

come about, be given? The tacit assumption is that since order, unity, meaning are constructed, then nothing! There was never anything in it, behind it, whatever. It was just—made up! *Constructedness* is the answer, the alpha and omega, the origin, what there was "in the beginning." So it is an illusion, we seem to be assured, to look for anything more.

This is *not* the lesson imparted by Derrida's texts, always obsessed by the address and by its "something more." We may very well concede that this voice and calling are (whatever else they may also be) "effects of discourse," but who (certainly not Derrida) "knows" what discourse is, or whose? Care belongs in the first instance to the address being attended to before any decision can be made as to the ontological status of sendings and sender. Existential claims (there exists an x . . .) and existential denials (e.g., God does not exist, there is no unified or original sense) are from this point of view subordinate to and comprehended within the event of the address in language. An awareness of being addressed existentially precedes, or is, in any case, equiprimordial with, any specific determination as to the meaning of a communication.

Our being addressed, if we allow it to, speaks with a prior claim under which reality is already subsumed, such that our very notion of what counts as real depends on our sense of a dialogical context.[53] This situational reality is assumed before it is even possible to begin making conscious judgments as to real existence or lack thereof. The notion of any statement's being warrantable or not depends on the possibility of confirmation from a partner in dialogue (or at least on the iterability of its affirmation in dialogue with oneself). This situation may be considered as neither real nor unreal but as simply the condition for any discrimination between the two, and to this extent the address, and poetic and religious discourse (or prayer) *as* address, are more ontologically uncommitted than any constatives that might be deployed to "deconstruct" them.

Though it demands effort, the tension toward truth is worth maintaining, for it might actually give something significant, as Dante's struggles show. Dante already envisages the message, the allegorical meaning, as to-be-determined in conjunction with the situated, factical being of reading. But this does not necessarily imply that therefore no message can get through, that any claim to true understanding is a sham. Dante already sets his poetic signifiers free to produce meanings autono-

53. Giambattista Vico imagines man primordially, by universal human nature discoverable in the modifications of our own minds, as in a dialogical relation with the reality around him, interpreting natural phenomena as "wanting to say something." The poet-theologians who first created a human culture are said to have been moved in particular by the phenomenon of lightning. They imagine the sky to be the body of Jove, and that this first of the gods" "col fischio de' fulmini e col fragore de' tuoni volesse loro dir qualche cosa." *Principi di scienza nuova*, ed. P. Rossi (Milan: Rizzoli, 1971), 2, i, 1.

mously (see sec. 2 above), but that does not prevent them from finding meanings in this very process that may also be in some other way or perspective antecedently given, "predestined." Even through all the mediations of artifice and constructedness, which he deliberately exposes and foregrounds, the tension toward truth is sustained. Shall we say, in the modern way, that it is just this tension itself which counts? Or should we rather allow that the tension might possibly reveal itself from a broader or more multifaceted perspective as a response, not only an autonomous exercise in "free play" but actually a response to a claim, to being addressed?[54] Dante risks personally addressing a message to his reader. He does so in such a way as to imitate and participate in the traditional structure of address of the word of God to the individual heart or conscience. Can the reader risk responding accordingly? This may mean, in application, not simply accepting Dante's orthodoxy so much as searching to respond, after Dante's example, to the truth or passion, and in any case the disclosure, that claims one.

The address is not just a point of arrival, any more than its message is just a content. The address, rather, is the very structure of the discursive world that is in question in the claim the poem makes. And the message it addresses to the reader is not decidable in abstraction from the actual existence of the reader here and now ("Se tu sei or, lettore")—which motivates its being unspecified per se but having to be sought out by the reader (in some sense *as* the reader involved as a locus taken up and occupied in an event of disclosure). Some such necessity of application and appropriation seems quite generally to constitute the motivation for allegory in Western tradition,[55] and it is often expressed in the form of an imperative to maintain secrecy. Indeed, the inherent secretiveness of the allegorical text can be understood as a precursor to the necessary errancy implied in "différance."[56] The allegorical method built into Dante's hermeneutic addresses to the reader in fact presupposes a *lack* of evident sense in the narrative. For the application to one's own life in which a text's meaning is appropriated requires an open-endedness

---

54. In Derrida's own readings especially of literary texts the analysis of play in its unending freedom leads persistently to responsibility to "the call of the other." Consult, for example, selections in Jacques Derrida, *Acts of Literature,* ed. Derek Attridge (New York: Routledge, 1992).

55. See, for example, Jon Whitman, *Allegory: The Dynamics of an Ancient and Medieval Technique* (Cambridge: Harvard University Press, 1987), or Hans Jonas, "Myth and Mysticism: A Study of Objectification and Interiorization in Religious Thought," *Journal of Religion* 49 (1969): 315–29.

56. A brilliant contemporary handling of the problematic of sending and transmitting truth, stressing its inherent deferrals and differences, in traditional hermeneutic terms, dealing particularly with the interpretation of the Bible, is Frank Kermode's *The Genesis of Secrecy: On the Interpretation of Narrative* (Cambridge: Harvard University Press, 1979).

and indefiniteness or even downright obscurity of meaning in the text it-self in order that its meaning might originate anew in a unique life situation.[57]

What is sent to the address of the reader comes in the form of a truth, a "dottrina," a meaning. But meaning, as Heidegger points out in *Sein und Zeit* (sec. 32), is precisely the "upon-which" ("Woraufhin") of a pro-jection. The meaning is not wholly other than or unrelated to readers, but rather correlative with their projection of the possibilities of their own existence. This is a decisive reason why Dante cannot make it ex-plicit but must resort to allegory. It also reveals allegory as inherently temporal in structure, hiding at the same time as it discloses, disappoint-ing by its deferrals and recurrent relative *in*significances, given that the significance never arrives neatly objectified in a package, but comes, if at all, with the projection of a structure like faith that can never be fulfilled *within* the conditions of the world, since it has to do with our very way of having a world that is significant. In Dante's poem meaning is emphat-ically the upon-which of a projection. This is first and foremost evident in that the world of the *Commedia* in its entire meaning is nothing if not that upon which the individual existence and life story of Dante Al-ighieri, and through him those of the poem's reader, are projected. In such a case, the sending of meaning is not unilateral; and the address is at the same time a place of receiving and an initiative, an act of giving.

Dante as author—according to an etymology for his name that goes back to Boccaccio, namely, "dante," that is, "giving," present participle of *dare*, "to give"[58]—lends himself to our construing the locus from which the address issues as a giving and a Giver.[59] When we consider

57. Similarly concerned for the uniqueness of the literary in each of its repetitions, Derrida emphasizes, instead of appropriation as one's own, the invention of the other: "[C]'est . . . de l'invention comme allégorie, autre nom pour l'invention de l'autre, que je voudrais parler aujourd'hui" ("It is . . . of invention as allegory—other name for the invention of the other—that I would like today to speak"). "Psyché: Invention de l'autre," in *Psyché: Inventions de l'autre* (Paris: Galilée, 1987), p. 13.

58. Giorgio Padoan, ed., *Esposizioni sopra la Comedia di Dante,* vol. 6 of *Tutte le opere di Giovanni Boccaccio,* ed. V. Branca (Milan: Mondadori, 1965), p. 8 f. Cf. also Guido da Pisa's version of this etymology having already become traditional in the fourteenth century: "Dante dicitur a *do, das;* . . . ita a Dante datur nobis apud istud altissimum opus." *Guido da Pisa's expositiones et glose super Comediam Dantis,* ed. Vincenzo Cioffari (Albany: State University of New York Press, 1974), p. 1.

59. Derrida's thoughts on the gift are unfolded in *Donner le temps* (Paris: Galilée, 1991). He begins from the impossibility of the gift—"Commençons par l'impossible"—in his approach to the "question transcendantale ou plutôt sur le transcendental" ("the transcendental question or rather the question about the transcendental"—p. 76). Exposure of constructedness, of how every purported gratuity is always already preceded by structures of indebtedness making it instead a form of exchange, Derrida well knows is not the answer to the question of a possible transcendence of such structures but only a way of opening the question.

that Dante as author is imitating the ultimate author of all, as has been ruminated in the critical heritage down to, and through, Singleton, the giving and sending that constitute the hermeneutic process may be linked with the view of the whole universe as a message or specifically a gift sent from its creator, which in the last section we saw emerging from the exegetical tradition and its speculation about signs. The metaphysics of theism, then, can perhaps be read in this key as cohesive with the hermeneutic nature of signification. Some such dependence is in fact strongly suspected by many of the detractors from hermeneutics, alias "onto-theology." [60]

The Christian conviction and ideology of Dante's poem challenge us to ask whether it might not risk reductiveness to restrict characterization of the giving to the "Es gibt" ("It gives") of Heidegger—and from there to the even more minimal "trace" and "effect" of Derrida—and whether letting the Giver give might not mean accepting a given historical and even institutional revelation of its being that conditions and makes demands upon individual interpreters, but nevertheless involves them in a more demanding and responsive relation with what gives. All the institutions that have been socially constructed and the belief systems that have been culturally fabricated nevertheless *are* (if we recognize them as being), and their very artifice, their having been deliberately made, far from excluding such a possibility, itself suggests that they may be intending and addressing a message to us. At all events, they create possibilities for us to respond.

Only the experience of peoples can demonstrate in a public way what constitutes authentic, life-receiving, life-giving response to 'what is', the miraculous fact 'that it is', and the message that this may address to us. Dante was responding to just such a message inhering in the miracle of constructedness in his otherwise absurdly circular reasoning in response to St. Peter's demand that he declare the proofs for his faith in Scripture and the miracles it attests:

> "Se 'l mondo si rovolse al cristianesmo"
>   diss'io "sanza miracoli, quest'uno
>   è tal, che li altri non sono il centesmo."
>   (*Paradiso* XXIV. 106–11)

> ("If the world turned to Christianity,"
>   I said, "without miracles, this one
>   is such that all the others are not one-hundredth of it.")

---

60. The term is originally Heidegger's, for example, in *Identity and Difference,* trans. J. Stambaugh (New York: Harper & Row, 1969). Heidegger plays a double role as fountainhead of both ontological hermeneutics and the destruction of the history of ontology and metaphysics.

It is perhaps most of all in the constructions of faith, like the Church, as in works of artifice, like the *Commedia*, that the miraculous possibility of an address from God is not merely constructed by, but also constructs, us.

4. A PHILOLOGICAL DEBATE: AUERBACH AND SPITZER

The addresses to the reader in the *Divine Comedy* became a crux for scholarship, if they had not always been such, in the criticism of Erich Auerbach. Auerbach's now famous essay on the subject (dedicated, incidentally, to Rudolph Bultmann) provoked a quick rejoinder from Leo Spitzer, criticizing Auerbach's sweeping generalizations as to the authoritative character of Dante's addresses and their prophetic voice. Spitzer examined the addresses one by one, reducing the list to nineteen from Auerbach's twenty, itself a reduction from Gmelin's twenty-one, to show that they more often bring out "Dante's friendly closeness to his truly 'Beloved Reader.'"[61]

A few years later Auerbach returned to the topic and defended and extended his argument.[62] Auerbach's second effort on the addresses to the reader comes in a different and much more convincing context. Rather than in an article on an apparently self-contained subject in *Romance Philology*, the addresses are treated as a "key problem" in a great synthesis of European literature and culture, *Literatursprache und Publikum*

61. Articles by Auerbach, Gmelin, and Spitzer cited in notes 1 and 2 of this chapter. Quotation from Spitzer's article on p. 162. See, further, Dante Della Terza, "Auerbach e Spitzer: Itinerario dell'esilio e *Lecturae Dantis*," in *Da Vienna a Baltimora. La diaspora degli intellettuali europei negli Stati Uniti d'America* (Rome: Riuniti, 1987), pp. 37–52.

62. Auerbach, *Literary Language and Its Public in Late Antiquity and in the Middle Ages*, trans. R. Manheim (New York: Pantheon, 1965); originally published as *Literatursprache und Publikum in der lateinischen Spätantike und im Mittelalter* (Bern: Francke, 1958). A review of the debate together with further reflections on the social identity of the reader can be found in Vittorio Russo, "Apelli di Dante al lettore: Quale?" in *Esperienza e/di letture Dantesche tra il 1966 e il 1970* (Naples: Liguori, 1971). Russo stresses that Dante is addressing to a laicized, citified, diversified new public a doctrine with content of a sort formerly reserved for a much more homogeneous clerical class. The four-fold allegorical method, Russo suggests, enables Dante to meet different levels of readerly preparation and demand.

It is difficult, however, to see much specification of the *Commedia*'s readers on Dante's part in sociocultural terms. He tends more to divide them into two groups like sheep and goats: "voi altri pochi," "voi che avete li intelletti sani." Something monolithic in his vision corresponds to a genericity and essentiality of his appeal to the reader. Surely these addresses are sensitive to the sociocultural changes in progress as Dante writes, but this is reflected more indirectly in his voice than in any actual characterization of his reader as to class either in the poem or readily inferable from it. The "quale" of the reader addressed in the poem is perceptible more as a "come," and Dante's "lettore" figures basically as an everyman or every Christian, though admittedly the vernacular poet addresses himself to this generic reader in ways that become newly possible in Dante's bourgeois world with its new middle class.

in der lateinischen Spätantike und im Mittelalter. In the *Literatursprache* it became patent that Auerbach was using the subject of the addresses as a "point of departure" for a particular kind of philological effort that aspired to bring into focus "something more general" than any isolated phenomenon in a text. "My purpose is always to write history," Auerbach writes, though the historiography he propounds, coinciding with "philology" and in the end with philosophy too, is far from scientific and is even consciously inflected by personal prejudice. He candidly avows: "I address a question to it, and my question, not the text, is my primary point of departure" (p. 20). Auerbach's taking it up in this way points to the potential of the topic of the address to become a key not only to the relationship of Dante to his audience and therewith to the meaning of the *Divine Comedy,* but to the whole nature and method of philology and even to the destiny of European civilization.

Auerbach brings out how Dante is "intent on influencing the reader and drawing him into the magic circle of his vision" (p. 310). The address to the reader "compels him to participate intensely" (p. 302). Auerbach's emphasis on "personal involvement" in the poem as solicited by the addresses and his reading them through his own involvement in larger questions of human and historical existence demand to be examined in light of recent reflection on method and particularly on objectivity in philology.[63] Such reflection is encouraged by Spitzer's having used this exchange as an occasion to define his own philological method in contrast with Auerbach's. "Speaking in terms of my personal method of the 'philological circle,'" writes Spitzer, "I would say that Mr. Auerbach has taken his point of departure from his unsurpassed encyclopedic knowledge of the whole of the *Commedia,* neglecting the exact analysis of the detail chosen in this article to represent the whole, while I would prefer to start with the analysis of a detail" (Spitzer, "Addresses to the Reader," p. 164).

Spitzer's philological method presupposes that it is possible to work neatly from the detail to the whole. Yet the whole is always already there. We can suspend belief in ideas, but some global structures still imperceptibly govern what we perceive in reading a text, beyond our conscious awareness and control. Moreover, after the foregoing considerations in the first section of this chapter, it is apparent that the addresses to the reader cannot be considered adequately as just one more figure within the fabric of the poem, nor as one of the "technical devices" that make up Dante's "artistry" and distinguish his "masterly manner" (Spitzer, "Addresses to the Reader," p. 143). We saw that they are not

---

63. See articles, especially those by Gabrielle Spiegel and Lee Patterson, in special issue on the "New Philology," *Speculum* 65 (January 1990).

just present within the text; they also, and more momentously, present it. To this degree they operate metatextually, situating the text within an enunciatory occurrence. They make happen articulately what inevitably happens when a reader takes a poetic text in hand and reads: the poem begins happening for him or her as an event with incalculable meaning that can in principle reach out referentially to embrace the whole of a civilization, as is emphatically the case with Dante's *Commedia*.

The addresses are a formidable challenge to philology and a revealing test case of its capacities and limitations, for they defy treatment as a "neatly circumscribed philological subject."[64] Spitzer proposes to consider the addresses "from a most factual point of view" (p. 146). He considers them as functions within the text, as technical devices, whereas they more importantly define the function *of* the text in a pragmatic context of enunciation. The addresses to the reader address an extratextual reality. They do figure this reality, most fully, with body and in a specific ambience in *Paradiso* X. 22 ("Or ti riman, lettor, sovra il tuo banco"), as Spitzer points out; to this extent the invoking of the reader indeed produces a literary figure. Yet it is a figure oriented toward what surpasses figuration as its ground: it is *for* a reader that the meaning of the figurative content of poetry can "happen" and be realized. The addresses are a contact point with reality, and they declare that the purpose of the poem is to take place within a context of reality rather than to be "merely" fiction.

The addresses create an ontological density in poetic discourse in which it emerges from the relative flatness of textuality and representation in order to take on the dimensions of an event. Of course, poetry has such ontological depth in effect, whether addresses to the reader appear in it or not, simply by virtue of its eventually being read by someone. What happens newly in the *Divine Comedy* is that this aspect of poetry as history-making event comes to be consciously exploited and made conspicuously manifest. This does not automatically make Dante's poetry superior, but shows it to be a watershed in the development of poetry and reveals something essential about the sort of significance poetry can attain.

Spitzer himself cannot keep from eroding the boundaries of his "neatly circumscribed philological subject," limited in principle to precisely nineteen passages, by his avowals that all the similes, such as those involving geographical references, "appeal to the reader's memories" and

---

64. Spitzer, "Addresses to the Reader," p. 145. It is ironic, and perhaps betrays a sense of what is at stake here, that Spitzer should begin his article on precisely this topic by announcing that "philology," which insists on close adherence to the text and on comparison of sources, "has thus reconquered its due place in Dante studies" thanks to the elucidation of medieval manners and techniques by such scholars as Faral, Schiaffini, Curtius, and Auerbach (p. 143).

so "could be considered as containing a hidden address to the reader" (Spitzer, "Addresses to the Reader," p. 153). He also admits that "it would not be entirely wrong to include all the passages containing the 'possessive of human solidarity' [e.g., the word 'nostra' in *Inferno* I. 1] among the addresses to the reader" (p. 151). Such philology is far from insensitive to impulse toward generalization inherent in the addresses and to the speculative problematic that they engender.

The real source of disagreement in this tidy philological debate is much less circumscribed, and more philosophical than philological. Spitzer emphasizes the "this-worldliness" of Dante's appeals and poem. Auerbach stresses their source in a vision of transcendence. The divisive question is not whether the appeals are friendly or authoritative,[65] but whether they proclaim the *Commedia* as divine or as merely human. And behind this lies the question of language: is it to be taken as a humanly manipulable tool, an instrument of communication, or as a disclosure of being transcending the world of beings that first comes to be in its light? This is no tidily delimited philological question of identifying sources and schematizing rhetorical characteristics of a certain set of passages.

For a narrowly philological sort of scholarship, what is important is not necessarily the interpellative essence of the address, but rather the literary convention of addressing a "reader." This, however, is only secondary in relation to the response the poem solicits; it comes from *un*involvement, and constitutes an attitude of detached analysis of a literary specimen. On the "positive" side, this attitude aims to avoid indulging in merely personal, subjective responses. Nevertheless, a hermeneutically complete reading will aim to render intelligible and precisely communicable the possibilities inhering also in this "subjective" dimension of response. Such reading must respond, or at least account for the possibility of responding, to the irreducibly personal appeal poetry can make.

It needs to be remembered that the text's being addressed to a reader, and having the reader's participation be determinative of its meaning, does not mean that the text is subject to the reader as an object to be invested with any significance whatever, according to the reader's arbitrary caprice. The address to the reader signals the reader's interpellation, the reader's being addressed by an other, the reader's being placed in the

---

65. Auerbach actually does not emphasize authoritativeness at the expense of solidarity; he rather links the two together: "But only in the *Commedia* does the accent of authoritative leadership and urgency reach its full strength—and it is there linked to the expression of brotherly solidarity with the reader. . . . Dante is much nearer to the reader [than Horace in *Favete linguis*]; his appeal is that of a brother urging his fellow brother, the reader, to use his own spontaneous effort in order to share the poet's experience and to *prender frutto* of the poet's teaching" (Auerbach, "Dante's Addresses," p. 273).

position of a hearer vis-à-vis an authoritative voice, an *auctor*. In the end, philology's object is not an object, and this perhaps holds in a peculiar sense for the literature of Christian revelation. It may assume the role, the voice, the initiative of an Other. Again, the biblical model of the author who precedes human authors and of a God who calls a people to himself, putting humanity in the position of a respondent, serves as the enabling paradigm. This faith of Israel in its God as always preceding and anticipating it, as having the initiative rather than abiding in the attitude of an object to be placated or aroused according to the exigencies of humans, has been isolated as the radically differential element in biblical religion.[66] The Lord of history first addresses before being addressed, and all human activity can be but a response or a refusal to respond to his summons and plan.

Philology assumes an analogous posture, and gains an analogous openness, by recognizing that poetry, literature, language, rather than being only a passive object for scientific investigation, speaks. The "It" of poetic language is a speaker that addresses its messages to readers—this is at least a view of poetry and literature that receives emphatic assertion in Dante's poem via its addresses to the reader. Of course, it is *Dante* who is peremptorily addressing the one to whom his poem speaks. But more fundamentally, there is an active dynamism in the poem itself and in its language, indeed, in language itself as it occurs in the poem, which comes forward as speaker, as addresser, above and beyond the authorial persona projected within it.

It was language considered essentially as poetry of which Heidegger wrote, "Language speaks" ("Die Sprache spricht"). We need not shrink from discerning and naming a certain metaphysics of poetry as personal and "authoritative" voice and agency that is operative in the phenomenon of the poem that addresses its reader. Dante's figuring himself as scribe (*Paradiso* X. 27) or as amanuensis (*Purgatorio* XXIV. 51–53) grows out of a sense of the poem's being or embodying some authority superior to his own. But in whose image is such poetic language made, and what or who may be speaking in it? Surely the most pertinent model for Dante's discourse of address must be found in the word of God, the Bible, which can be interpreted, as indeed it has been by Gerhard Ebeling, as in every part address, appellation: "[T]he content of what God says always unconditionally concerns the person and the hearer. . . . God's Word rightly understood is never statement but always address."[67]

66. See especially the pioneering work of Gerhard von Rad, *Theologie des Alten Testaments* (Munich: Kaiser, 1965–66).

67. Gerhard Ebeling, *Word and Faith*, p. 211. Most any traditional Christian theology, of course, stresses that the biblical Word is addressed to humanity. This understanding is only further sharpened by the focus on the Word as event in contemporary theology under the

The Word speaking in Scripture is the inevitable guide, from Dante's point of view (and why not ours too?), to what or whom is speaking in Dante's, in his poem's, in poetry's, address. If Spitzer is right that Auerbach exaggerates the "authoritativeness" of Dante in the addresses, might this not be because Auerbach senses the importance of the address as a channel not only for Dante's didacticism but also for a revelatory event in which the language of the poem speaks from beyond Dante, from God, in addressing the reader? It may be the opening to this possibility that is ultimately implied in "hearing" Dante's address to the reader.[68]

5. PETRARCH, BOCCACCIO, AND THE FICTION OF PHILOLOGY

The fiction of treating the past "philologically," from an absolute historical distance and with the presumed objectivity that this confers, arguably originates with Dante's successors, Petrarch and Boccaccio. So far from walking shoulder to shoulder with Virgil in all familiarity and sharing his horizon, Petrarch and Boccaccio begin contemplating the classical world with the kind of detachment that comes to characterize philological science. It is with them, among the first of the Renaissance scholars styled "humanists," that philology in any modern, protoscientific sense can be said to be born.

This new discipline turns a new kind of attention to the artifacts and documents left as the positive traces of past life and experience. Petrarch's letters, for example, to Giovanni di San Vito, recounting his walking through the Roman forum, fasten upon the fragmentary ruins as all that is left of that epoch-straddling civilization. The sense of discontinuity, of no longer being within the past and its consequential unfolding, of being able only to weakly re-evoke it from these inert, disintegrating remains is expressed in what Thomas Greene characterizes as Petrarch's "archaeo-

---

banner of the New Hermeneutic. Some limitations of such an understanding of the Word as address are argued by Amos Wilder, "The Word as Address and the Word as Meaning," in *The New Hermeneutic*, ed. J. Robinson and J. Cobb, Jr. (New York: Harper & Row, 1964), pp. 198–218.

68. The problem of how to hear the word of God in human words, a problem Dante certainly wrestled with, is further pursued by Ebeling in *God and Word;* originally published as "Gott und Wort," in *Wort und Glaube,* vol. 2. The essential openness and "answerability" of human being as itself linguistic in character—features highlighted in provocative ways also by Dante's address to the reader—help account for the possibility of God's word breaking into human discourse. Cf. also Ebeling's "Wort Gottes und Hermeneutik," in *Wort und Glaube,* vol. 1.

logical" attitude toward the cultural heritage of Rome, his "'archaeologi-cal' scrutiny, a decipherment of the latent or hidden or indecipherable object of historical knowledge beneath the surface."[69]

Thus science (archaeology, philology) and its "method" begin to come between past and present. The past no longer speaks except in an ersatz voice. It is an object for scientific analysis rather than a subject speaking with the wholeness and authority of an "auctor," for the hu-manist is positioned outside it and its hermeneutic horizon. He may "res-urrect" the past within his own present, but as something sham. Human-ism in its relation to the past is dominated, Greene suggests, by the im-agery of necromancy. Manipulative technologies of magic and science, which are hardly distinguishable at this stage, operate on objects in ways illustrative of the "necromantic superstition at the heart of the humanist enlightenment" (Greene, *Light in Troy,* p. 93). According to Greene, "the image that propelled the humanist Renaissance and that still determines our perception of it, was the archeological, necromantic metaphor of *disinterment,* a digging up that was also a resuscitation or a reincarnation or a rebirth" (p. 92). In a letter to Giovanni Colonna, Petrarch actually ventriloquizes the ruins ("ruinae") of Rome, as each step stirs tongue and mind: "Aderat . . . per singulos passus quod linguam et animum exci-taret" (p. 88). He is bodily taken over by the past, but in a step-by-step, fragmentary fashion, in what is clearly an image of magic as opposed to hermeneutic conversion and its transformation of the whole man through an altering of his horizons and his structural framework of self-understanding.

The image of necromancy suggests how close humanism remains to the ideal of a living relation with the past, even while in possession merely of its corpse, now reanimated only by tricks and techniques of magic or science. Certainly in some ways Petrarch's philology is still more hermeneutic than scientific, more a continuation of an active past than its reconstruction and containment in a supposedly objective repre-

---

69. Thomas M. Greene, *The Light in Troy: Imitation and Discovery in Renaissance Poetry* (New Haven: Yale University Press, 1983), p. 93. See also the account of the transition from medieval to modern historical consciousness by Anthony Kemp in *The Estrangement of the Past: A Study in the Origins of Modern Historical Consciousness* (Oxford: Oxford University Press, 1991). For Kemp this turning hinges on the collapse of two supporting columns that make a last stand, so to speak, in Dante's *Commedia,* though the first, a belief in redeemed secular history under the guidance of church authority, is perhaps already poised to topple: "The decline of the medieval model of the past and the rise of the modern is an untidy process, one that takes perhaps four hundred years to reach completion. There are, however, two intellectual changes in themselves quite simple, that are the modes from which a new historical configuration must emerge: the identification of the institution of the papacy with antichrist . . . and the rejection of the *translatio imperii,* the doctrine that the Holy Roman Empire was identical with its classical model" (p. 66).

sentation.[70] Kenelm Foster shows the extent to which Petrarch is a partisan of a rhetorical culture as against the dialectical culture on the rise in his day, with which he entered into acrimonious confrontations. Indeed, Petrarch's detachment is clearly that of the man of letters rather than that of the scientist: "Nothing weighs less than a pen, and nothing is more cheering"; "of all earthly delights none is nobler, sweeter, more lasting and dependable than that afforded by books."[71] However, literature here is no longer conceived of as an ontological event but as out of the way of events and their risks and consequences. Petrarch prizes it not for its ontological import but for its virtual weightlessness. At most, his literary production is burdened with the confession of a self become a vain and empty cipher, not with any sense of address from an other. Petrarch retains an openness to the past, with which he is intimately conversant and on behalf of which he assumes a vital role: nevertheless, this role may best be defined as that of being a sort of cultural curator.

The pretense of an objective science of the past reduced to the inert contents of a museum obscures the way in which we are always in the past, which manifests itself in us in more ways than we can possibly be aware of. This is something that Boccaccio and Petrarch had not yet really forgotten, although they began to forge the fictions that would eventually make its forgetting possible. The potential for a detached, objective analysis of documents begins to be discernible in their erudite works. Boccaccio as mythographer continually shows himself to be conscious of the enormous historical distance that separates him from his material. His work of encyclopedic salvaging is predicated on the nonpresence and noncontemporaneity of the antique world. In *Genealogia deorum gentilium* he figures himself in the guise of Aesculapius reconstituting the *disiecta membra* of the Hippolytus of classical mythology. The relation to the past literally becomes one of "recollection," rather than one of living in uninterrupted communication with it. Antiquity is at an absolute remove; it is no more alive and immediate for him than for his mentor as humanist scholar, Petrarch. Significantly, Boccaccio's primary model shifts from Dante to Petrarch as he moves from poems such as *L' amorosa visione* in terza rima to the works of erudition. Rather than, as for Dante, a present horizon and living vision, antiquity has become a

70. This, in fact, is what is emphasized by Gerald Bruns in *Hermeneutics: Ancient and Modern* (New Haven: Yale University Press, 1992), who on the basis of Greene's research describes Petrarch's hermeneutics as "reawakening an antique spirit instead of reconstructing original meanings" (p. 198).

71. Petrarch, cited in Kenelm Foster, *Petrarch* (Edinburgh: Edinburgh University Press, 1984), p. 141.

heap of documents in fragmentary form needing to be deciphered and reconstituted.[72]

To reach Dante we must turn back the page of the scientific age in the history of reading and literary criticism. Dante's hermeneutic procedures stridently violate the principles of scientific philology (well-known emblematic instances of this, to be examined later, are found in appropriations of Virgilian texts in *Purgatorio* XXII and XXX), and to draw near them we need other models and paths. This is why recently renewed speculation in hermeneutic thought is so important for the opportunities it affords for reading Dante with a critical perspective on customary philological frameworks and their inevitable biases.

This remark is by no means intended as a dismissal of Dante scholarship or even of traditional Dante scholarship. It is an attempt to point out that what is so often brilliant in the readings of Dante's interpreters today no less than in the critical classics surpasses the scope of positive, demonstrable science or its literary-critical emulation aiming to produce the "definitive" reading. The massive and in varying degrees necessary and useful philological work done on the *Commedia* finds its genuine value when deployed within interpretive projects that do more than simply ascertain facts, even newly discovered facts, about the poem or its context as a subject of archaeological research. Searching criticism of the poem enables it to react upon contemporary literary, intellectual, social, and religious history. It interrogates the poem in correspondence with what are experienced as genuine questions today. This is how it can be "true" to its source, the poem that inspires all this labor, granting continuation to the event of disclosure that the poem originates.

What Renaissance humanism did in alienating classical antiquity (even while fashioning itself in its image) has been carried on with regard to the Middle Ages by modern philology. The illusion of being able (and of needing) to attain verifiable knowledge of some object, a notion likely picked up by "attraction" from the scientific norms reigning in academic institutions where philology is pursued, has governed especially medieval studies, typically marginalized as having to do with something very remote and perhaps no longer comprehensible. The so-called "New Philology" is at least in part an effort to take account of the critique of traditional philology's scientific methodology and historicist presuppositions. It aims to revamp the discipline so as to preserve traditional virtues of painstaking manuscript study and careful attention to documentary details while at the

---

72. Susan Noakes, in *Timely Reading: Between Exegesis and Interpretation* (Ithaca: Cornell University Press, 1988), has effectively analyzed "Boccaccio's humanistic quest for the perfectly reconstituted text" (p. xiii) as a paradigm of "exegesis," contrasting it with Dante's stories of reading more oriented to "interpretation."

same time adapting to rapidly shifting theoretical foundations in the wake of such currents as poststructuralism, hermeneutics, and new historicism.

In this vein, Lee Patterson argues that medieval philology's historical expertise and conscience can challenge postmodern "theory" and its universalist claims, calling scholarship back to a respect for the particular, but only on condition of engaging the issues of our time and treating medieval texts in their contemporary relevance. Howard Bloch delineates the New Philology's turn away from a kind of scientific positivism that dominated the discipline of philology from after what he fixes as its modern origins in Vico to recent times of crisis and questioning. Philology must be construed, more accurately than by its traditionally positivistic self-understanding, as a "cultural hermeneutics à la Vico," to borrow Stephen Nichols's phrase from the introduction to the *Speculum* issue dedicated to the New Philology.[73]

Patterson, moreover, contends that the Middle Ages did not lack historical consciousness but simply had a kind of historical consciousness different from that which has prevailed since the Renaissance. The Middle Ages, in this revised assessment, embody an authentic appropriation of the past as continuous with the present. Patterson has paid close attention to two Old French readings of Virgil, the *Roman d'Eneas* and Chrétien de Troyes's *Erec et Enide,* to show how they recuperate Virgil's text, with perspicacity and persuasiveness, in ways lost to modern historical science and research.[74] These twelfth-century works may serve to exemplify a sort of dialogic engagement with the past that Dante's poem develops and that speaks, engaging even future historical contexts, most distinctly out of its direct addresses. Such precedents help us gain a perspective on philology, a relative freedom with respect to its methodological consciousness, which can de-objectify the addresses and let them speak as a genuine voice of an other so as to actually address their reader today.

Even a discipline as strictly bound and beholden to the ideal of fidelity to an original meaning as textual criticism is making efforts to assimilate these ideas. For it has become increasingly clear that the text cannot be established except as it is addressed to a reader and that any reader reads it as addressed to her rather than reading it "objectively," that is, as existing independently and as an object for positive, pure, impersonal, disinterested science. In recognition of this, Jerome McGann stresses "the interpretive force of all editorial interventions." He explains, "These essays

73. *Speculum* 65 (January 1990) contains inter alia Lee Patterson, "On the Margin: Postmodernism, Ironic History, and Medieval Studies" and Howard Bloch, "New Philology and Old French."

74. Lee Patterson, "Virgil and the Historical Consciousness of the Twelfth Century: The *Roman d'Eneas* and *Erec et Enide,*" in *Negotiating the Past: The Historical Understanding of Medieval Literature* (Madison: University of Wisconsin Press, 1987).

[on method in textual criticism] show repeatedly, and in a variety of contexts and ways, that 'meaning' in literary experience is a function of a dialectical exchange between the imperatives of the past and the insistencies of the present. Moreover, in this exchange many individuals are involved, as well as many groups and institutions, and all of these groups and individuals represent various centers of interest. As such, they participate actively in the production of literature, in the 'literary work' (properly so called). This complex network of past and present exchanges and investments both in and between the past and the present—*is* the mode of existence of the literary work of art."[75]

In our perspective this suggests how Dante's discovery of the poetic word as address is being rediscovered today in the theory and practice surrounding literature. The crucial question is whether we can be authentically addressed out of the past or whether every text must be for us simply an object. The answer Dante gave, the answer he is as "giving"—*dante,* opens as a hermeneutic horizon stretching down to our own time, to us latter-day readers of the *Commedia,* recipients of its address. It is not so much an answer as an invitation to abide within the questioning, the calling for response, of the address.

Nevertheless, there is always a strong temptation in outlining and programming any discipline to fall back on the common denominators of what seem to be objectively verifiable grounds for a positive consensus. This is why the hermeneutic perspective opened by Heidegger's fundamental ontology quickly devolved into reception-aesthetics. It is surely safer and easier to talk about man than about Being, and, indeed, once the moment that breaks open new insight passes, the uncanny language it coined cannot help but go bankrupt in a hurry. This is clearly the case with the language of Being in the general currency of cultural exchange today, though that should not rule out efforts like the present one to restore to it some value in a specifically delimited appropriation and employment. The value of this language can be assessed only from within its own verbal event. This gives it the structure of faith, that is, of a circle between understanding and belief, between value and intelligibility. Though it is vulnerable to assessments from the outside that will find it wanting, its value cannot be sifted through except in its own terms. This might seem an elected isolation and fruitless incommunicability, were it not at the same time lucidly illustrative of the predicament of understanding and interpretive inquiry as such. Should we become skeptical enough to accept this, we might be in a position to find with Dante a rationale for a mode of cognition open to penetration by religious faith.

75. Jereome McGann, *Textual Criticism and Literary Interpretation* (Chicago: University of Chicago Press, 1985), pp. xiii–xiv.

T W O

Dante's Hermeneutic Rite of Passage: Inferno IX

Lettor, tu vedi ben com'io innalzo
la mia materia; e però con più arte
non ti maravigliar, s'io la rincalzo.
(*Purgatorio* IX. 70–71)

1. BLOCKAGE

*I*n *Inferno* VIII. 64–IX. 105, before the gate of the city of Dis, Dante's journey risks being brought to an abrupt halt. Why this particular step of the way should turn out to be so singularly difficult may have to do with the transition to the "basso inferno" or with the entry within the walls of the hellish city (VIII. 75–78). As indicated by these and other border signposts, Dante stands at the passage to the *inside* of Hell, effectively imaged by the house metaphor of Virgil's exclamation: "chi m'ha negate le dolenti case!" (VIII. 120) This threshold (actually termed "l'orribil soglia" in IX. 92), with its attendant metaphorics of depth and innerness, is chosen by Dante for intensive problematization of the pilgrim's progress, which is treated as fundamentally a hermeneutic problem and linked to that of getting inside the meaning of the poem.

The parallel between the progress of Dante and Virgil on their journey through the other world and the progress of the reader's understanding of the poem begins to emerge when, just as Dante and Virgil are threatened with an abortive end to their venture, the narrative itself is interrupted for the first time in the *Divine Comedy* by a direct address of Dante as poet to his reader:

Pensa, lettor, se io mi sconfortai
nel suon de le parole maladette,
ché non credetti ritornarci mai.
(*Inferno* VIII. 94–96)

(Think, reader, whether I was not dismayed
at the sound of the accursed words,
as I believed I should never return here again.)

These words follow directly upon the words of the demons who stop Dante and Virgil dead in their tracks, threatening to send Dante back along the foolhardy path he has come by and to keep Virgil with them (VIII. 84–93). Performative in character, the verses effect a break in the narrative by shifting suddenly from diegetic to apostrophic discourse and from an indicative to a vocative mood. Taken together, the parallel interruptions—the one *within* and the other *of* the narrative—preliminarily enact the two-fold interpretive dynamic that is to be worked out decisively in Canto IX.

At the beginning of Canto IX, the progress of Dante and Virgil is blocked not only by the hostility of the inhabitants of Dis; obstacles also crop up in their communication with one another, hermeneutic obstacles. Virgil stifles what seems to be a worry as to whether he and Dante will win out against the furies ("se non . . ."), and Dante sees that he is covering up ("I' vidi ben sí com' ei ricoperse"). But Dante's reading between the lines, by his own admission, may be a misinterpretation of Virgil's reticence, attributing to the suppressed sentence a meaning even more ominous than whatever Virgil actually held back ("io traeva la parola tronca / forse a peggior sentenzia che non tenne"—IX. 8–15).[1] Furthermore, Dante responds by dissembling his own meaning, inquiring obliquely, via a circumlocution that belies the urgency of the situation and his own present fear, whether Virgil is experienced in such descents into the infernal depths. He asks whether anyone (meaning Virgil) from the "primo grado" (meaning the first circle of Hell, or Limbo) has ever before descended to the stage of Hell now before them.

Thus the blockage that Canto IX as a whole introduces into the journey through Hell is first intimated as hermeneutic difficulty in the relation between Virgil and Dante, normally so immediate and perspicuous that hermeneutic instruments like words are often superfluous, as when Virgil simply reads Dante's mind (e.g., at *Inferno* II. 36; X. 18; XVI. 118–23; XIX. 39; XXIII. 25–27; *Purgatorio* XV. 127–29). This twist in the verbal action of the story suggests how the hermeneutic problematic pervades the whole episode, and closer examination will unveil in virtually every aspect of the conflict and action narrated in this canto images of hermeneutic procedure. But the deeper and more dynamic way in which Dante-protagonist's problem is fundamentally a hermeneutic problem consists in its being fundamentally the reader's or interpreter's problem. Hence it is precisely at this juncture that the didactic status of Dante's narrative fiction is made fully explicit, in the poem's most imperious hermeneutic injunction:

1. The word "sententia," it should be noted, was actually a technical term used in medieval schools for a third level of reading: beyond grammatical comprehension of the "littera" and a grasp of the "sensus" (content), the higher doctrinal significance of a text was termed "sententia." Dante does not necessarily use it in this technical sense here, but the word's connotation and

O voi ch'avete li 'ntelletti sani
  mirate la dottrina che s'asconde
  sotto 'l velame de li versi strani.
                              (*Inferno* IX. 61–63)

(O you who have sound intellects,
  look at the doctrine which hides itself
  beneath the veil of the strange verses.)

At the literal level, the protagonist's progress is impeded by the devils and furies (and potentially the Medusa) that gather to mock and threaten him at the top of the city's gate and tower. However, we are enjoined not to stop short with this reading alone, but to seek out the doctrine beneath the veil of the "strange verses." The summons to hermeneusis interrupts the narrative at a climax of dramatic tension, thus undermining the value of the narrative, together with the events it recounts, in and for themselves, and effectively preventing the reader from becoming too involved in the fictive situation. The focus of attention shifts instead to the poem as poem, with its opaque meaning and teaching, and to the hermeneutic event of reading it, a task reserved for "sound intellects." A leap in seriousness of tone, signaled by the rhetorically monitory 'O', prioritizes *this* struggle as the one for the sake of which the other is being carried out.

Immediately prior to the directive addressed to the reader, another imperative, this time within the narrative fiction, also directing sight, was enunciated, and compliance manually effected, by Virgil—here called teacher ("maestro")—upon his protégé:

"Volgiti 'n dietro e tien lo viso chiuso;
  ché se 'l Gorgon si mostra e tu 'l vedessi,
  nulla sarebbe di tornar mai suso."
Così disse 'l maestro; ed elli stessi
  mi volse, e non si tenne a le mie mani,
  che con le sue ancor non mi chiudessi.
                              (*Inferno* IX. 55–60)

("Turn yourself around and cover your eyes;
  for if the Gorgon should appear and you see it,
  never more would you return above."
So my teacher said; and he himself
  turned me, and did not trust to my hands,
  but also with his own covered my eyes.)

Virgil's superimposition of his outside help, not trusting in Dante's own self-help, is strikingly like, and virtually reproduces, Dante's very hands-

---

the context it evokes contribute to the suggestion that this exchange concerns hermeneutics. See F. Paré, A. Brunet, and P. Trembly, *La Renaissance du xii*ᵉ *siècle: Les écoles et l'enseignement* (Ottawa: Ottawa University Press, 1933), pp. 116–17.

on obtrusion of hermeneutic direction into his text, imposing it on his reader.

Just as Dante would be turned to stone if he gazed directly at the Medusa rather than turning away and suffering various sorts of mediation figuring the detour of interpretive procedures, so the poem would become the tombstone of mere writing as a dead-end-in-itself if there were no hermeneutic access to the doctrine beneath the veil of the verses, and hence no progress beyond the "scritta morta" (*Inferno* VIII. 127). The inscription seen earlier on the *outside* of the Gate of Hell is here recalled and can now be understood as a dead letter in a sense referred to the interpretive journey of the reader. For it was presented from the beginning, the very first textual edge, of Canto III without any hermeneutic mediation, such as narrative enframement or a discursive transition, as the very words seen by the pilgrim (i.e., this situation was approximated, since the reader sees the same words written, though obviously not on the same surface).

These "found" verses are poetry pretending not to be poetry but rather the thing itself, and such poetry is deadly in its illusory immediacy, for it denies hermeneutic passage through its own literal-mimetic surface to spiritual, life-giving meaning in the form of saving doctrine. The form of death specific to interpretive impasse, namely, petrification, was intimated earlier in Canto III when the inscription was said to be impenetrable because too hard or stony ("duro"—III. 12). Thus the danger involved in reading is fully analogous to the Medusa danger,[2] and both need to be met by hermeneutic wherewithal. In this way, hermeneutics comes forward as the only means by which both Dante's journey as protagonist and his poem can make genuine progress, though the effect of hermeneutics is precisely to collapse these two together, revealing the one as the meaning behind the other.

It is no accident, then, that the author's hermeneutic intervention

2. John Freccero has explored the petrification figure and its hermeneutic import in "Medusa: The Letter and the Spirit," in *Dante: The Poetics of Conversion*. According to Freccero, the Medusa threat constitutes for Dante a temptation to return narcissistically and nostalgically to his past as a poet of dark eros, specifically in the "rime petrose." To yield to such a temptation would amount to petrification (one might even say "Petrarchification," since the end of the *Canzoniere* confirms quite convincingly that a narcissist's love object essentially turns out to be a Medusa). For the love involved would be terminal and idolatrous, refusing to pass beyond into the infinite love of Christian *caritas*, toward which the trajectory of the *Commedia* and the main thrust of Dante's career, the stony rhymes excepted, is directed. The Medusa thus lines up, in Freccero's reading, with the letter that kills, according to the Pauline phrase (2 Cor. 3.12–16), while the Pauline image of lifting the veil, or "revelation," figures a hermeneutic procedure whereby the spirit gives life. The significance of the unmediated inscription at the head of Canto III is discussed by Freccero in "Infernal Irony: The Gates of Hell," in *Dante: The Poetics of Conversion*.

should occur at just this juncture where the continuation of the journey is in jeopardy, if the progress of the protagonist and the poem alike constitutes a single hermeneutic problem. Just where surface vision has been precluded for the protagonist, the author breaks into the text and breaks up the continuity of the narrative, explicitly advising the reader that the fantastic story exists for the sake of something that is supposed to be learned from it. The exhortation makes a break in the narrative, even while it calls the reader to break through to another level of meaning beyond all naive fascination with the literal narration and to seek a teaching hidden beneath it. Thus it enacts at the metanarratological level the same sequence of impasse-calling-forth-interpretation that is illustrated within the narrative.

The principle of impasse on the surface requiring a move to another depth and sense was, of course, fundamental to the scriptural hermeneutics of the fathers of the Church: a millenary tradition stands behind Dante's representation of impasse as the situation out of which the need for and call to hermeneusis arises. Typically, the fathers taught that certain passages of Scripture were deliberately nonsensical or otherwise unassimilable at the literal level in order to invite or even coerce the reader to seek out a spiritual sense beneath. According to Origen, building on the theories of Philo, who was himself indebted to the Stoa, the search for allegorical meaning takes its departure from some logical absurdity ("alogon") or impossibility ("adunaton") in the literal sense.[3] Precisely a stumbling block to interpretation, something that apparently contradicts the context, or an accepted truth, or the presumed perfection of the author, gives the cue for hermeneutic penetration of Scripture. Augustine formulates a broadly equivalent principle—"Quidquid in sermone divino neque ad morum honestatem ad fidei veritatem proprie referri potest, figuratem esse cognoscas" ("Whatever appears in the divine Word that can be referred neither to virtuous conduct nor to the truth of faith must be taken to be figurative")—in his tractate on scriptural hermeneutics, *De doctrina Christiana* (3, x, 14; see also 2, vi, 7–8, 29), a title that actually happens to echo in the verses of Dante's address to the reader in *Inferno* IX.[4]

In line with this tradition's privileging of an invisible, spiritual meaning over literal, corporeal meaning, Dante consistently figures hermeneutic *aporiae* as a blocking specifically of the sense of sight. This is so in miniature, in verbal detail, as well as in the structural design of Canto IX as a whole. A tableau near its outset depicts Virgil, after his setback at

3. Cf. Jean Pépin, *La tradition de l'allégorie: De Philon d'Alexandrie à Dante* (Paris: Études Augustiniennes, 1988).

4. See discussion of this work and Augustine's interpretation theory generally by Graziano Ripanti, *Agostino teorico dell'interpretazione* (Brescia: Paideia, 1980), p. 60 ff.

the furiously defended gate, striking the quintessentially hermeneutic posture of waiting attentively upon, of hearkening to, what must be revealed:

> Attento si fermò com' uom ch'ascolta;
> ché l'occhio nol potea menare a lunga
> per l'aere nero e per la nebbia folta.
>
> (IX. 4–6)

> (Attentive, he stopped as a man who listens,
> since his eye was not able to travel far
> through the dark air and thick mist.)

In this simile, the obstacle consists in the thick fog and impenetrable darkness that block vision. In the episode of Canto IX as a whole, the obstacle is constituted by the recalcitrance and menace of the inhabitants of the city of Dis who bar Dante and Virgil's way. But on this larger scale as well, what calls for hermeneutics is figured by the sense of sight, since that is the channel through which the Medusa freezes up progress in perpetuity.

The sense of sight operates both in the simile and in the whole narrative sequence as a metaphor for immediate knowledge, in which one simply "sees" what is before one without having to interpret or lift any veils. This sort of knowledge seems to come first naturally and needs to be checked in order for hermeneutic resources to be mobilized. The Medusa motif chillingly epitomizes the perils inhering in the immediacy of outer vision and its adherence to the aesthetic-erotic surface turning to frozen death. Within the fiction, Dante risks losing message and meaning alike when he allows his outer eye to be seduced, even just episodically:

> E altro disse, ma non l'ho a mente;
> però che l'occhio m'avea tutto tratto
> ver' l' alta torre a la cima rovente. . . .
>
> (IX. 34–36)

> (And he said more, but I do not remember it,
> for my eye had taken me entirely towards
> the high tower with its glowing top. . . .)

The hermeneutics required for the advance of both protagonists and readers seems, then, to be represented in terms of an antithesis between seeing and hearing, which stand for different aspects of the process of knowing, for its moments of fixation on the immediately present phenomenon and of attentive hearkening in the absence of any actual object of perception, respectively. However, here we are confronted with a paradox: the kind of knowledge to be gained through hermeneutic media-

tion is also figured in terms of the sense of sight, right from the herme-
neutic exhortation itself, which commands healthy intellects to *look* at
the hidden doctrine ("*mirate* la dottrina che s'asconde").

The same metaphorics of sight, where, precisely, nonimmediacy and
looking beneath or beyond to an invisible, spiritual, or at any rate allegor-
ical truth are aimed at, recurs at a juncture of the *Purgatorio* that corre-
sponds symmetrically with *Inferno* IX, namely, the sacral representation,
also a symbolic rite of passage, just before the entry from Ante-Purgatory
into Purgatory proper in Canto IX. Although this instance of the address
to the reader was examined as exemplary in chapter 1, it was not empha-
sized there that the reader is commanded to sharpen specifically his *eyes*
to the truth:

> Aguzza qui, lettor, ben gli occhi al vero,
>   ché 'l velo è ora ben tanto sottile,
>   certo che 'l trapassar dentro è leggiero.
>   (*Purgatorio* VIII. 19–21)

> (Here, reader, sharpen well your eyes to the true,
>   for now the veil is so thin,
>   certainly, that passing within is easy.)

Indeed, throughout the poem Dante consistently figures understanding
or insight, whether in a discursive, rational, or intuitive sense, as a kind
of seeing. By 'vision' reasoning is apprehended ("Or drizza 'l viso a quel
ch'or si ragiona"—*Paradiso* VII. 34), and by 'vision' the eternal design of
things, even when discursively exfoliated, can be scrutinized:

> Ficca mo l'occhio per entro l'abisso
>   de l'etterno consiglio, quanto puoi
>   al mio parlar distrettamente fisso.
>   (*Paradiso* VII. 94–96)

> (Now drive your eye into the abyss
>   of the eternal counsel, as far as you can,
>   riveted strictly to my speech.)

Thus vision (and the kind of immediate knowledge that it figures) has
not been transcended—and in fact will not be throughout this whole
journey to the ecstatic vision of the deity. But vision, from the herme-
neutic juncture of *Inferno* IX forward, in conformity with a well-worn
convention of gnoseological representation, has been set on a higher
hermeneutic plane, a new foundation, and presumably represents a pro-
founder seeing into things, no longer surface gazing of the sort so easily
associated with the fatal fixation of the erotic gaze, but rather an intellec-
tual seeing that is healthy ("'ntelletti sani") in a spiritual sense, a kind of

higher immediacy. Dante is envisaging a hermeneutically achieved vision of a type that will eventually lead to Blake's definition of poetic vision as "Allegory addressed to the Intellectual powers." To the degree that Dante passes within Hell's inner domain, his seeing is in-sight, as is the reader's doctrinally aware comprehension of the poem.

Mere outward vision was associated in the exegetical tradition, at least since the school of Alexandria, with myth.[5] Even Hellenistic interpretation of the Homeric poems distinguished between the outwardly apparent *muthos* and a rational meaning to be grasped by the intellect through allegorical interpretation. The strange verses composing the mythologically wrought and fraught episode of encounter with the furies and the Gorgon epitomize the entire strange myth of Hell that envelops the *Inferno,* all of which after all stands in need of interpretation. To this extent, what Dante moves beyond in his hermeneutical (and Christian doctrinal) movement is classical myth.

A conspicuously mythological iconography is used to depict, in an almost unbearably spectacular description, the blood-red, hydra-girdled, serpent-coiffed furies. Here language approximates pure ostension as Virgil designates them one by one with demonstratives ("Questa . . . Quella . . .") and the imperative "Guarda," only pointing out and naming each, "e tacque a tanto" (IX. 45–48). This careful naming with names culled from Latin learning (Megera, Aletto, Tesifone) seems calculated to control the scene's delirious phantasmagoria by just enough doctrine to keep all hell from breaking loose through the power of the image. The threat of visual overkill comes to a head in the Medusa, in which myth and the visual unite forces, almost slaying Dante but for Virgil's doctrine and direct intervention.

The same alliance between myth and the visual is marshaled by the *Inferno*'s next major hermeneutic transition to a still more inward region, the descent to the Malebolge on the back of Geryon. There Dante overtly ironizes upon the absurdity at the story level of his "comedía," insisting that despite its preposterousness, it is true. Extravagance of mythological fantasy is "obviously" designed to make the reader look for a meaning behind the verses about Geryon—just as strange as those about the Medusa—that have the face of a lie but cover some truth: "quel ver c'ha faccia di menzogna" (XVI. 123). In his transition to yet a deeper penetration of Hell by means of this unlikely form of transportation, Dante is deprived of, or limited in, his corporeal sense of sight—"e vidi spenta / ogni veduta fuor che de la fera" (XVII. 114); "E vidi poi,

5. See Jean Pépin, *Mythe et allégorie: Les origines grecques et les contestations judeo-chrétiennes* (Paris: Montaigne, 1958) and "L'Herméneutique ancienne," *Poétique* 23 (1975): 291–300.

ché nol vedea davanti" (XVII. 124); instead he feels the wind and hears
the rushing of water at a distance. What he can as yet only hear, on the
right-hand side, makes him strain his eyes to see to the bottom:

> Io sentía già da la man destra il gorgo
> far sotto noi un orribile scroscio,
> per che con li occhi 'n giù la testa sporgo.
>   (XVII. 118–20)

> (I heard already on the right hand the torrent
> making beneath us a horrible roar,
> so that, eyes straining downward, I crane my neck.)

Similarly, in Canto IX we have seen that Dante's outward vision must
be blocked as he makes, or emblematizes making, a hermeneutic transi-
tion. And the same goes for the reader, whose immediate vision, or literal
reading, encounters a veil that hides deeper truth. Indeed, the reader, no
less than the protagonist, has been absorbed in the spectacle of Hell as
Dante has vividly depicted it up to this point, but is then called upon to
see through to the doctrine veiled beneath the myth. Although Dante-
protagonist is confronted with mythological enemies, to understand them
as such is really the reader/interpreter's victory, and in this sense the
burden of the journey shifts to the reader's interpretive journey, the ad-
ventures of Dante-protagonist reducing, at least in this one respect, to
the dimensions of a heuristic fiction.

It is characteristic of Dante's methods that this reduction is only half
the truth and is paired with assertions of literal truth pronounced in the
most peremptory tones. This paradoxical linkage between the claim
to truth and a foregrounded fictiveness is wrought almost to a breaking
point in the Geryon passage. Dante stridently exposes the fabrications
that go into the making of his poem, while at the same time swearing to
the veracity of the experience it recounts: "e per le note / di questa com-
edía, lettor, ti giuro, / . . . ch'i' vidi" ("and by the notes / of this comedy,
reader, I swear to you, / . . . that I saw"—XVI. 127–30). The ironic tone
of the passage unmasks the fiction as a sort of fraud that nevertheless
participates in the poem's action of revealing an ever so true experience.

To unveil his narrative as myth at the literal level is to de-objectify it,
revealing how it belongs to the reader-interpreter and the significances
this latter (which first of all includes the author himself) projects upon
his world. The danger is that of objectifying what is being interpreted,
of separating it from the interpretive activity involved in its production,
making it a strange object ("li versi strani"). For all this is exactly what
petrifies understanding. The practice of allegorical exegesis, common-
place in Dante's day, programmatically avoids objectifying as myth, or
rather looks through the objectification of signifying relations, which

myth intrinsically is,[6] revealing it as effect and expression of a signifi-
cance, be this psychological, existential, or theological, projected onto
the world of objects. In our time it may be called "demythologization,"
as exactly the reversal of the objectification that characterizes and in fact
defines myth, for example, for Rudolph Bultmann.[7]

In his management of the Medusa scene, Dante expressed with maxi-
mum compression and clarity the way in which the reification of signi-
fying relations into a face no longer seen through but itself taken as ter-
minal object threatens to petrify understanding. The modern analyses
of mythic semiosis and religion help to suggest how myth needs to be
understood as stymieing progress not simply because it belongs to primi-
tive or pagan times of the "dèi falsi e buggiardi" (*Inferno* I. 72), but spe-
cifically because of how, from the point of view of historically reflective
cultures like Dante's and our own, when taken naively it impedes the
process of interpretation, the veritable "altro viaggio" ("other way"—I.
91) that leads Dante toward his goal of total vision.

Countering the tendency of the *muthos* or story toward opaqueness
and self-enclosure, Dante instigates the interpretive process from within
his own text, which in the scene in *Inferno* IX that we have examined
demands to be understood, from beginning to end, as figuring an inter-
pretive event. The opening up of the narrative as an allegory of reading
or interpretation, as it takes place decisively in Canto IX, in fact opens
the whole of the *Inferno* to being understood as representing the basic
problems, the death struggles, of interpretation in a world ordinarily
devoid of grace. The basic experience of hermeneutic blockage, so in-
cisively imitated by the textual performance of this passage, arguably
becomes, with building thematic concentration, the main issue of the
Inferno. This conspicuous instance of the narrative's representing in im-
ages the drama of its own interpretation, which is being performed meta-
narratologically by its reader, is illustrative of how the entire journey of
Dante through the other world represents a journey of interpretation
built into the narrative as its deep structure. Interpretation operates con-
stantly upon the narrative in textually determined ways, such as we have
begun observing in relation to the address to the reader in *Inferno* IX,
and is coordinately coded into the narrative throughout its entire extent.

6. Roland Barthes, in "Le mythe, aujourd'hui," *Mythologies* (Paris: Seuil, 1957), explains
myth as a semiological system freezing the signifier together with its signified into a form taken
not as a historically forged relation, arbitrary and contingent, of signifying one thing by another,
but as itself a natural object.

7. "Myth intends to talk about a reality that cannot be objectified, observed, and con-
trolled. . . . Mythological thinking, however, naively objectifies what is thus beyond the world
as though it were something within the world." Rudolph Bultmann, "On the Problem of
Demythologizing," *New Testament & Mythology and Other Writings,* pp. 160–61.

The *Inferno,* understood in the light (or rather shadow) of the impasse reached in Canto IX, can be taken as a demonstration of the impossibility of merely human interpretation winning through to truth. In the event of a revealed truth such as the poem posits, everything merely human, rational, and rhetorical remains blocked. Interpretation is blocked not only by a literal sense acting as a veil but much more fundamentally by the human condition represented in the *Inferno* as alienated from God. Thus, beyond the consideration already touched on of how perception must be interpretively mediated to yield its truth, the dialectic of seeing and hearing as played out in this scene of interruption by an authorial, prophetic voice opens onto a larger issue concerning the possibility of a prophetic discourse, or true, divinely guided interpretation, in the *Inferno* as a whole, an issue not to be resolved within its own covers.

In the end the *Inferno* must be understood as a dramatization of the death of interpretation, as well as the necessary prelude to its resurrection in the *Purgatorio,* particularly in the form of poetry: "la morta poesì resurga" ("let dead poetry arise"—*Purgatorio* I. 7). The pretense to prophetic powers of interpretation, on the part of Virgil and of Dante himself, is continually weighed in the balance and found wanting, as much as this subject itself becomes an inexhaustibly rich mine for poetic interpretation of characters like Manto and Ulysses, alongside Dante and Virgil. Movement through the *Inferno* leads to progressively greater depths of uninterpretability and insignificance sunk in impenetrable materiality. This sets up a nicely ironic counterpoint to the programmed penetration to increasingly greater depths of understanding. While Dante and his reader are granted, exceptionally, a passageway of interpretation through the *Inferno,* Hell itself presents a reality devoid of interpretive openings, fixed in increasingly gross, corporeal, and, by the end, literally frozen physical fact. From this point of view, hermeneutic blockage—together with the need for transcendence it implies—becomes the main theme and the provisional conclusion, with a dying fall, of the entire *cantica.*

Hell as Interpretive Impasse in the Wake of Inferno IX

If the *Divine Comedy* as a whole represents a journey of interpretation, the *Inferno* in particular concentrates on the potential—and all too often actual, final, and literal—dead-end of this journey. Generalizing from what becomes especially evident in Canto IX, we can see that throughout the *Inferno* Dante's difficulties as character depict *aporiae* of interpretation. This happens programmatically in the setbacks of Dante as a character within the story that converge upon and represent his difficulties in telling it. Even the raw physical action of the journey, which proves increasingly difficult as Dante labors over the ruined ridge connecting the pouches of the Malebolge, becomes allegorically significant, in exquisitely suggestive ways, of the increasing difficulty of interpretation and, specifically, of poetry or, more generally, writing as the vehicles and modes of interpretation.[8]

Dante brings into thematic focus the difficulty of writing that is part of, nay, that thoroughly pervades, the story of his *katabasis* in explicit statements, for example, at the openings of cantos XXVIII ("Chi porìa mai pur con parole sciolte") and XXXII. The latter canto marks the third major structural division of Dis, the well of Cocytus, the ninth circle of the Inferno, and so here, naturally, the hermeneutic thematic once again comes into prominence with Dante's express reflection on the problem of writing his *Inferno* as he bears down upon its end, daunted by the difficulty of describing that hard place of which it is hard to speak ("loco onde parlar è duro"). Writing is here reduced to mere description ("discriver fondo a tutto l'universo"), as if at this stage it could have only a literal sense. By representing his purpose as simply one of literally "describing the bottom of the universe" in a purely factual way ("sì che dal fatto il dir non sia diverso"), Dante may even insinuate that he is betraying his own interpretive mission and principles. For he has shown— and we have seen in *Inferno* IX—how this sort of literalization in representation is itself a form, perhaps *the* literarily realizable form, of damnation.

The treachery, furthermore, inhering specifically in narrative form is realized compellingly and with devilish ingenuity in the following canto by Ugolino's story, motivated by revenge and totally missing the meaning, Christological in essence, of his sons' offering their own flesh to the father who gave it to them, so that this sacramental gesture can have no redeeming value for him, as he literally "petrifies within" ("Io non piangea, sì dentro impetrai"—XXXIII. 49). All natural emotion and meaning are frozen by his vengeful, treacherous determination, which solidifies precisely in the form of narrative—the rhetorical form Dante has relied on throughout his own revenge poem, at the risk of association with Ugolino's eternal damnation, and at any rate assuming even this abysmal human horror into his own experience on the way through it towards a possibility of redemption.

The interpretive means Dante employs as poet, notably, writing, had already been radically called into question at just the juncture where, ironically, he boasts of his unprecedented mastery in this medium, crying silence to Lucan and Ovid with regard to their now inferior descriptions

8. The intimate connection between Dante's difficulties as character and the difficulty he faces as writer and poet has been examined in detail by Robin Kirkpatrick in *Dante's Inferno: Difficulty and Dead Poetry*, pp. 227–379. Among much else, these provocative pages track the breakdown of confidence in rational and discursive means of interpretation in the Malebolge in the face of a progressively visual hell.

of metamorphoses as formal but not material change (XXV. 94–102). The boast concerns Dante's ability to represent precisely *change,* and yet this phenomenon of mutability is just what threatens every writer and indeed any human achievement whatsoever with oblivion. The canto just before the boast, Canto XXIV, had begun with a hint of the utterly ephemeral nature of writing, the primary means of attempting to stabilize all human culture including Dante's poem, in the mention of how the frost imitates the image of its white sister on the ground, but not for long, since as it melts in the sun its "pen" does not remain sharp ("ma poco dura a la sua penna tempra"—XXIV. 6). It was perhaps not without an implicit acknowledgment of a kind of complicity, then, that Dante described the vanity and vanishing into ashes of Vanni Fucci through a metaphor of inscribing letters:

> né O sì tosto mai né I si scrisse,
>   com' el s'accese e arse, e cener tutto
>   convenne che cascando divenisse. . . .
>
> (XXIV. 100–102)

> (neither *o* nor *i* was ever written so fast
>   as he was ignited and burned, and all to ashes
>   it was meet that, falling, he should turn. . . .)

Surely it was not accidental either that the difficulty of the physical journey, its path becoming "ronchioso, stretto e malagevole, / ed erto più assai che quel di pria" ("rocky, narrow and difficult, / and a good deal steeper than before"—XXIV. 62–63), was most heavily underscored precisely in Canto XXIV, just where writing and its difficulty, its inadequacy with respect to the dynamism of the physical world, become a main concern.

However, not just writing but every human means of interpretation is thrown into check during the descent into the Inferno. All the difficulties encountered in the difficult descent through Hell reflect at least indirectly on the interpretive dilemmas of the author (and by extension of the reader); they demand to be read as hermeneutic difficulties. Even the sins and torments depicted or described in the *Inferno* embody variations on the theme of the blockage inherent in any human act of interpretation without grace. For every sin, as Infernal images so often and so poignantly recall (e.g., "la cara e buona imagine paterna" of Brunetto), causes or coincides with a deformation of the image of God in humanity, and thus represents an obstacle to knowing God and to interpreting oneself truly.

While the *Inferno* presents humanity in a state devoid of grace, the presentation itself, despite the programmatic claims to prophetically reveal the judgments of God, participates in that very state. To show this,

Dante contrives to call into question his own interpretation, at the same time as he offers it, by juxtaposing authorial assertions of the prophetic voice, like that in the address to the reader in Canto IX, with the humiliations and defeat experienced by the protagonist so as to suggest how the poet himself is undercut. The way the character is presented pertains, at least obliquely, to the self-presentation of the poet, who, like the pilgrim, swings from prophetic to impotent postures. The Malebolge particularly is punctuated, as Kirkpatrick has brought out in finely sifted detail, by affirmations of Dante's prestige turned to mockery and farce by the compromising incidents and indignities to which he is subjected.

Canto XIX, for example, begins with the ringing jeremiad of denunciation, "O Simon mago," with which Dante chastises the popes. But, as is typically the case, this instance of the prophetic voice of the author is ensued by a comeuppance within the narrative that threatens to turn its resounding aura into pretentious airs. Dante's identity is completely shaken a little later in this canto by his being mistaken for Pope Boniface VIII; he is capable only of a negative, stuttering reply ("Non son colui, non son colui che credi") given him verbatim by Virgil. Although he manages to recover his poise in this encounter, it is only to be even more radically insulted and undermined in the following cantos. Such vicissitudes of Dante's fictive persona gain their most powerful motivation from the way they bear indirectly upon the real, historical Dante and on the difficulties and presumption of his interpretive enterprise.

As in cantos VIII and IX, again in cantos XXI–XXII devils threaten to block a fearful Dante and a Virgil who again loses mastery of the situation. Here, too, the narrative depicts impasses that stand for interpretive blockage in relation to the narrative. The story becomes farcically exciting and spectacular in a way that invites speaking of "the obsessiveness of the fiction" (Kirkpatrick, *Dante's Inferno*, p. 274) that blocks interpretation through to any more edifying significance. Dante is reduced to defenseless vulnerability by the devils threatening to "skewer him in the rump" ("in sul groppone"). Once we have learned to read the narrative as reflecting back upon the interpretive act that creates it, all this with its indignity hints that there may be something ambiguously ridiculous in Dante's attitude as prophetic poet with a message of the ultimate seriousness.

In these cantos of the Malebolge, Dante himself accepts becoming a ludicrous figure within his own comedy or, rather, farce. For the authority for his interpretation cannot rest on his own intellectual prowess or rhetorical accomplishment. Precisely this must be broken down if Dante's poem is to become a vehicle of a divine Word bearing a transcendent address. The human voice and prophetic persona belong to the veil needing to be pierced for the truth to be revealed or take place. In other words, Dante refuses to forget that his poem cannot achieve prophetic revelation simply by claiming or pretending to do so, or on the basis of any classical, human, or rhetorical resources of his art of poetry. The divine truth revealed through the poem is not identical with what Dante himself, however skillfully and earnestly, says in his work.

Only by the breakdown of all his art and by its being broken open to other voices, only through "comedy," that is, a mixture and multiplicity of styles, as opposed to Virgil's "high tragedy," is it possible for Dante's poem to become a vehicle of something beyond himself and beyond the whole human range of interpretation. Indeed, in Canto XIX, it is the words of Scripture that jut through Dante's own discourse excoriating the popes, as in the echo of Christ's words to Peter, "Viemmi retro" ("Follow me"—XIX. 93; cf. also line 105), letting that Other who alone can make the poem truly prophetic be heard in it, not in rhetorically elaborate speech, but in the biblical *sermo humilis*. More than any high art these plain phrases (which are nevertheless described as notes that Dante sings—"io li cantava cotai note") constitute what Virgil too, evidently, can recognize as "words truly expressed":

> I' credo ben ch'al mio duca piacesse,
>   con sì contenta labbia sempre attese
>   lo suon de le parole vere espresse.
>   (*Inferno* XIX. 121–23)

> (I well believe it pleased my guide,
>   who with so satisfied an expression
>   listened to the sound of the true words expressed.)

Immediately after this, Virgil has nothing to say; his rhetoric, his "ornata parola," is irrelevant as he leads Dante on by his physical presence and affection alone, embracing his companion in silent humanity:

> Però con ambo le braccia mi prese;
>   e poi che tutto su mi s'ebbe al petto,
>   rimontò per la via onde discese.
>   (*Inferno* XIX. 124–126)

> (And so with both arms he took me;
>   and when he held me full against his breast,
>   climbed back up the way he had come down.)

The very next canto, ostensibly an encomium of Virgil, actually turns to subtly undermining all the authority that this greatest of human *auctors* can command. Canto XX is devoted to the punishment of the divines and to an examination of Virgil's pedigree as prophet, with its inset recounting the founding of Mantua, Virgil's own home city and origin, by the damned prophetess Manto. The peril of Virgil's and even Dante's being confounded with such prophetic perversions is most seriously contemplated. Retrospectively we are given to wonder whether Dante's sermonizing against the popes in the preceding canto, although approved by Virgil, cannot but be tainted by the human poet's arrogating a prophetic authority to himself in defiance of the ordained clergy.

This process of self-questioning is necessary if a divine voice is to be heard and transcendent truth be allowed to occur through the representations of the poem. The *Inferno* relentlessly undermines Dante's claims to a conventional, classical prophetic authority after the fashion of Virgil in order to make way for the possibility of authentically prophetic revelation in the event of the poem beyond the author's control, in which he and his work are taken up to become the vehicle of divine revelation. The blockage inherent in human understanding without grace is worked out with particular intensity, and in a way that stands symbolically for damnation and the whole of the *Inferno,* precisely in the portrayal of Virgil. Virgil represents human, rational, rhetorical understanding at its best and highest development, including a certain ambiguous capacity for prophecy, which may genuinely prefigure revealed truth but nevertheless remains in and for itself desperately lost.

Most importantly, as we are now in a position to grasp, the nature of Virgil's limitation as guide for Dante is shown to be precisely hermeneutic. Fundamentally, Virgil is incapable of understanding—for lack of which grace he is condemned to Limbo—the Christ event. In *Inferno* XII. 38–39, Virgil describes the *Descensus Christi* to Limbo and the earthquake that announced it as if he were describing the daring exploit of a Homeric hero; the souls are lifted from the clutches of Hell as if taken captive or freed in a raid:

> "ma certo poco pria, se ben discerno,
>   che venisse colui che la gran preda
>   levò a Dite del cerchio superno,
> da tutte parti l'alta valle feda
>   tremò sì, ch'i' pensai che l'universo
>   sentisse amor, per lo qual è chi creda
> più volte il mondo in caòsse converso."
> (XII. 37–43)

> ("Certainly but a little earlier, if I perceive aright,
>   than the one who lifted the great booty
>   from Dis out of the highest circle came,
> On all sides the deep, fetid valley
>   so quaked that I thought the universe
>   felt love, the cause for which some think
> the world at times has turned back into chaos.")

Virgil interprets the event through reference to a cosmogony ascribed by Aristotle to Empedocles, a patently pagan view of the universe as cyclically returning to a state of chaos. Although he may be uneasy about accepting this view himself ("è chi creda"), clearly Virgil ignores or is at least confused about the decisiveness of the advent of Christ. Augustine's schematizing of pagan time as circular, in contrast to the linear time of the Bible, will be shown in the following chapter to be too simplistic for Dante's purposes, yet the notion nevertheless serves him here to hint at Virgil's hermeneutic shortcomings.

Virgil's supposedly prophetic powers of interpretation are called into question, especially in the Malebolge, by the breakdown of discursive forms of knowing before the startling immediacy of ocular evidence. Rationality and discursive order, the virtues of Virgil and of pagan philosophy and rhetoric generally, need to be radically undermined in order to re-establish foundations on a Christian basis, from a transcendent source. By this means, the dialectic between visual-perceptual and discursive modes of knowledge inscribes itself within the question of Virgil's and ultimately of Dante's own prophetic authority, its channels and their grounds. The poem's prophetic claims—such as in the decidedly prophetic voice that addresses the reader in the hermeneutic injunction in *Inferno* IX—are tested, dismantled, and recomposed in a most exacting fashion by the carefully calculated vicissitudes of discourse and vision especially in this part of the poem (cf. Kirkpatrick, *Dante's Inferno*, p. 236 ff.).

Virgil's whole way of understanding and interpreting, based on general principles and examples, and on smooth rhetorical glosses, "ragionamenti," is undermined perhaps most arrestingly by the particular test of the vision of the cross in Canto XXIII. For what confronts Dante and Virgil in the *spectacle* of Caiaphas crucified on the floor of the bolgia of the hypocrites is a parodic image of the unique event that is the ultimate interpretive key in a Christian universe. But this Virgil cannot comprehend:

> Allor vid' io maravigliar Virgilio
> sovra colui ch'era disteso in croce
> tanto vilmente ne l'etterno essilio.
>
> (XXIII. 124–46)

> (Then I saw Virgil marveling
> over the one who was stretched out in a cross
> so vilely in eternal exile.)

Indeed, human, rational, discursive understanding per se is found to be wanting in this scene (as through the overall movement of the *Inferno*), showing the need for some higher source, some transcendent basis of true interpretation, intervening into the darkness of a lower world. The "etterno essilio" of rationality without God is what Virgil later in *Purga-*

torio XXI. 18 names as his own fate. Moreover, Dante's own words are broken off by the sight of Caiaphas, of *one* crucified before him:

> Io comminciai: "O frati, i vostri mali . . .";
> ma più non dissi, ch'a l'occhio mi corse
> *un,* crucifisso in terra con tre pali.
>
> (XXIII. 109–11)

> (I began: "O brothers, your ills . . .";
> but I said no more, because to my eye came
> *one,* crucified in the earth with three stakes.)

Whether they were to be words of pity or of prophetic denunciation of the hypocrites in this circle, Dante's speech was itself liable to fall into hypocrisy, as is human language in general as used by any of the sons of Adam this side of Paradise regained. This singular ("un"), excruciating vision brings Dante's words up short, as is ineluctably the case when he assumes prophetic tones and postures in the *Inferno,* and particularly in the Malebolge. In this way, the opposition of seeing and hearing, which in Canto IX was seen to encode literal versus interpretively informed understanding, is transposed and its valence reversed. The polarization of speech and sight still functions as a mechanism for demonstrating the necessarily transcendent grounding of prophetic interpretation. But in the Malebolge, sight, now no longer associated with the deceptive veil and surface of the letter, stands over and against human discourse for the interruptive event that checks superficially rational, glibly discursive assimilation, and thus at the same time points to the need for transcendence.

This latter exigency characterizes the hermeneutic dynamic of Dante's entire project, which admits of no stable formulas such as that sight is always superficial or rational discourse invariably veridical. Indeed, later in the *Inferno* the theme of how the eye deceives, that is, of "quanto 'l senso s'inganna di lontano" (XXXI. 26), returns to preside over the descent via the giants, seeming towers, to Cocytus. And at this point Virgil has just had to snap Dante out of the visual inebriation ("le luci mie sì inebriate"—XXIX. 2) that has enthralled him to the hallucinatory vividness of the scenes of bodily schism and disease in the ninth and tenth bolgias, with stinging reproofs: "Che pur guate? / perché la tua vista . . ." ("What are you looking at? / why does your sight . . ."—XXIX. 4–5), and again "Or pur mira, / che per poco che teco non mi risso" ("Now just keep looking, / and I would almost have a row with you myself"— XXX. 131–32).

The *Inferno* constantly eschews univocal determination of values in rational, human terms, and so all pat solutions to questions such as whether the damned can be possessed of dignity, even tragic heroism, or are to be viewed uncompromisingly as contemptible, or again whether pity is the humane reaction to them or a form of complicity and refusal of God's wholly good will, or even whether Dante's questioning curiosity concerning the other world is praiseworthy or importunate.[9] On such issues, this deliberately didactic text surprisingly generates unresolved dialectic. Rather than consistent positions, the *Inferno,* despite certain appearances, offers only shifting images of the insufficiency and instability of all human judgments. It is in the necessary oscillation between interpretive options that the *Inferno* depicts the inescapable human predicament, and only the continual onward drive of the narrative can embody the promise of eventual resolution of such antinomies. Truth comes through time and the quest for disclosure with its orientation toward transcendence, rather than being given in any general principles.

2. PASSAGE

Just as hermeneutic impasse is the situation reached within the narrative in *Inferno* IX right before the hermeneutic injunction to the reader, so its removal and the journey's continuation, effected by the heaven-sent messenger, ensues immediately upon the imperative address. Indeed, the syncopated resumption of the narrative ("E *già* venía"—IX. 64) makes it overlap and interpenetrate temporally with the address itself. The appeal to the reader for interpretation seems virtually to be efficacious even within the narrative, bringing free passage in its train in the shape of a personification of the hermeneutic principle. Thus the application of Dante-protagonist's journey through Hell to the reader's journey through the poem is structured into the canto by the juxtaposition of the disruptive address to the reader with, on the one hand (the forehand), the protagonist's being blocked in a perceptual channel analogous to literal reading, namely, sight, and, on the other (the posterior), with his being liberated by an event featuring a Hermes figure. Such is the parallelism of hermeneusis at work within and upon the narrative.

Upon return to the narrative sequence, after the interruption of the single but absolutely decisive *terzina* addressed to the reader, mythological motifs continue to be employed, but they no longer represent obstacles to progress. Once it has, through the hermeneutic process, been given its due doctrinal weight, myth comes to represent a means of revelation rather than a dangerously seductive veil. Instead of demonish obstacles to progress, the stores of myth bring forth a celestial deputy or "messenger": "elli era da ciel messo" (IX. 85). The descent of the figure is reminiscent of similar descents of Hermes in Statius's *Thebaid* (VII. 65)

9. On this last point, one could begin by comparing *Inferno* III. 79–81; X. 19–21; XIV. 133.

and in the *Aeneid* (IV. 416 ff.). But now myth is no longer perilously fascinating in and for itself; it is rather the bearer of a message from above and beyond. Whether the figure is to be strictly identified with Hermes, and so as a personification of hermeneutics, or not, clearly hermeneutics is what makes this difference between myth's functioning first as a deceptive veil, then as disclosure, ushering in the continuation of the journey and the entry deeper into Hell.

Once hermeneutic help arrives, and once the summons to interpret has been heeded, most importantly by the reader who looks over the shoulder of the fictive persona of Dante-protagonist, eyes can again be used to good purpose; accordingly, Dante's eyes are uncovered, and he is directed to use them:

> Li occhi mi sciolse e disse: "Or drizza il nerbo
>   del viso su per quella schiuma antica
>   per indi ove quel fummo è più acerbo."
>
> (IX. 73–75)

> (He let go of my eyes and said: "Now direct the nerve
>   of sight upon that ancient foam
>   in the place where that smoke is most acrid.")

The "antique foam" of mythological representation can "now" ("Or") be looked at as a surface that taken for itself is obscure, but out of which a clear and luminous message emerges. Hence the celestial messenger's role within the narrative includes clearing the air that obstructs vision ("Dal volto rimovea quell'aere grasso"—IX. 82).

The celestial messenger's embodiment of the hermeneutic principle is also suggested by his hurry to get beyond what is immediately before him—perhaps to return to the hidden region of fullness of meaning from which he has come, like Beatrice in *Inferno* II ("vegno del loco ove tornar disio"—71); but, in any case, his anxiousness is provoked by *other* intents and purposes, by unwillingness to be confined to what is present at hand. As soon as his mission is accomplished, that is, as soon as his role within the narrative has been performed, without further ado he passes onward "like a man whom other cares press and gnaw at / than those of the one in front of him" ("non fe' motto a noi, ma fe' sembiante / d'omo cui altra cura stringa e morda / che quella di colui che li è davanti"—IX. 101–3).

Even more hermeneutically significant—since it opens a whole new level of significance—than any particulars of how he is represented within the narrative, the messenger is a transparently allegorical figure representing some kind of event of grace. The mechanism at work would seem to be typological, for the messenger is said to walk dry-shod across the waters, evoking a famous passage from the Gospels and hinting at a Christological dimension to this hermeneutic savior. The words "un ch'al passo / passava" (IX. 80–81) have puzzled commentators, whose explanations are all found to be inadequate by Natalino Sapegno.[10] But if the phrase can be interpreted as referring to a textual passage—"one who in that passage passed"—the redundancy turns out to be motivated by a provocative double entendre. Not just a passing, overdescribed detail in a narrative, but rather a doctrinal text that can function quasi-typologically as a scriptural precedent for this fictive, or perhaps rather figural, savior-event, would be signified by that seemingly unaccountable, but in fact deliberately redundant phrase.[11]

Indeed, reference has already been made to a previous descent into Hell, that of Christ, which opened, and by that very fact left open, the gate:

> "Questa lor tracotanza non è nova;
> ché già l'usaro a men secreta porta,
> la qual sanza serrame ancor si trova."
>
> (VIII. 124–26)

> ("This arrogance of theirs is nothing new;
> for already they used it at a less secret gate,
> which still remains without a lock.")

In this relation, the episode is presented as a repetition of another that offers a paradigm and makes the immediate situation comprehensible in a positive light, within the horizon of Christian victory. The typological apparatus of the scene has in fact been demonstrated in detail by Amilcare Iannucci, who offers a reading based on the *Descensus Christi ad Inferas* related in the apocryphal Gospel of Nicodemus.[12] Iannucci notes how Dante's account of a descent into Hell early Saturday morning in the year of our Lord 1300 forms a radical synthesis of sacred and profane traditions, as it is prefigured not only by Christ's temporally coincident visit to Limbo, recalled in *Inferno* VIII. 124–27, but also by Hercules'

10. "[T]utte spiegazioni che non soddisfano appieno. Credo si tratti soltanto di un'espressione ridondante." Natalino Sapegno, ed., *La Divina Commedia,* vol. 1, *Inferno* (Scandicci [Florence]: La Nuova Italia, 1985), p. 107.

11. On some of the looser uses of biblical types as moral examples to be followed and fulfilled by extrabiblical protagonists or even by readers in their own future, rather than only in connection with a biblical antitype, or what has been called "postfiguration," see A. C. Charity, *Events and Their Afterlife: A Dialectics of Christian Typology in the Bible and in Dante.* Developing such a position, Mark Musa in *Advent at the Gates: Dante's Comedy* (Bloomington: Indiana University Press, 1974) interpets the messenger as Dante's re-enactment of the First Coming of Christ, to be followed by the Second Advent, which according to St. Bernard's scheme occurs daily in the lives of men, and would be represented by the angels in the Valley of Princes.

12. Amilcare A. Iannucci, "Dottrina e allegoria in *Inferno* VIII. 67–IX. 105," in *Dante e le forme dell'allegoresi,* ed. Michelangelo Picone (Ravenna: Longo, 1987), pp. 99–124.

liberation of Theseus from Hades, triumphing over Cerberus, associated in *Inferno* IX. 91–99 with the victory of the messenger over the demons. Such intertextual typological connections cannot but underscore the interpretive essence of the messenger's event in the text.

But, even more importantly, we must remember that Christ's descent is not only the prototype of a heroic foray into the nether realm; the Christ event is the hermeneutic key to all events in a Christian universe. It is the type not just for the epic action of Dante's victorious passage but also for the universal Christian struggle against darkness in the battle to understand. It prefigures the reader's victory in that "passo" through which he passes in this particular reading, descending into a hell, a darkness, an unconscious populated by fears and furies, but along a path opened by Christ and lighted by that true light, typologically reflected. Undoubtedly, Christ and, specifically, his descent into Hell form the basis for the Christian understanding Dante attempts to inculcate through this scene.

The hermeneutic event of the poem is ultimately grounded on the Christ event, and the violence of the latter, gruesomely displayed in the Crucifixion, unfailingly invades the act of interpretation as represented in the poem. This literally "crucial" aspect of the hermeneutic model Dante is working with, one that reflects on all the others and even threatens to throw them into check, is dramatically stamped upon the description of the celestial messenger's descent. The eruption of this figure onto the scene unmistakably manifests the violent side of hermeneutics; it follows in the tracks of Christ's harrowing of Hell, which is still legible in traces of structural damage pointed out at several reprises in the course of the descent (*Inferno* V. 34; XI. 2; XII. 34–36; XXI. 108; XXIII. 136). Terror and destruction make up the keynotes of the scene as Dante composes it. Before anything can be made out visually, the imminent arrival is announced by a dreadful uproar of noise:

> E già venìa su per le torbide onde
> un fracasso d'un suon, pien di spavento,
> per cui tremavano amendue le sponde.
> (IX. 64–66)

> (And already along the torbid waves came
> a fracas of noise, full of fright,
> on account of which both banks quaked.)

A more violent entrance could scarcely have been imagined than that of this celestial messenger, like an impetuous wind that wounds the forest, ripping away branches, as it goes proudly ("va superbo"—IX. 71). The simile of the frogs escaping in terror from the hostile serpent likewise dramatizes the role of this personification of hermeneutics as aggressor.

The disruption and obstreperousness that confront Dante and Virgil externally in the main plot of the episode are here carried inside the symbol of the hermeneutic process itself. Not only is hermeneutics called forth, then, by obstacles to continuation and to communication; such rupture constitutes the hermeneutic process intrinsically. This must be so if hermeneutics is to be a procedure for reaching or being reached by an otherness, as the calling in (or down) of an absolute other, one "sent from heaven," suggests.

Inimical to the protagonists' progress and to the whole hermeneutic process, the demons jealously defend their realm against all intrusion of otherness. Indeed, Dante and Virgil are stopped at the entry to Dis specifically because of Dante's otherness, for the demons are outraged that Dante, being one who is not dead ("sanza morte"), should be going through the realm of the "morta gente" (VIII. 84–85). This resistance to otherness is just what must be overcome if the hermeneutic event is to take place. But this, it seems clear, cannot be done without violence.[13]

Dante, of course, is about to pass into the zone of the *Inferno* where the "violenti" (XI. 28) are punished. But, as always, he participates in what he visits and knows, this being the condition of all knowing as hermeneutically understood, and the transition to this segment of Hell underscores precisely the violence that belongs as a constitutive principle to hermeneutics. What Dante sees here in the seventh circle of Hell reflects upon what he does in creating it: upon the violence, for example, of the interpretation of Brunetto Latini as a sodomite, against all historical or traditional knowledge and even, presumably, against Dante's own feelings toward "la cara e buona imagine paterna" ("the dear and good paternal image"—XV. 83) of his own teacher or at least favored author. Dante's interpretive violences are fully of a piece with the violences that are manifest in the sinners, as in Pier de la Vigna's interpretation of himself as a thing whose life can be broken off by physical violence as if it were a tree. The fact that Dante is enacting, interpretively, the violence

---

13. For a contemporary perspective on the violent side of the hermeneutic phenomenon, see "Violence du visage: Entretien avec Emmanuel Lévinas," *Hermeneutica* 5 (1985). The logic of violence intrinsic to the interpretive act has also been stressed, somewhat one-sidedly in my view, by Michel Foucault: "Il n'y a jamais, si vous voulez, un *interpretandum* qui ne soit déjà *interpretans,* si bien que c'est un rapport tout autant de violence que d'élucidation qui s'établit dans l'interprétation. En effet, l'interprétation n'éclaire pas une matière à interpréter, qui s'offrirait à elle passivement; elle ne peut que s'emparer, et violemment, d'une interprétation déjà là, qu'elle doit renverser, retourner, fracasser à coups de marteau" ("There is never, as it were, an *interpretandum* that is not also already *interpretans,* so that the relationship established in interpretation is as much one of violence as of elucidation. In fact, interpretation does not illuminate a matter that passively offers itself to be interpreted; interpretation can only seize, violently, an interpretation already there, which it can reverse, bend, hammer to bits"). "Nietzsche, Freud, Marx," in *Nietzsche: Cahiers du royaument* (Paris: Minuit, 1967), p. 189.

that is his theme belongs rigorously to the realization of the poem as a hermeneutic event, that is, as a knowing that fundamentally proceeds not from disinterested representation but from existential involvement.

The note of violence so pronounced about the celestial messenger's descent is again struck forcefully in the flight of Geryon in Canto XVII, already indicated as the next major hermeneutic transition after Canto IX:

> "Ecco la fiera con la coda aguzza,
>   che passa i monti e rompe i muri e l'armi!"
>
> (XVII. 1–2)
>
> ("Behold the beast with the sharpened tail,
>   who crosses mountains and shatters walls and arms!")

This time, however, it is a violence not so much of nature, as in the celestial messenger's descent and throughout the seventh circle (with its river of blood, rain of fire, and bleeding trees) entered almost immediately thereafter, but of human artifacts and artifice. Geryon is an unnatural concoction and evinces all the "fraud" that artifice can trump up. This "sozza imagine di froda" ("loathsome image of fraud") reads, among other ways, as a figure for Dante's *Commedia* itself.[14] For Dante's act of interpretation in his poem as symbolized by Geryon is not only violent; it is also fraudulent. Dante's own involvement in fraud at just this juncture, as he enters into the eighth circle, where ten-fold sins of fraud are punished, is first hinted at by the description of his own and Virgil's path as having to be twisted a little to approach the wicked beast:

> "Or convien che si torca
> la nostra via un poco insino a quella
> bestia malvagia che colà si corca."
>
> (XVII. 28–23)
>
> ("Now it is necessary to twist
> our way a little, even up to that
> malicious beast that is lying over there.")

We observed in the preceding section how in this episode Dante foregrounds the contrived, not to say mendacious, aspect of his "comedía"—whether to protect or to subvert its literal truth claim. The *Commedia's*

---

14. Franco Ferrucci, in *Il poema del desiderio: Poetica e passione in Dante* (Milan: Leonardo, 1990), develops the fundamental point that Geryon "è anche la personificazione della menzogna poetica" (p. 99). See, further, Zygmut Barański, "The 'Marvelous' and the 'Comic': Toward a Reading of *Inferno* XVI," *Lectura Dantis: A Forum for Dante Research and Interpretation* 7 (1990): 72–95, and John Kleiner, "Mismapping the Underworld: Essays on Error in Dante," (Ph.D. diss., Stanford University, 1991), p. 148.

own complicity in fraud receives further concentrated development in
the Ulysses canto, where Dante becomes acutely conscious of the dan-
gers of rhetorical deceptiveness, sharply figured in the spectacle of Ulysses
being consumed by a flaming tongue—dangers in which Dante himself
is perilously close to his classical foil and alter ego. This risk is felt in the
self-monitory lines that constitute a hermeneutic enframement, delineat-
ing its interpretive bearings in the author's own autobiographical drama,
for this absorbing encounter:

> Allor mi dolsi, e ora mi ridoglio
>   quando drizzo la mente a ciò ch'io vidi,
>   e piùlo 'ingegno affreno ch'i' non soglio,
> perché non corra che virtù nol guidi. . . .
>
> (XXVI. 19–22)
>
> (I grieved then, and now again I grieve
>   when I direct my mind to what I saw,
>   and my genius I rein in more than I'm used to,
> that it not run without virtue as guide. . . .)

The Ulysses encounter, moreover, points to yet a further, and a unify-
ing, element absolutely vital to interpretation in Dante's reflection upon
it at this stage in the phrase "com'altrui piacque" ("as pleased another"—
XXVI. 141), so resonant up and down the *Commedia* and in all Christian
tradition. Hermeneutics, called forth to comprehend something alien, is
ultimately an endeavor to reach or be reached by an other; accordingly,
for Dante all human interpretation can find its sufficient ground only
in a divine "Altrui." Unlike Ulysses, deaf to the exigencies of all others,
including son, father, wife, companions, and also Diomedes, with whom,
unacknowledged, he shares the same forked tongue of flame, Dante
is reached by a divine otherness, and this makes all the difference. The
other who was pleased to intervene on Dante's behalf in an act of grace—
"com' altrui piacque" (*Purgatorio* I. 133)—saves him from perishing on
the sea that devoured Ulysses, from which no man was ever "expert,"
however great his own powers, to return.

Interpretation is a question of life or death, and Dante represents it as
such. It is even a question of eternal life or death if we consider that the
inhabitants of Dante's Inferno are consistently shown to be damned by
their own self-interpretations, their eternally stubborn resistance in refus-
ing to understand themselves as God sees them. Witness Francesca's ro-
mantic idealizations of her sin or Brunetto Latini's undying yet deadly
humanistic illusions. All this with its intense pertinence for Dante him-
self is concentrated especially in the figure of Ulysses. Although Dante
broaches the hermeneutic question in a didactic guise, it becomes pro-
gressively clear that much more is at stake in the hermeneutic junctures,

given the way they determine the meaning of the whole poem, and that what we have to do with is an existential hermeneutics. The hermeneutic process in its radical form involves shaking one's self-understanding and identity to their existential grounds. The self is taken up into a larger circle of understanding that shatters and redefines it, yanking it out of its own familiar sphere. What is ultimately required is a transformation of existence, not just a shift in perspective or change of ideas.[15]

The structural affinity between the Geryon sequence in XVI–XVII and the Ulysses episode in XXVI as "narrative transitions" has been examined in detail by Teodolinda Barolini in "Ulysses, Geryon, and the Aeronautics of Narrative Transition."[16] We now need to grasp the intimate connection between the two passages from the point of view of their hermeneutic function. The *Inferno's* pivotal transitions to a hermeneutics of violence (VIII–IX) and to a hermeneutics of fraud (XVI–XVII), as well as to a more overtly personal, self-reflexive, and existential hermeneutic (XXVI), have been flagged by Dante as specifically hermeneutic in nature through a carefully managed symbolism of directions. A code of left and right turnings is consistently applied throughout the *Inferno* (and even beyond, I believe, albeit with greater complications). In the course of their physical descent through the Inferno, Dante and Virgil always turn to the left, as is stated, for example, by Virgil:

> "Tu sai che 'l loco è tondo;
> e tutto che tu sie venuto molto,
> *pur a sinistra,* giù calando al fondo
> non se' ancor per tutto 'l cerchio vòlto."[17]

(XIV. 124–127)

> ("You know that the place is circular;
> and although you have come far,
> *always toward the left,* dropping down to the bottom,
> still you have not revolved around the whole circle.")

---

15. See John Freccero, "The Prologue Scene" (especially the section "The Wings of Ulysses") and "Dante's Ulysses: From Epic to Novel" in *Dante: The Poetics of Conversion,* on Dante's uncompromising demand for Christian conversion as opposed to mere intellectual illumination on a Neoplatonic model.

16. Teodolinda Barolini, *The Undivine Comedy,* pp. 48–73. John Freccero dwells on these connections from the standpoint of their significance for the structure of allegorical autobiography in the *Inferno* in "Introduction to *Inferno,*" in R. Jacoff, ed., *The Cambridge Companion to Dante.*

17. Cf. XXIII. 68: "Noi ci volgemmo ancor pur a man manca." Also, at the conclusion of Canto X, when Dante has been counseled by Virgil to not yet try to interpret the ominous prophecy of Farinata regarding his future, but to wait until he reaches Beatrice, linear narrative progress, with this deferral of interpretation, is resumed on the left foot—"Appresso mosse a man sinistra il piede" (X. 132)—just as it began, abortively, in Canto I on the "piè fermo," that is, the left foot (see Freccero, *Dante,* p. 34 ff).

But Canto IX—exceptionally—ends with a sharp turn in the opposite direction, to the *right*—"E poi ch' *a la man destra* si fu vòlto / passammo" (132–33)—just as again, in order to mount Geryon, a rightward detour has to be taken: "Però scendemmo *a la destra mammella*" (XVII. 31).

These unexpected changes of direction have caused a good deal of puzzlement and confusion among commentators. Allen Mandelbaum remarks on IX. 132: "This is one of only two points in Hell where the poets head to the right, the other being at Canto XVII. 31. Normally the poets head left in Hell and right on the Mountain of Purgatory. The deviation here seems to indicate some special intent, but no commentator has defined it convincingly."[18] But having identified the two passages in question as pivotal hermeneutic transitions, we need not remain clueless upon finding them set off in this way as traversed by a movement contrary to the normal direction of movement in the narrated journey. Interpretation, as a reflexive doubling back upon literal sense, is aptly figured by the image of a turn back in the direction opposite that of the regular progress within the narrative.

The same connection between rightward turning back upon one's tracks and deep, reflective interpretation, such that the former becomes an image for the latter, is also made in another text, seemingly a cue for allegorical interpretation that has likewise remained highly enigmatic to commentators, *Inferno* XV. 97–99:

> Lo mio maestro allora *in su la gota*
> 　　*destra si volse in dietro* e riguardommi;
> 　　poi disse: "Bene ascolta chi la nota."

> (My mentor then *turned his head back*
> 　　*around to the right* and looked at me;
> 　　then he said: "He listens well who takes note.")

And when we read that the celestial messenger "led with his left" though it was tedious ("menando la sinistra innanzi spesso; / e sol di quell'angoscia parea lasso"—IX. 83–84), might this not encode how the literal sense always comes first even at the expense of delaying the disclosure of the true meaning of the episode and, in this case, of the messenger himself? Such a coding of left and right, moreover, can be derived from such canonical sources as biblical wisdom literature: "The heart of the wise inclines to the right, but the heart of the fool to the left" (Eccles. 10.2).[19]

---

18. Allen Mandelbaum, *The Divine Comedy of Dante Alighieri: Inferno* (New York: Bantam, 1980), p. 359.

19. A yet broader anthropological basis can be inferred from Robert Hertz's classic essay "La prééminence de la main droite: Étude sur la polarité religieuse," in *Mélanges de sociologie religieuse et folklore* (Paris: Librairie Félix Alcan, 1928): "La droite représente le haut, le monde supérieur, le ciel; tandis que la gauche ressortit au monde inférieur et à la terre" ("The right

Dante's virtually obsessive references to directions throughout the poem are hardly casual, nor can they be treated merely as matters of fact and circumstance objectively given by the journey. Surely they have a systematic (or at least pseudosystematic) significance: they stake out the poem's deep structure as an interpretive itinerary, constantly operative in relation to the reader, but also surfacing in the narrative itself, which is indeed marked and measured as interpretive each step of the way. This particular key for decoding unlocks the meaning of a wealth of telltale details, as, for example, the leftward direction of Ulysses' "folle volo, / sempre acquistando *dal lato mancino*" ("mad flight, / always gaining on the left side"—XXVI. 125–26). Ulysses' sticking unswervingly to the course of his mad flight, letter-blind and leftward-bound, prevents him from achieving the hermeneutic distance, through the ability to turn back reflexively and hermeneutically (rightward), that saves Dante, perhaps by a narrow margin, but in a decisively different direction, that of interpretation, in which he is led by his guide.[20]

3. AMBIGUITIES

Within a hermeneutic perspective, the violence and fraud manifest exteriorly in Hell become ways of exploring the violence and fraud that are internal to the interpretive process of the *Inferno*. Both are quintessentially characteristics of the demonic, and the *cantica* indeed evinces awareness at certain points of being an exploration of the demonic not only on the thematic level but in its own interpretive techniques as well. The metaphor in which the demons over the gate of Dis first appear describes them as "raining from the sky" ("dal ciel piovuti") onto the doors or ramparts of the city. The close resemblance of this imagery to that used for the messenger from the sky—who erupts onto the scene out of heavy weather and saves the day at the end of Canto IX—makes this heavenly

---

represents height, the upper world, heaven: while the left belongs with the lower world and the earth"—p. 114); "La droite est *le dedans* . . . le bien-être et la paix assurée; la gauche est *le dehors* . . . l'hostile, la perpétuelle menace du mal" ("The right is *the inside* . . . well-being and assured peace; the left is *the outside* . . . the hostile, the perpetual threat of evil"—p. 115); "Puissance sacrée, source de vie, vérité . . . côté droit" ("Sacred power, source of life, truth . . . right side"—p. 116).

20. Being guided is, of course, another necessary condition of sound hermeneutic procedure, as Dante conceives it. Without a guide, one remains, like Guido Cavalcanti, cut off from higher powers; Cavalcanti's fatal error was to disdain a necessary conductor to the transcendent, regardless of whether "cui" in *Inferno* X. 63 refers to Beatrice or to Virgil. Guido's very name, juxtaposed to this relative pronoun in "forse cui Guido vostro ebbe a disdegno," means, fatefully, "*I* guide." And it is precisely that unwillingness to accept guidance from an *other,* bound up with the denial of any being transcending the self, that seems to be the final ground on which Dante judged him.

Hermes look something like a version or inversion of the demons. The parallel would seem to be reinforced by the curiously, or even shockingly, cantankerous attitude of the celestial messenger, who is full of disdain— "Ahi quanto mi parea pien di disdegno!" (IX. 83)—not unlike the demons who speak spitefully out of their "gran disdegno"(VIII. 88).

Despite his liberating and saving function, there is something unmistakably demonic about the celestial messenger, especially in his sinister and terrifying entrance, precisely like a serpent, the enemy, that the text stridently insists on, however incongruous it may at first seem. The demonic may be defined, as suggested by Paul Tillich in his *Systematic Theology,* as the raising of some finite structure of creation to the status of an absolute. It is perhaps not so incredible, then, that hermeneutics should be found complicitous in what has an at least ambiguously demonic side. For an interpretation always arbitrarily begins somewhere in its effort to understand in their relations all the elements of an ensemble. Something particular is made to serve as the key for the explanation of things more general, and so to take on a universal significance. Although the tendency of interpretation is to seek to establish an all-encompassing, stable explanation of the whole, its own preconditions are in finite, temporally conditioned being. Therefore, these bases must be forgotten or hidden in the interest of the claim to universal validity. This builds a devilish sort of dissimulation into the hermeneutic process. It finds archetypal expression in the arch-demon and father of lies, Satan, who is also the emblem of the tendency of finite, created being to usurp the status of infinity.

Gadamer's hermeneutic theory brings out the finitude of hermeneutics as a specifically linguistic practice, and yet also its speculative projecting of totality. Every word speculatively mirrors the whole of language, on the hermeneutic principles of the linguistic ontology spelled out in part 3 of *Wahrheit und Methode.*[21] Although every interpretation is only a perspective, it must necessarily strive to efface the untruth of its partiality, if the criterion of its adequacy is wholeness. This built-in tension is what makes hermeneutics regularly tend to resemble the demonic. There appears inevitably to be something potentially self-assertive and God-denying about interpretation, by virtue of which it risks substituting itself for what really is, recreating everything after its own image.

Dante's sense of the dark side of the force that triumphs in *Inferno* IX expresses itself vigorously in the destructive, violent characteristics of the heaven-sent messenger. The dramatization of the violence latent within hermeneutics, just when hermeneutics is called in and exalted as savior,

---

21. Gadamer is of course developing Heidegger's thought as well as Schleiermacher's insight that "Language is infinite because every element is determinable in a special way by the other elements."

witnesses to the strength of Dante's imagination of this awesome power in its radical ambivalence. He had reason to be so aware, considering the God-like powers of interpretation he assumes in his poem. His interpretations of his contemporaries and of God's judgments upon them have never ceased to expose him to charges of Satanic presumption. Much too near and dear to Dante for him not to be cognizant of it lies the hermeneutic power that emerges from his whole poem as a supreme, creative and destructive, pseudo-omnipotent agency, potentially demonic in nature.

The very phrase "heaven-sent" actually recurs in one of the most audacious interpretations of the entire poem, a sort of emblem of the interpretive arbitrium on which his whole career is founded, Dante's transfiguration of his adolescent passion for a Florentine girl into a mystic marriage of biblical resonance:

> e un di loro, *quasi da ciel messo,*
>   "Veni, sponsa, de Libano" cantando
> gridò tre volte, e tutti gli altri appresso.
>   (*Purgatorio* XXX. 10–12)

> (and one of them, like a messenger from heaven,
>   singing "Veni, sponsa, de Libano"
> shouted thrice, and all the others right after.)

The lexical link back to the less hallowed scene in *Inferno* IX helps to remind us of the sinister side of the interpretive power Dante wields even at this most triumphal moment. The poet's power of declaring what is sent from heaven renders possible a prophetic vocation but at the same time creates a crisis of legitimacy that Dante is constantly at shifts to try and manage.

Another example of ambivalent language used for crucial hermeneutic events is the phrase "rent the veil before me," which introduces Ugolino's haunting dream in *Inferno* XXXIII and then recurs in a splendid vision that bathes in the light of Christ's transfiguration, in *Purgatorio* XXXII. 71–72: "dico ch'un splendor mi squarciò 'l velo / del sonno." Whereas sleep is here the veil, in Ugolino's speech sleep's dream-consciousness is what ruptures the veil of the future: "'l mal sonno, / che del futuro mi squarciò 'l velame" (*Inferno* XXXIII. 26–27). But in either case, the unveiling that constitutes the essential figure of the hermeneutic moment is figured as a violent tearing. As such, it reveals both the terror and the glory, the whole range of the hermeneutic phenomenon as Dante maps it from the nether parts to the peaks of the universe.

Like the veil, the imagery of lightning is also consistently exploited by Dante for crucial hermeneutic events, thanks to its established association with revelation. Earthquakes and lightning, as stereotyped images of apocalypse, punctuate the journey's passage points and threshold cross-ings. The first of them, Dante's crossing of the Acheron to enter Hell, is cataclysmically signaled by an earthquake in darkness traversed by a violet flash:

> Finito questo, la buia campagna
>   tremò sì forte, che de lo spavento
>   la mente di sudore ancor mi bagna.
> La terra lagrimosa diede vento
>   che balenò una luce vermiglia
>   la qual mi vinse ciascun sentimento. . . .
>   (*Inferno* III. 130–135)

> (After this, the darkened land
>   trembled so violently, that fright
>   bathes my mind again in sweat.
> The tearful earth gave vent to wind
>   that flashed a vermilion light
>   which overwhelmed my every sense. . . .)

Since religious revelation itself, as an unveiling, is first and foremost a hermeneutic event, this imagery helps configure the hermeneutic di-mension and essence of Dante's transitions. His progress is quite generally by means of an unconcealing or an apocalypse, even when this event is microcosmically concentrated in the overwhelming power of beauty beaconed from Beatrice's eyes. Each breakthrough for understanding is accompanied by some kind of shattering violence. The violence inherent in hermeneutics is the means of a certain breaking down and shaking out that characterizes an uncompromisingly radical interpretive apocalypse such as Dante sets out to achieve, beginning in the *Inferno*.

Even in Paradise, Dante's passages from heaven to heaven and to the final vision given in a stroke of lightning ("la mia mente fu percossa / da un fulgore in che sua voglia venne"—XXXIII. 140–41) are marked by the violence of blinding and rending that are simply part of the event of genuine understanding which bursts asunder one's world and its order, that all may be comprehended anew. In the case of apocalypse this de-structiveness manifests divine power, but it can also belong to the vio-lence against whatever is other that Dante discovers as a potential within acts of interpretation generally. Hermes is after all a god and in some respects perilously close to being a demon. It is perhaps only under the controlled conditions of a rite of passage that the violence released by the hermeneutic event can be expected to do good rather than harm, to be freeing rather than obliterating.

So much should suffice to demonstrate that the hermeneutic prob-lematic pervades the entire episode of *Inferno* IX—and not just its single

most peremptory tercet—with implications for the whole poem. Theo-
retically informed analysis shows how Dante touches on the most crucial
themes of hermeneutic thought as it has evolved even down to our own
day. Although Dante's concerns are not primarily theoretical, his repre-
sentations embody basic hermeneutic assumptions in a primordial form,
and his text is in turn revealed by later theory, which can bring out its
implicit problematic. The venture I propose, of applying modern herme-
neutic theory in the reading of Dante's text, and vice versa, is predicated
on a belief in the "hermeneutic productivity of temporal distance" and
the view that understanding a text is never merely a reproductive but
always also a productive activity.[22] In this sense, and not in a narrowly
exegetical sense, I endeavor to engage Dante's probing dramatization of
the hermeneutic problem hermeneutically.

4. APPENDIX: HERMENEUTICS, PHENOMENOLOGY, AND THE MEANING OF A MODERN UNDERSTANDING OF DANTE

The task of hermeneutics as evoked by Dante in the injunction in *Inferno*
IX is not to explain discursively in the manner of an exegesis. It rather
consists in disclosing, literally unveiling, something that can be seen,
some phenomenon. In this sense, Dante's is a phenomenological herme-
neutics. The metaphorics of seeing more deeply and inwardly bring
Dante's hermeneutic close to the phenomenological hermeneutics of
more recent times: both adhere to the primacy of perception, even while
passing hermeneutically beyond first impressions or immediate percep-
tion. Indeed, this paradoxical quality of a "primary" perception that is
not perceptible at first sight (because not thematically focused) compli-
cates the history of the phenomenological movement as markedly as it
complicates Dante's text. Maurice Merleau-Ponty's recapitulation of the
history of this movement in the avant-propos to *La phénoménologie de la
perception* stresses the seemingly contradictory phenomenological task of
arriving at immediacy, but not through immediacy.[23]

There is a deep paradox in Dante's hermeneutic injunctions, which

22. Gadamer, *Truth and Method:* "Not just occasionally but always, the meaning of a text
goes beyond its author. That is why understanding is not merely a reproductive but always a
productive activity as well. . . . [W]e understand in a *different* way, *if we understand at all*" (p. 296).

23. Maurice Merleau-Ponty, *La phénoménologie de la perception* (Paris: Gallimard, 1945):
"C'est une philosophie transcendantale qui met en suspens pour les comprendre les affirmations
de l'attitude naturelle, mais c'est aussi une philosophie pour laquelle le monde est toujours 'déjà
là' avant la réflexion, comme une présence inaliénable, et dont tout l'effort est de retrouver ce
contact naïf avec le monde pour lui donner enfin un statut philosophique" ("It is a transcenden-
tal philosophy that places within brackets, in order to understand them, the affirmations of the
natural attitude, but it is also a philosophy for which the world is 'always already' there before

presumably direct attention to invisible, supersensory, doctrinal meaning, but nevertheless are cast in the form of a command to metaphorically sharpen our eyes and look at what (the metaphor of sight suggests) should be immediately evident. The spiritual or allegorical truth he would have us see may indeed be what is most self-evident of all, and what is most immediately knowable in the order of things, once our intellectual vision has been cleansed or made "sane." This paradox—that what is most immediate in perception is ordinarily least and last known—can be illuminated by following certain paths of recent hermeneutic and phenomenological philosophy.

While initially the phenomenon was identified with appearance, as in Kant, by the time of *Being and Time* it had become precisely what does not appear "proximally and for the most part," but rather is nonthematically present in what is given. It therefore needs to be brought into view by careful hermeneutic work. It is "behind" or "within" the ordinary objects that clutter perception, with the result that it cannot be directly seized upon. "Phenomenon" in Heidegger's "distinctive sense" is defined as "something that proximally and for the most part does *not* show itself at all: it is something that lies *hidden*, in contrast to that which proximally and for the most part does show itself; but at the same time it is something that belongs to what thus shows itself, and it belongs to it so essentially as to constitute its meaning and ground" (Heidegger, *Being and Time*, p. 59).

The phenomenon, according to Heidegger, is Being itself as it shows itself in, yet is covered up by, beings. It is not a discrete, isolable object at our disposal. It is hidden by these objects to the extent that they claim to exclusively dominate perception and assert themselves alone as what is. As a consequence, we no longer even realize that Being *is:* "Yet that which remains *hidden* in an egregious sense, or which relapses and gets *covered up* again, or which shows itself only '*in disguise*', is not just this entity or that, but rather the *Being* of entities (das Sein der Seiende), as our previous observations have shown" (p. 59).

The question about the meaning of Being, Heidegger laments, has been forgotten, and it is the task of phenomenology to make the Being of beings a phenomenon that is "taken into its grasp thematically as its object" (p. 59). "In the phenomenological conception of 'phenomenon' what one has in mind as that which shows itself is the Being of entities, its meaning, its modifications and derivatives" (p. 60). Accordingly, phenomenology is concerned with the Being of entities, and the objective of phenomenological hermeneutics is to bring this Being into view.

---

reflection, like an inalienable presence, and which makes every effort to recover this naive contact with the world in order to give it at last a philosophical status"—p. i).

Heidegger brought about what can be termed the "ontological turn" in the history of interpretation by merging phenomenology with hermeneutics in such a way as to restore priority to Being as that which makes meaningful, beyond the self-reflective focus on a subject's perceptual apparatus or on method in the endeavor to secure epistemological certainty. For Heidegger, the phenomenological method becomes just the opposite, in crucial respects, of what it was for its creator, Husserl. Husserl (following Descartes's inaugural move of doubting all but his own clear and distinct perceptions) used it as an epistemological razor, a way of putting reality within brackets, so as to deal only with the immediate, indubitable evidence of appearances before consciousness. But Heidegger's phenomenology seeks to bring Being as it is manifest in the phenomenon into view—not appearance nor an inner world of subjective perception but the Being of beings, which was understood classically as presence or presencing.

Red color on a face, for example, might announce fever, embarrassment, and so on. But redness would be only an epiphenomenon of such a psychological state; it does not make it directly accessible as phenomenon. What phenomenological analysis, according to Heidegger, is interested in is the Being of the redness in so far as this is manifest. This is no more a question about whether the color exists in the object perceived or in the perceiver, the second option of which might lead to a causal explanation of color as a "secondary quality," than it is a question about the psychological causes of blushing. All such things lie somewhere behind and beyond the color as phenomenon. Rather, what is directly manifest in the being-colored of the face is presence. This coloredness brings presence into view, as present visibility. Coloredness is present in the face; it perdures and changes. It reveals the temporality of something that is present at hand or before one. Temporality cannot help showing through in this way, though nonthematically.

Temporality is also what shows itself in acts of consciousness like understanding, although in a different way, and in fact as a different temporality, no longer that of an object present at hand but that of the human being who exists and is called by Heidegger "Dasein" ("Being-there"). In Dasein, Being is revealed as "there," as in fact already existing whenever reflection begins, as if it had been "thrown" so as to have its existence always already dispersed in time. Dasein's mode of being is to gather itself out of the possibilities that it projects: it *is* understandingly this thrown-projectedness of Being. In the phenomenon of understanding, what is manifest is that Dasein projects its Being upon possibilities. Thus, in the case of Dasein, too, phenomenology's subject matter is the Being of an entity as a phenomenon present nonthematically whenever anything is understood or experienced.

Just as the phenomenon of Being, according to the analysis of *Being and Time,* is revealed within the horizon of temporality, so too Dante brings truth into view by interrupting the objective temporality of narrative, the temporality of myth that is objectifying, and calling rather for temporalization on the part of the reader, that is, the individual human existence that serves as site for the happening of the poem. The summons to hermeneusis is after all a summons to recapitulate the narrative in a temporality that reorders its elements in accordance with a meaning or truth that, as a whole, they reveal. This is precisely the temporality of human existence as it can be realized by the reader.

The Cartesian, Kantian, and at least sometimes Husserlian project of bracketing reality in order to talk just about phenomena as they appear seems antithetical to hermeneutics until it emerges that what is bracketed is only a certain conceptualization of the real, precisely in the interests of letting the real reveal itself in its own Being. For once such presumed realities as the conscious subject and the objective world have been dismantled as abstractions from the primordial phenomena of experience, what is revealed in phenomena alone can claim to be underived, concrete reality. Thus phenomenology involves no renunciation of access to the reality of things, but rather the opposite. It shows how by giving up our preconceived notions about what is real we can become consciously participant in the actual self-revelation and realization of Being.

This suggests how phenomenology arrives at its claim to attain to knowledge of "the things themselves," to quote Husserl's slogan. It has implicitly redefined the notion of the thing-in-itself and by consequence that of the real. This is no longer taken to be what is self-subsistent or what exists independently (i.e., independently of appearing to a subject). Reality in that sense is left lying on the other side of the Kantian epistemological gulf that divides appearances ("phenomena" for Kant) from things themselves. Rather, things themselves, realities (and this includes their being understood) are given prior to any split between subject and object. This being given is an appearing in which being and appearing are one. It is the self-showing of Being, the primordial phenomenon of Being as time.

The breakthrough of phenomenology is enacted in a primordial way by Dante's project of writing a poem whose fiction is that it is not a fiction, in the formula Singleton made famous. The bracketing of the reality question, which is the initial move of Husserl's phenomenology, amounts to a fiction, or at least a hypothesis, that the appearance is not (just) appearance. As what appears in the sense of showing itself, the phenomenon is taken in and for itself, as if it were an independent entity, as if it were itself reality. But this turns it immediately into a sort of reality, the reality of what shows itself. Once no claim is any longer made to being real in any other sense, indeed, the phenomenon *is* what really shows itself. Moreover, it really is *as* it shows itself. As phenomenon, it is truly revealed; indeed, its true Being is revealed. And to this extent it can even be said, to the satisfaction of Husserl and Descartes, that it reveals an indubitable truth.

The realities or things themselves discovered by the phenomenological method really are what they are because they are purely phenomenal—they are what they appear to be. There may be further hidden realities behind them. But this does not detract from the reality of the phenomenon qua phenomenon. The latent, nonphenomenal reality that may be supposed or inferred is not the reality of the phenomenon. It is something else that can be signified or indicated by the phenomenon taken as a symptom or index. But all that is inference and guesswork in comparison with the immediate evidence of what the phenomenon itself is. The phenomenon has a reality of its own independent of what it signifies, and this reality is fully manifest in it. And, most importantly, this fundamentally is the reality of Being itself. Though it may be but the surface of deeper structures within schemes of causal explanation, the phenomenon is the open manifestation of Being. It *is* just as much as, and more evidently than, whatever realities may after all underlie it.

What is transformed in phenomenology and, I propose, in Dante's gnoseological method and presuppositions are the relations between immanence and transcendence of what is known as real or true with respect to the phenomena that manifest it. If phenomenology claims to go back to the things themselves, then truth or true being must be immanent within the phenomenon and its manifest showing. Similarly, if Dante claims in the world of his poem to reveal the true world of Christian faith, not only to comment upon Christian revelation but to mediate it more directly, to make it occur historically, then the Christian truth must be capable of being manifest immanently within the phenomenon that the *Divine Comedy* is or can become in reading.

Now does this mean that there is supposedly no reality outside the phenomenal realm? Would any transcendence of the truly real with regard to the phenomenon not deprive phenomena of their status as things themselves and hence true reality? Though we (and this includes Heidegger most of the time) are generally inclined to think so today, this need not be the case. An incisive critique of Heidegger in the name of "la philosophie de l'être," that is, Thomism, by Géry Prouvost is based on the distinction between "the being of beings," understood exclusively as phenomenal being, and the transcendent being of God as pure act in itself independent of beings. The latter is unpacked as "*Esse subsistens* dont l'être n'est l'acte d'aucune détermination définie, car il subsiste hors d'un étant ou, si l'on veut, il est l'*esse* de l'étant qu'il est lui-même" ("*Esse subsistens,* the being of which is not the act of any definite determination, because it subsists outside of a being or, if you will, it is the *esse* of the being which it itself is"). By contrast, and falling short of Thomas's metaphysical insight, "Heidegger s'est tenu à l'être des étants qui, découvert irréductible aux étants, ne subsiste qu'en eux" ("Heidegger kept to the being of beings, which, discovered to be irreducible to beings, subsists only in them").[24] For Dante, as for Thomas, its reality as phenomenon still leaves room for the transcendence of Being. This paradoxical form of affirmation is in fact fundamental to the Christian theology of the Incarnation.

Thanks to its phenomenological transmogrification, hermeneutics can claim to attain the real, to experience it interpretively, to look at and see truth, rather than following endlessly frustrating methods of seeking to certify certainty. It is not by accident that we discover "affinities" in this with Dante's own mind-set, for we learn how the basic constituents of his intellectual framework function to make sense in ways that we cannot but understand and make sense of in our own terms. The affinity therefore does not present itself purely by chance; but neither is it just an arbitrary imposition. It stems rather from a higher necessity inherent in the nature of historical understanding, the necessity of a fusion of present and past in the event of understanding, an issue that will be pursued further in chapter 4.

With the qualifications that this discussion implies, then, it may be affirmed that Dante's hermeneutic injunction, even with its didactic accent, by exhorting the reader to *look* at some phenomenon even while a superficial looking is exactly the danger hermeneusis must avoid, illustrates what amounts to a "phenomenological" type of hermeneusis. The true "dottrina," like Being itself, is really the most immediate of all phenomena, even though, in the ordinary way of experiencing or reading, it may not be discerned as such. What Heidegger and Dante both urge us to see is not any new object or field of objects, but rather the meaning and truth of what we already see objectively, and ultimately the meaning of Being. This truth reveals itself within the horizon of a specific temporality that for Dante is constitutive of Christian conversion.

24. Géry Prouvost, "La constitution ontothéologique de la métaphysique chrétienne," *Revue Thomiste* 90 (April–June 1990): 244.

THREE

The Temporality of Conversion

Casella mio, per tornar altra volta
là dov' io son, fo io questo viaggio.
(*Purgatorio* II. 91–92)

I. INTERPRETATION AS ONTOLOGICAL REPETITION AND DANTE'S FATEDNESS

S' io torni mai, lettor . . .
(*Paradiso* XXII. 106)

*T*he removal of obstacles in order that progress may be resumed along a linear trajectory does not exhaust the contribution of hermeneutics to furthering the advance of Dante's journey. We saw a transposition to a higher level of meaning encrypted in the passage to a lower region of Hell in Canto IX. Hermeneutics displaces the journey more than it sends it along its original way, opening further spheres of significance rather than simply supplying solutions to problems as they present themselves in the sequence of narrated events. Most importantly, we saw, the protagonist's journey turns into, or at least converges upon, the reader's journey, in programmatic ways at the hermeneutic junctures where the reader is explicitly addressed.

This shift into a vertical, interpretive dimension crossing the narrative itinerary was also implicit in Dante's representation of the proclivity of hermeneutics to become demonic, evincing an awareness of hermeneutics as a speculative activity, mirroring a totality of meaning, beyond being merely a practical means or "organon" for overcoming ad hoc difficulties of comprehension. The epoch-making step from the one conception of hermeneutics to the other in modern intellectual history is generally credited to Friedrich D. E. Schleiermacher. Comparison with this latter-day "Copernican revolution," thanks to which we are able to talk about hermeneutics as a properly philosophical discipline, rather than as just an assortment of guidelines for interpretation specific to separate fields like theology, jurisprudence, and philology, will help us to define with greater precision the far-reaching hermeneutic significance of Dante's address to the reader.

Schleiermacher evokes the conception of hermeneutics as an activity called for only episodically, in response to some contradiction or absurdity disturbing the normal progress of reading, in order to label it the "traditional view" and to distinguish it from his own. In the Aphorisms of 1805 he writes: "Two divergent maxims for understanding. (1) I am understanding everything until I encounter a contradiction or non-sense. (2) I do not understand anything that I cannot perceive and comprehend [konstruieren] as necessary. In accordance with this second maxim understanding is an unending task."[1] Schleiermacher goes on to identify the first maxim with traditional hermeneutics and the second with the radically reformed hermeneutics that he proposes. In the traditional view, hermeneutics is called in only where some special problem for interpretation arises; for the rest, comprehension of the text is taken for granted. Schleiermacher's revolution basically consists in showing how all understanding is interpretive, so that the hermeneutic problematic determines the reading of texts from beginning to end quite apart from whatever special difficulties may or may not present themselves.[2]

Schleiermacher focused attention on the act of understanding as the basis for all knowledge as interpretive in nature. He did so out of epistemological preoccupations like those of the Kantian critique in search of the a priori conditions of all knowledge. He wished to establish the principles and rules by which the act of understanding constituted a sort of a priori condition of interpretation. It was left to Heidegger to concern himself with the *being* of understanding ("Verstehen") and to describe it as one of the fundamental structures of being-in-the-world. Nevertheless, an ontological orientation toward knowledge had already been taken up by Schleiermacher, even without being advertised as such. The act of understanding as a process transpiring in time and embedded in language, unlike Kant's pure categories of the understanding, was recognized as the basis of knowledge in fields in which interpretation operates. Interpretive knowledge was thereby viewed as grounded in historical being.

Like Schleiermacher's second maxim, Dante's metanarratological gesture in *Inferno* IX presupposes that nothing has been truly understood prior to interpretive operations. The contradictions or obstacles encountered occasion an interpretive redefinition of the meaning of the whole sequence of verses in accordance with the doctrine found underneath. That everything was understood up to the impasse is a naive assumption undermined by Dante's allegorical method no less than by Schleiermach-

---

1. Friedrich Schleiermacher, *Hermeneutics: The Handwritten Manuscripts,* p. 41.

2. Of course, the revolutionary importance of the "is" in this statement that all understanding *is* interpretive has become apparent especially since Heidegger. For an account of Heidegger's radicalization of the hermeneutic problematic, see Karl-Otto Apel, "Heideggers philosophische Radikalisierung der 'Hermeneutik' und die Frage nach dem 'Sinnkriterium' der Sprache," in *Die hermeneutische Frage in der Theologie,* ed. O. Loretz and W. Strolz (Frieburg: Herder, 1968), pp. 86–152.

er's critique of eighteenth-century hermeneutic theory and practice. According to Schleiermacher's "more rigorous practice of the art of interpretation," "misunderstanding occurs as a matter of course, and so understanding must be willed and sought at every point" (Schleiermacher, *Hermeneutics*, p. 110). The misunderstanding that occurs as a matter of course for Dante consists in merely literal reading. The piercing of the veil to which Dante exhorts in direct addresses concerns the reinterpretation of the entire fiction and not merely the clearing away of an incidental obstacle. The whole ensemble of the poem's verses is liable to being understood in a new and truer way, leveraged from the breaks created by the hermeneutic directives. And this involves understanding the verses not simply as text but as event, after the fashion explored in the preceding chapters and introduction.

Furthermore, according to Schleiermacher's maxim, understanding in the second and more adequate sense entails the ability to reconstruct what is understood and to see its necessity. This involves being able to deduce it ("ableiten"). To understand what is given, and not just perceive its existence as an opaque fact, is to comprehend its necessity. Understanding moves from the modality of the purely given to that of possibility and necessity. Later hermeneutic reflection brings out how it is in the projection of possibilities that meaning arises. But the projection of a possibility is already a recapitulation. In the speculative tradition in which hermeneutics was destined to assume the dimensions of a general philosophical paradigm, interpretation always involves a recapitulation of the phenomenon, that is, the event that is being subjected to interpretation, in such a way that its meaning can be disclosed. This idea was to be developed influentially by Wilhelm Dilthey, under the heading of "Nacherleben." For Dilthey, "the highest form of understanding in which the totality of mental life is active" is "re-creating and re-living."[3] The idea receives its most probing treatment in the theory of repetition as intrinsic to the hermeneutic process, and especially in *Being and Time*, with its claim that "By repetition [Wiederholung], Dasein first has its own history made manifest."[4]

---

3. From Wilhelm Dilthey's "Critique of Historical Reason," in *Dilthey: Selected Writings*, trans. H. P. Rickman (New York: Cambridge University Press, 1976), p. 226.

4. Martin Heidegger, *Being and Time*, p. 438. "Repetition" is being used in a sense sharply different from, indeed diametrically opposed to, that of a slavish copying or of a circle closed to the possibility of anything new. Repetition is a retrieval not just of a past fact that is over and done with but of a possibility the past contains and which can be broken open in the present with a view to opening possibilities for the future: "[I]n repetition the 'force' of the possible gets struck home into one's factical existence—in other words . . . it comes toward that existence in its futural character" (p. 447).

According to Heidegger, only in recapitulation does Dasein (the being that we are) exist understandingly. "Dasein has already in every case gone astray and failed to recognize itself. In its potentiality-for-Being it is therefore delivered over to the possibility of first finding itself again in its possibilities" (Heidegger, *Being and Time,* p. 184). Its possibilities are always already gone by, and whenever Dasein actually grasps them, it is through a repetition. This is entailed by Dasein's existential thrownness, its being always already, no matter where one begins, "Nel mezzo del cammin."

Dante's poem begins from just such a position, its protagonist like a shipwrecked man thrown up on shore, having narrowly escaped from death, who looks back over a perilous pass and past:

> così l'animo mio, ch'ancor fuggiva,
>   si volse a retro a rimirar lo passo. . . .
>   (*Inferno* I. 25–26).

> (in this way my mind, which still was fleeing,
>   turned behind to look back at the pass. . . .)

Texts as distant in origin as Dante's poem and Heidegger's treatise can gloss each other reciprocally on the deployment of repetition as a deep-seated hermeneutical structure of narrative and even of temporal and historical experience per se. Repetition properly belongs to the temporality of human existence and thereby to the whole construction of "the historical" in the Western conception.

Dante's journey is presented from the very first, indeed it is proposed, as a repetition. Paul and Aeneas are mentioned as models for the prospective visit to the other world: "Io non Enea, io non Paolo sono" (*Inferno* II. 32). And even though they are mentioned in the context of Dante not daring to emulate the world-historically significant missions of either, Dante's journey nevertheless becomes, in its peculiar significance, conceivable only in relation to the precedents set by these paradigms. But again these images of repetition within the narrative are most significant, hermeneutically speaking, for their imitation of relations that frame the narrative, placing it in relation to the author and his reader. The hermeneutic injunction essentially invites the reader to repeat the elements of the narrative in accordance with a significance that the narrative as such does not make explicit but which the reader can find within it. This amounts to a repeating of the narrative in a temporality that will be the reader's own, determined and reordered by the meaning the reader finds there. The narrative in being thus repeated is grafted onto the existence of the reader.

The address to the reader is in essence a summons to repeat the pro-
tagonist's experiences, recapitulating the narrative sequence in light of
the meaning that it takes on in the reader's own experience. According
to the whole speculative tradition of hermeneutics, it is by repeating and
reconstructing experience that its meaning can be appropriated, which is
the same as understanding it in accordance with that meaning, and in
this relation, as "necessary." Dante's inclusion of the interpreter within
the poem in his addresses to the reader implicitly acknowledges this com-
plex structure of mutual dependence between the meaning of the poem
and the reader's understanding of it; indeed, the address conspicuously
announces the relation to the reader, determinable specifically as the re-
capitulation of the narrative in accordance with a meaning found therein,
as constitutive of the poem.

Heidegger characterizes repetition in terms of a condition of "re-
soluteness," or taking a stand existentially, and of fated existence. He
writes, "We characterize repetition as a mode of that resoluteness which
hands itself down—the mode by which Dasein exists explicitly as fate"
(Heidegger, *Being and Time*, p. 438). Now both resoluteness and fate
become fundamental structures of Dante's pilgrimage within his poem.
For Dante has to become resolute in order to begin his journey in
the first place. He has to overcome the mood of irresolution that tram-
mels him:

> E qual è quel che disvuol ciò che volle
>   e per novi pensier cangia proposta
>   sí che dal cominciar tutto si tolle,
> tal mi fec'io 'n quella oscura costa,
>   perché, pensando, consumai la 'mpresa
>   che fu nel cominciar contanto tosta.
>
> (*Inferno* II. 37–42)

> (And as one who unwills what he willed
>   and with new thoughts changes his mind
>   so that from the beginning everything is taken away,
> such I myself became on that dark shore,
>   because, thinking, I consumed the enterprise
>   which was so precipitous in beginning.)

And when by the end of the canto Dante achieves resoluteness, it is
expressed precisely in figures of repetition. As at the return of day blos-
soms that have been bowed down and closed by the night's chill rise
up and open again, so Dante announces, "ch'io son tornato nel primo
proposto" ("I have returned to my first purpose"—II. 138).

The conception of fate ("Schicksal"), Heidegger further explains, "is

how we designate Dasein's primordial historizing, which lies in authentic
resoluteness and in which Dasein *hands* itself *down* to itself, free for death,
in a possibility which it has inherited and yet has chosen" (p. 435). He
adds that "in the depths of its Being Dasein *is* fate" (p. 436). This notion
of fate as built into the very structure of the existence of a human being
as historical involves an explicit process of "handing down," or tradition:
"The resoluteness which comes back to itself and hands itself down, then
becomes the *repetition* of a possibility of existence that has come down to
us. *Repeating is handing down explicitly*—that is to say, going back into the
possibilities of the Dasein that has-been-there" (p. 437).

Repetition defined in these terms, as mediated by a handing down
of possibilities, accurately describes the working of specifically literary
tradition and therefore of a process carried forward exemplarily in the
Commedia. For the poem gives its reader just such a possibility of going
back to the possibilities of the "Dasein" (i.e., human being, being that is
self-interpreting in its very being) that has been there, in Hell, and so
forth. Heidegger himself conceives the relation of Dasein to its past by
means of a literary metaphor, and in so doing conflates the relation of
Dasein to itself through repetition with the relation between reader and
protagonist: "The authentic repetition of a possibility of existence that
has been—the possibility that Dasein may choose its hero—is grounded
existentially in anticipatory resoluteness; for it is in resoluteness that one
first chooses the choice which makes one free for the struggle of loyally
following in the footsteps of that which can be repeated" (p. 437). Taking
up these terms, we may say that the poem invites the reader to choose
Dante-protagonist as hero, to follow in his footsteps, repeating his possi-
bilities in anticipatory resoluteness, or, to put it in a Christian idiom,
in conversion.

The protagonist represents a past that can be projected as the reader's
future. What is above all necessary, within this perspective, is that the
reader assume the possibilities of existence revealed by the protagonist as
his or her *own,* rather than as objective and external, or, in other words,
as myth. In this way, the kind of being that emerges as a possibility for the
reader through the experiences of the protagonist constitutes a specific
application of the authentically historical being that Heidegger describes
as Dasein's own and ownmost possibility: "only an entity which, as fu-
tural, is equiprimordially in the process of *having-been*, can, by hand-
ing down to itself the possibility it has inherited, take over its own
thrownness and be *in the moment of vision* for its time" (p. 437). The mo-
ment of vision, which pierces the flatness of the temporality of everyday-
ness for Heidegger, is for Dante the moment of seeing through the veil
of the myth to its application in one's own life, of taking in hand one's
past, both one's personal past and one's cultural heritage as handed down

through such means as the poem, and understanding all this as coinciding with the possibilities of one's own future.[5]

The meaning of Being, as inquired into by the existential-hermeneutic analysis of *Being and Time,* is revealed within the horizon of temporality, and Dante, concordently, brings the deep meaning his poem searches for into view, as we have seen, by interrupting the objective, mythifying temporality of narrative fiction and calling rather for temporalization on the part of the reader, that is, the human existence that serves as site for the happening of the poem and its truth. The summons to hermeneusis is after all, by the effect it ideally if not inevitably produces, a summons to the reader to recapitulate the narrative in a temporality that reorders its elements in accordance with a meaning or truth that they, as a whole, reveal.

The horizontal repetitions within the *Inferno* of Aeneas's, or in the *Paradiso* of Paul's, journey, or again at the culmination of *Purgatorio* of Man's original state of justice, as well as the projections of the journey's (and thereby of all history's) end, are most importantly images of potential repetition from successively higher levels of hermeneutic enframement. The move to these higher-order levels of interpretation characterizes Dante's procedure as hermeneutic in the speculative, Schleiermacherian sense. Dante introduces a metanarratological dimension through his hermeneutic interventions calling for a repetition of the narrative in its significance at another level, by the interpreter, in his own existence, projecting its possibilities as his own. In doing this the reader simply follows after the example of the author, in some sense the poem's first interpreter.

---

5. Heidegger scholarship has cautioned against misinterpreting his doctrine as concerned with a subjective, "existentialist" choice. Hence Ricoeur: "Ce qui importe ici, ce n'est pas le moment existentiel de la responsabilité ou du libre-choix, mais la structure d'être à partir de laquelle il y a un problème de choix. Le *ou bien . . . ou bien . . .* n'est pas premier, mais dérivé de la structure du *projet-jeté*" ("What counts here is not the existential moment of responsibility or free choice, but the structure of being on the basis of which there is a problem of choice. The *either . . . or* is not primary, but derived from the structure of the *thrown-project*"—*Du texte à l'action,* p. 92). Ricoeur depends to some extent on Gadamer, *Truth and Method,* p. 99. Indeed, Heidegger is concerned not with psychological but with ontological structures. And yet the ontological structure of resoluteness surely is not separable from the concrete state of being resolved that is phenomenally experienced by the agent. Heidegger's point is that this "authentic" existential orientation is a choice simply to be what one already is—but one *is* this nonetheless in choosing it existentially. Admittedly, not the choice itself but its possibility, given in the structure of projection, is what belongs essentially to Dasein's way of being. But since the structure of Dasein is nothing apart from the phenomenal event of being-in-the-world, such phenomena as decision and commitment cannot be divorced from the very structure of existence. Hubert Dreyfus, *Being-in-the-world: A Commentary on Heidegger's* Being and Time *Division I* (Cambridge: MIT Press, 1992), points out how the structure of being-in-the-world is equated by Heidegger with "Dasein's taking a stand on itself and significance" (p. 192).

The structures of repetitiveness and fatedness, disclosed by existential-hermeneutic analysis as fundamental to the historical existence of human being, comprise the gist of the message enunciated by the celestial messenger in his speech in *Inferno* IX, reproving the vain recalcitrance of the denizens of Dis, and clearing the way for Dante and Virgil's passage:

> "Perché recalcitrate a *quella voglia*
>   a cui non puote il fin mai esser mozzo,
>   e che *più volte* v'ha cresciuta doglia?
> Che giova ne *le fata* dar di cozzo?
>   Cerbero vostro, se ben vi ricorda,
>   ne porta ancor pelato il mento e 'l gozzo."
>
> (IX. 94–99)

> ("Why do you buck against *that will*
>   *of which the end can never be cut off,*
>   and which has *several times* increased your pain?
> What's the use of colliding with the fates?
>   Your Cerberus, if you remember well,
>   for that still has his chin and throat peeled.")

These lines rehearse a formula reiterated at every potential impasse along the way through the *Inferno*. They refer to God's omnipotent will as sanctioning Dante's journey: "Vuolsi così colà dove si puote / ciò che si vuole" (III. 95–96). The formulation in *Inferno* IX, on the lips of the celestial messenger—"quella voglia / a cui non puote *il fin* mai esser mozzo"—is particularly apt for purposes of bringing out the hermeneutical structures of historical existence, since it verbally crystallizes and throws into relief the end, the terminus, as the source and focus of historical being and envisages the potentiality for completion, that is, for being-a-whole, as the foundation for authentic temporal existence. This end, in Heidegger's thinking, is ultimately death, which must be assumed as *one's own*, rather than as pertaining to "someone," the "they" ("das Man"). Chapter 5 of part 1 of *Being and Time* argues that Dasein can achieve its being-a-whole only by embracing death as its end, in which alone its being is complete. For Heidegger, fate refers to the fact of mortality and its finality. For Dante, being free for death belongs to the structure of conversion, wherein the old self dies freely. And the paradox of being given and yet choosing the new self is a universal condition of Christian moral conversion, possible only by grace, yet grace that makes free.

By hearing the words about his fated journey repeated every major step of the way, having first heard in more detail before beginning the journey how the relay of three blessed women had rescued him and set him this course (*Inferno* II. 43–126), Dante-protagonist is empowered to reconstruct the precedents and sanctions for his journey, giving it a certain structure of necessity that sustains him along his way. Such is the sense of the insistent repetition of formulas of Dante's election and of reminders regarding "lo suo fatale andare" (*Inferno* V. 22). It seems strange, at least prima facie, that Dante should write of his journey as "fated," since that is generally not part of the Christian code he adheres to, and it would even seem to compromise the Christian moral drama of conversion.[6] It almost appears to be a sort of atavism reverting to the fate of the hero in pagan tragedy. The term seems equally out of place in as (supposedly) secular a discourse as Heidegger's Dasein-analytic. Yet both Heidegger and Dante have sensed the appropriateness of just this term for the structure and dynamic of human being's recapitulation of its ownmost possibilities of existence in the resolve to be them. In anticipatory resoluteness or conversion what one discovers and is free to embrace—one's ownmost possibility of existence—demands to be described as one's fate, since it brings to one's life the finality that only death can give. Heideggerian anticipatory resoluteness and Dantesque conversion converge upon the fate of death, which at the same time marks also their divergence, since death is for Heidegger the possibility that is not to be outstripped, while for Dante it is rather the obligatory passage towards resurrected life.

Dante the writer repeats the protagonist's experience and sees the whole arc of the journey in its necessity from the standpoint of its completion. From the standpoint of the reader, finally, all this represents a possibility of existence offered through the poem. Its repeatability opens a way to a temporality and a future in which the meaning revealed through the poem can be incorporated into and so be repeated in the reader's own life. In this way, what the narrative offers in the form of strange myths and images presented in "li versi strani" can be taken over and appropriated into the reader's own experiential reality. By shifting from the temporality of objectified, mythic narrative to the reader's own temporality of looking into and through a narrative, seeing there the reader's own history or historicality, Dante shifts from flat, linear time as well as from cyclical time to an ecstatic and repetitive temporality, which we will presently attempt to unfold as being, from a certain point of view, the essence of Christian doctrine. The true "dottrina" that is given out to be the deep meaning of his narrative in the hermeneutic injunction in *Inferno* IX, and that Dante discloses narratologically, resolves into a specific, revealed understanding of the temporality of human existence.

6. See Karl Löwith, *Meaning in History* (Chicago: University of Chicago Press, 1949), chap. 9, for Augustine's qualified acceptance of the term "fate" into Christian discourse in the *De civitate Dei*. See Theodor Haecker, "Fatum," chap. 7 in *Virgil: Vater des Abendlands* (Bonn am Rhein: Jakob Hegner, 1933), for the etymological sense of fate as "what has been spoken."

2. ECSTATIC AND REPETITIVE TEMPORALITY

Or ti riman, lettor, sovra il tuo banco,
dietro pensando a ciò che si preliba . . .
(*Paradiso* X. 22–24)

It is commonplace in intellectual historiography to stress the revolution-
ary conception of time inaugurated by Judeo-Christianity. But this pro-
found transformation is usually described simply as a breaking out of the
circle of fate that governed ancient myth into the linearity of historical
religion. This commonplace—together with a sense of its inadequacy—
can readily be found in the most able criticism of the *Commedia*. Thus
Giuseppe Mazzotta rehearses the canonized approximation: "The *cir-
cuitus temporum*, where events repeat themselves and fall upon themselves,
flatly contradicts the view of time having a beginning and an end, and
also contradicts implicitly the Incarnation, the radically new event which
breaks open the pagans' circle. Dante dramatizes his conception of the
linearity of history."[7]

A certain rhetorical effort ("flatly contradicts") betrays what may be a
lurking suspicion that the flat contrast between linearity and circularity
does not quite get at what is unique about Christian temporality, as famil-
iar and as little challenged as these schemata have become in standard
accounts of Christian intellectual history. A circle, after all, does not flatly
contradict a line, but itself *is* a curved line bent around to its own point
of origin. Even if one wishes to emphasize the *straightness* of a (straight)
line, this hardly makes it coincide with the course of Christian history,
articulated, as it is, by backslidings and bindings up, conversions, rever-
sals, falls, and risings again. Even the stress on the "radically new" in the
Incarnation hardly lines up with the image of the line, which instead
features continuity. Of course, the "point" about the line is its termini,
the beginning and the end that it connects together. But if "in my begin-
ning is my end," as in Christian poetry and story, where Christ is the new
Moses (Matt. 5.7) and the new Adam (1 Cor. 15), then the line seems to
be beside the point. Admittedly, steady development and unequivocal
directionality govern segments of Christian history; but the shape of
these segments does not work as a general schema for the whole Chris-
tian vision of time, and much less of time and eternity together.

Freccero, too, contrasts the time of classical antiquity, which "moved
in an eternal circle," with the "new linear conception of time" brought
by the coming of Christ. The Incarnation makes possible an advance
from "continued repetition" to "an absolutely new event."[8] This basic

---

7. Giuseppe Mazzotta, *Dante. Poet of the Desert*, p. 20.
8. John Freccero, *Dante: The Poetics of Conversion*, p. 136.

contrast, which Freccero treats with a touch of skepticism ("Whatever the accuracy of such a dichotomy") in applying it to pre-Christian Ulysses literature, yields results such as the following: "There can be misfortunes or disasters, monsters and sirens, but from beginning to end the game is fixed and both the reader and the protagonist, confident by tradition about the eventual outcome of the adventure, are more concerned with the 'how' of it than with the 'why' of the universe in which it is enclosed" (Freccero, *Poetics of Conversion,* p. 137). But what could be more "fixed" than a Christian narrative like the *Divine Comedy* or *Paradise Lost?* In the Christian story the end has always already been disclosed in the Christ event. Creating dramatic tension is notoriously a problem for Christian narrative, where the providence of an omniscient God is omnipotently in control from beginning to end. Freccero himself notes how inadequate the disjunction is for dealing with Dante: "At the beginning of this essay, I suggested a distinction between the circular and the linear forms of human time and of narrative structure and said that Dante's poem could be characterized by neither figure because it partook of both" (p. 150).

Dante reveals that contrary to the customary assumptions of scholarship, due perhaps in part to a rather narrow focus on a famous polemical passage from Augustine,[9] the authentic Christian understanding of time is not based on linearity. More profoundly, or more exactly, the temporality that structures the existence of human beings is revealed in the *Divina Commedia,* as in the New Testament, to be ecstatic (in its etymological sense of "standing outside") and repetitive. Dante's text discloses with maximum clarity that if Christian temporality is linear, it is so only preliminarily, and precisely in order to delinearize time. What distinguishes Christian temporality is its ecstatic openness, a specific way of living historically that contemporizes past and future by repeating what has been accomplished in Christ while at the same time anticipating the *eschaton.* This ecstatic structure whereby everything is at once already and not yet defines the originality of Christian time. Paradoxically, for the Christian, "the hour is coming, *and now is* . . ." (John 4.23; 5.25; 16.32).

9. *De civitate Dei* 12.10–20. See also Hugh of St. Victor, *Expositio in Hierarchiam Coelestem,* Patrologia Latina, vol. 175, col. 144. Oscar Cullman, *Christ and Time,* trans. F. Filson (Philadelphia: Westminster, 1949; originally published as *Christus und die Zeit* [Zurich: Evangelischer Verlag, 1945]) is an influential advocate of the circle/line dichotomy, but nevertheless shows how complicated the "Linear Conception of Time in the Revelation of the Bible as Contrasted with the Cyclical Conception of Hellenism," as a chapter heading has it, really is. Karl Löwith, *Meaning in History,* in chapters on "Augustine" and the "Biblical View of History," offers subtly nuanced versions of the received views. Thus he writes of a "linear, but centered, movement" in which "a progressive condensation and reduction takes place, culminating in the single representative figure of Christ, to be followed by a progressive expansion of the central event" (p. 182).

Salvation already is, but is also not yet. The Christian is called upon to exist out of a future that is not yet, pending the time of the end, but that has been definitively anticipated in the Christ event. The New Testament as a whole enjoins Christians to stand outside the world and history into the end time of salvation, or, in other words (and in another vocabulary), to "temporalize" their existence.[10]

Christianity has fostered a speculative tradition that works out this temporality in the notion of "repetition," which distinguishes itself from the temporalities of both cyclical recurrence and linear progression (even while repeating them). Specifically, it is the existentialist tradition of reflection on the Christ event that furnishes a conceptuality of repetition and ecstatic openness adequate to what is really unique and "radically new" about the Christian experience of history and existence in time. In this view, temporality that is authentically human, which also means divinely graced, derives rather from the historizing of existence by the anticipation of a future that regains possibilities of existence that have been.

In this perspective, the narratology of the *Commedia* can be seen to unconceal, through the particular significance of its addresses to the reader, the specificities of Christian temporality as discovered first in the New Testament and eventually elucidated, most overtly, by the Christian existentialism of the nineteenth and twentieth centuries. It is worth paying some attention, then, first of all to the emergence in the New Testament of the conception of a temporality that is ecstatic and repetitive, if this is what is really distinctive about Christianity and its own peculiar historicity.

In New Testament terms: as Christians, "ye are dead, and your life is hid with Christ in God." This declared fact is also a hypothesis that finds its meaning in an imperative to live according to a salvation event that is both already and not yet. "If ye then be risen with Christ, seek those things which are above, where Christ sitteth on the right hand of God" (Col. 3.1–3). The same paradox of the declarative that is at the same time an imperative is compressed into a single verse in Galatians 5.23: "If we live by the Spirit, by the Spirit let us also walk," and again in Romans 6.12: "Even so reckon ye also yourselves to be dead unto sin, but alive unto God in Christ Jesus. Let not sin therefore reign in your mortal body, that ye should obey the lusts thereof."

10. The vocabulary of "temporalizing" like that of "historizing," as well as of the temporal "ecstasies," most directly invokes Heidegger's use of such terms. Dasein is constituted by "the unity of a future which makes present in the process of having been; we designate it as 'temporality'" (*Being and Time*, p. 379). In general, these terms may be understood to indicate interpretive phenomena that are constitutive of time and of history, giving them their meaningful structures.

This is a stubbornly persistent form of expression with Paul. The oscillation between declarative and imperative moods, between announcements and exhortations, grammatically reflects the ambiguity of ecstatic temporality that can be circumscribed within neither the already nor the not-yet. The fusion of announcement of an achievement—liberation from sin—with exhortation to achieve the very thing just announced as a fait accompli extends throughout Paul's writings. Its paradoxical quality hints that it expresses a revolutionary interpretation of temporality revealed in the New Testament and not comprehended without some strain within the categories available in the language and culture of the epoch.[11]

Paul's paradoxes simply expose in an insistent way the temporal logic of the gospel as announced by Jesus himself, for instance, in the Gospel of Mark: "Jesus came into Galilee, preaching the gospel of God, and saying, 'The time is fulfilled, and the Kingdom of God is at hand: repent ye, and believe the gospel'" (Mark 1.14–15). A time of imminence is here invoked in its ambiguity as containing something already in a manner present, fulfilled, and yet still (even twenty centuries later!) in arrival. This ambiguous time, open ecstatically in two directions, is precisely "fulfilled," for it is filled full of possibilities that neither a present nor a future in isolation from one another can contain.

Again, the meaning of the announcement of a state of affairs (a Kingdom) is to be grasped only in and by the action called for, namely, repentance and faith. Only from within this response of belief can what is announced as actual in effect be experienced as such. In other words, we are dealing with a claim to knowledge of a hermeneutic sort, in which what is known depends on and in part results from the involvement of the knower. It is not a truth that can be verified as true in abstraction from the existence of someone for whom it is true. Not to know positively what is present but to exist in a dimension of faith, of belief in possibilities that have been revealed, lending one's being to the event that

11. Frank Kermode, in *The Sense of an Ending: Studies in the Theory of Fiction* (New York: Oxford University Press, 1967), observes in Paul and John the "tendency to conceive of the End as happening at every moment," and remarks that "History and eschatology, as Collingwood observed, are then the same thing" (p. 25). Of course, the work of Rudolph Bultmann in interpreting the New Testament also needs to be mentioned as a seminal influence in this connection. See, for example, "Christian Faith and History": "It is the paradox of the Christian message that the eschatological event, according to Paul and John, is not to be understood as a dramatic cosmic catastrophe but as happening within history, beginning with the appearance of Jesus Christ and in continuity with this occurring again and again in history, but not as the kind of historical development which can be confirmed by any historian. It becomes an event repeatedly in preaching and faith. Jesus Christ is the eschatological event not as an established fact of past time but as repeatedly present, as addressing you and me here and now in preaching." *History and Eschatology* (Edinburgh: Edinburgh University Press, 1957), p. 108.

will reveal a future destiny—or, in other words, "inter-preting"—such is the temporality of existence prescribed in the New Testament, and we have seen it reflected in Dante's narratology with its implicit appeal for conversion as exposed especially by the address to the reader.

To the extent that we are in Christ, then, we too are saved, hearkening to the address in the New Testament. Yet to be in Christ, that is, to have died and risen with him, is not just a fact in our past; it cannot be achieved except in a project issuing forth from our future and embracing our entire existence from the moment of birth to death: "But if we died with Christ, we believe that we shall also live with him" (Rom. 5). Being in Christ means being out of the world, having overcome it (Matt. 28), but this can be so for us as we still live in world-time today only to the extent that we stand out of it ecstatically into the time of the end. This time is not to be waited for as something that will simply come along in the course of events, as does every thing that happens *within* the world. This much is clear from Paul's description of how he endeavors to "attain unto the resurrection of the dead" through knowing Christ, which means repeating Christ's death and resurrection in his own existence through "fellowship" in sufferings and being made "conformable" to Christ (Phil. 3.10). It is to be apprehended in an ecstatic anticipation of our future. So Paul writes of his effort to catch up with what has already been accomplished in him in advance:

> 12 but I follow after, if that I may apprehend that for which also I am apprehended of Christ Jesus.
> 13 . . . forgetting those things which are behind, and reaching forth unto those things which are before,
> 14 I press toward the mark for the prize of the high calling of God in Christ Jesus. (Philippians 3)

Paul forgets the things that are past *as* past, because in the temporalization of his existence—interpreting, realizing, and unifying it—he comes back to them from his future, in which the past comes to fruition and is finally to be achieved and fulfilled. It is in this sense that Heidegger too can write: "Anticipation of one's uttermost and ownmost possibility is coming back understandingly to one's ownmost 'been'" (Heidegger, *Being and Time*, p. 373). As a consequence, in the temporality Paul has discovered, the fashion of this world passes away and "all things are become new" (1 Cor. 15).

While Paul in 1 Corinthians, chapter 15, keeps in mind the past event (3 "how that Christ died for our sins according to the Scriptures") and the future expectation (24 "Then cometh the end, when he shall have delivered up the Kingdom to God, even the Father"), he brings all into the focus, or better, the repeated focusing, of daily death and resurrection (31 "I die daily"), which exceeds the boundaries of past and future alike and binds all three tenses together in ecstatic unity. Similarly, the author of Hebrews exhorts the faithful to "consider the end" in following "Jesus Christ the same yesterday, today and forever" (Heb. 13.8).

Every Christian is called to exist in a present ecstatically open to the "already" of the resurrection of Christ and the "not-yet" of the general resurrection. In Christ, all is already achieved. Indeed, for Paul the *eschaton* begins precisely with Christ's resurrection. Yet Christ's resurrection is inconceivable except as the first fruits of a general resurrection, such as is to be consummated at the end of all times. Paul cannot believe in it at all as just an isolated miracle. He conceives the Christ event as necessarily carrying on ecstatically in the existence of every Christian, which is to say, of everyone existing in the temporality of Christian salvation. Thus he views Christ's resurrection as absolutely inseparable from the general resurrection, which repeats it: "Now if Christ be preached that he rose from the dead, how say some of you that there is no resurrection of the dead? But if there be no resurrection of the dead, then is Christ not risen" (1 Cor. 15.12–13). Paul does not suggest that those who were denying the general resurrection may not have admitted Christ's resurrection as some special miracle. But the unique event of Christ's resurrection is inextricably connected in Paul's understanding with a resurrection that must be a possibility to be shared by further participants. This implies that the resurrected life lives through its own repeatability.

St. Augustine, in full accord with the understanding of the temporality of conversion in New Testament Christianity, also clearly articulates time in its ecstasies. The famous passage about the recitation of a psalm, which passes from existing in the mode of expectation to existing in the mode of memory, the lengths of the two respective segments being inversely proportional to each other at any given moment during the recitation, demonstrates that time can never be apprehended purely as immanent presence but only as being recollected or anticipated. The present, Augustine observes, disintegrates into nothing between the future that is expected and the past that is remembered, with nothing ever graspable as substantially present but only as repeated in memory and in expectation (*Confessions* 11. xxviii, 38). In this way, Augustine, too, temporalizes time, and in effect discovers its "ecstasies." Human being exists as the distension ("distensio") of one tense toward another, and time is nothing but the soul's stretching out toward the future in expectation and retaining of the past in memory ("inde mihi visum est nihil esse aliud tempus quam distentionem: sed cuius rei, nescio, et mirum, si non ipsius animi"—*Confessions* 11. xxvi, 33). Past and future things, which are not, nevertheless *are* "in animo," where they are repeated, opening the soul ecstatically to being outside itself and its vanishing present.

In modern times Kierkegaard resurrects the notion of repetition as a type of existential "movement," unmistakably Judeo-Christian in origin, to be sharply distinguished from the movement of "recollection" characteristic of the Greeks. "Recollection has the great advantage that it begins with loss; the reason it is safe and secure is that it has nothing to lose." To this ironic appraisal of recollection he contrasts repetition: "Repetition—that is actuality and the earnestness of existence."[12] What fundamentally distinguishes these two modes of relating to the past is that repetition is an ontological event, an actual reliving in one's own being of, particularly, the Christian story of death and resurrection, while recollection remains at the level merely of representation—a glance backward at what is no longer actually present and therefore no longer really involves one. Recollection has what is ironically called the advantage of incurring no risks because of its detachment from actual existence, its not placing any living being on the line where an experience needs to be existentially realized rather than just recalled or thought of and represented.

The ontological character of repetition in its opposition to a mode of representation forgetful of its own conditions and situatedness in being, pretending rather to operate on the basis of a priori epistemological categories, is brought out even more into the open by Heidegger. We have seen how, for Heidegger, repetition involves a retrieval of the past that fully activates it in and upon the present. Most importantly, this process of existential repetition is leveraged upon the future, resolutely anticipated. In this, too, Heidegger's thought coincides with Dante's placing of repetition within a prophetic perspective.

Heidegger stands in a tradition together with Dante by his giving priority to the future, the time not of objective fact, but rather the time out of which comes a calling and towards which conversion (or resoluteness) concentrates itself, in his account of the historicality of Dasein: "[H]istory has its essential importance neither in what is past nor in the 'today' and its 'connection' with what is past, but in that authentic historizing of existence which arises from Dasein's future" (Heidegger, *Being and Time,* p. 438). The poem's future rests with the reader, and in this case so does its history, in the sense that the history we care about is the one that will make our future. The futurity of the poem is written into

---

12. Søren Kierkegaard, *Repetition* (Princeton: Princeton University Press, 1983), pp. 136, 133.

it prophetically in its appeals to the reader and the influence they diffuse throughout its whole extent.[13]

3. PHENOMENOLOGY OF FEAR/ANXIETY IN *INFERNO* I

Com'io divenni allor gelato e fioco,
nol dimandar, lettor, ch'io non lo scrivo,
però che ogni parlar sarebbe poco.
(*Inferno* XXXIV. 22–24)

From its very beginning the poem discloses the temporality of conversion through a particular state of mind or mood, that of fear. Fear continually seizes the protagonist vis-à-vis an assortment of objects, like the three beasts in the first canto or the Gorgon's head in the ninth. These fearsome objects are conspicuously marked by a conventional iconology as allegorical, thus signaling meanings that reach beyond the narrative and its surface fiction into the moral lives and spiritual destinies of those "standing outside," at a higher level of hermeneutic enframement, for whom the story unfolds.

There is an obvious question, of the sort typically posed by undergraduates, that can actually be very revealing in this connection. Why does Dante continually fall prey to fear and panic before the monsters, furies, topological terrors, and other assorted frights that are summoned up as impediments along his path? Does he not already know that his journey has been foreordained by the Almighty? Virgil repeatedly de-

---

13. It should by now, incidentally, be evident why the hermeneutic passage of *Inferno* IX was described in the title of the last chapter as a "rite of passage." Since the pioneering work of Arnold van Gennep, *Les rites de passage: Étude systématique des rites* (Paris: A & J Picard, 1909), it has become increasingly clear that the "rite de passage" functions above all as a means of structuring time. Interpretation of existence right from the ritual exercises of primordial humankind has taken the form of efforts to temporalize and so to appropriate time, ever threatening with its annihilations. See, for example, Nicole Blemont, "La notion du rite de passage," in *Les rites de passage aujourd'hui: Actes du Colloque de Neuchâtel, 1981* (Lausanne: L'Age d'Homme, 1986): "Je crois donc que les rites de passage ont pour fonction essentielle de manipuler symboliquement le temps de toutes les façons essentielles de le retarder, de l'avancer, de le rendre plus rapide ou plus lent, de l'atomiser ou de le synthétiser, d'anticiper pour mieux revenir un arrière, ou de revenir en arrière pour mieux anticiper. Et la manipulation symbolique du temps donne aussi l'illusion qu'on le maîtrise, qu'on ne le subit plus dans l'impuissance" ("I believe therefore that the essential function of rites of passage is to symbolically manipulate time by all the essential ways of retarding it, advancing it, making it faster or slower, atomizing it or synthesizing it, anticipating in order better to return back, or returning back in order better to anticipate. And the symbolic manipulation of time also gives the illusion that one masters it, that one does not impotently suffer it"—p. 17).

clares in all confidence that the journey cannot come to grief or be ob-
structed because it is sponsored by the divine will. Are we supposed to
forget, and to suppose that Dante too forgets, this all-important point
every time the journey seems to run into trouble, all for the sake of
creating a certain impression of suspense in what would otherwise be a
dull story, ruined by having its denouement prematurely divulged?

Logically, fear on Dante's part is groundless, considering the divine
mandate by which his whole journey is sanctioned. But Dante is repeat-
edly thrown into crisis by the course of events; he loses his resolution
and his grasp of the necessary end of all his adventures in the other world.
In *Inferno* IX, as in the second canto, he wants to give up the quest and
go back home. Within the story and its presuppositions, fear hardly makes
sense. But if the story is understood hermeneutically as an interpre-
tive journey, then the fear has a perfectly intelligible significance beyond
considerations of the logical or psychological consistency of the narrative.
For it is not just fear in the face of external threats. Dante's forgetting
that his journey has an end that cannot fail, and his becoming susceptible
consequently to mere contingencies that begin to dictate his possibilities
once he has ceased to determine them for himself by choosing his final
end and destiny, signals the collapse of the distinctively human structure
of his existence as interpretive. He is reduced to existing as one intra-
mundane object among others, instead of resolutely assuming his exis-
tence as not contained within but rather as structuring, temporalizing,
historizing the world of meaning in which he lives.

In the first canto, Dante-protagonist flees in the face of three beasts,
but his flight figures a fleeing from the sort of existence—call it con-
version—that would eventually enable him to reach the mountain top
where his life's goal would be attained and his being be complete. The
beasts he flees from are not themselves frightful but only tokens of
the frightful and, more profoundly, of what is anxiety-arousing, namely,
nothingness. He is fleeing in the face of his own possibility of wholeness,
which comes through facing death (which he has in fact just narrowly
escaped), specifically in the mode of conversion: this possibility entails
losing all control over himself as a positive entity, dying to himself in re-
solutely accepting and embracing the nonbeing which intrinsically be-
longs to and conditions his creaturely existence as created ex nihilo, that
he might rise up again.

The protagonist's fear, inasmuch as it is directed to allegorical objects
that we are invited to demythologize by the text itself with its built-in
interpretive cues, signifies fear in a more fundamental, existential sense
for the writer or reader, what may be more appropriately termed "anxi-
ety," where anxiety is understood to occur in the face of no present

danger, no objective grounds for fear.[14] Interpreted as an objectification of anxiety, the fear represented in the narrative is referred to a structural rather than an occasional threat, not to the protagonist so directly as to the existence of the interpreter, whose being is at stake in reading the poem.

Descriptions of the protagonist's fear, thus, readily constitute allegorizations of the author's and reader's anxiety in the face of nothing. In a situation where the object of fear is not actually present, indeed, in the situation of reading or writing, fright is objectless and a projection from essential states, that is, from the constitution of the existence of the human being who reads/writes. Specifically, this existence is anxious because it is constituted by the nullifying agency of time.

Moreover, once we have understood Dante's fears, without denying their literal meaning, as figuring hermeneutic anxieties, this perspective reflects back into the narrative, for the protagonist himself is on an essentially interpretive journey, the risks and rewards of which are loss or fullness of understanding. Even for the protagonist, for whom it is literally a matter of life or death, everything depends on interpretation. Has he truly understood what he has been told and promised? Granted God cannot lie, is there not always still a factor of interpretation and of not knowing, or, in other words, of faith, in a religious quest such as that of Dante? Thus Dante's misgivings even at the narrative level seem not so senseless after all if it is remembered—and for this there is constant prompting—that everything in the poem, including promises and assurances, is interpretively mediated. And this makes it all, in crucial ways, a matter of time.

The journey is situated in spring, in a repetition of the time when divine love first moved the heavens, or, in other words, in the temporality of Creation. Accordingly, at the poem's beginning, and, in effect, as a condition of its beginning, Dante dramatizes the struggle between two temporalities, a time of origins, the originary temporality of creation, and the everyday time of our mundane and fallen existence, in which we are always already caught up. Dante's poetry as a ritual restructuration of time in the image of eternity aims to bring this fallen time back into

14. See Heidegger, "What is Metaphysics?" in *Basic Writings;* originally published as *Was ist Metaphysik* (Frankfurt am Main: Klostermann, 1969). See also *Being and Time,* sec. 40: "The basic state-of-mind of anxiety as a distinctive way in which Dasein is disclosed," where Heidegger affirms that "anxiety . . . is what first makes fear possible" (p. 230). Such a phenomenological interpretation in no way precludes also analyzing Dante's "timor" as a defective condition relative to the mean constituted by the virtue of fortitude within the Aristotelian economy of the passions, as explained by W. H. V. Reade, *The Moral System of Dante's Inferno* (Port Washington, N.Y.: Kennikat Press, 1909).

connection with originary time as its source and as the precondition of
the interpretive freedom and openness that characterizes human exis-
tence essentially. Ensuing narratively upon the protagonist's encounter
with the first beast, the "lonza leggera" that impedes his ascent toward
the summit of the mountain, evidently of Purgatory, wrapped in light,
so that he turns to go back down, Dante observes the time:

> Temp'era dal principio del mattino,
>   e 'l sol montava 'n sù con quelle stelle,
>   ch'eran con lui quando l'amor divino
> mosse di prima quelle cose belle;
>   sì ch'a bene sperar m'era cagione
>   di quella fera a la gaetta pelle
> l'ora del tempo e la dolce stagione. . . .
>
> (*Inferno* I. 37–43)

(The time was in the early morning,
  and the sun mounted on high with those stars
  that accompanied it when first divine love
moved those beautiful things;
  so that the hour of day and the sweet season
  caused me to hope well of that beast with the gay pelt. . . .)

This evocation, in a vocabulary of Aristotelian physics, of the first
cosmic motion ("mosse di prima"), that is, the beginning of time, with
its aesthetic aura ("cose belle") and divine agency ("l'amor divino") de-
scribed with touches from biblical sources such as the Book of Job (38.7),
sets the action of the poem into the frame of the primal time of Creation,
which its own creative-interpretive act can repeat. Dante finds himself
in that "ora del tempo" when it all began, the origin with respect to
which all time is repetition, whether in recovery or in loss. Although this
recovery of originary temporality, in which human being, in accordance
with its interpretive essence, is open toward the origin of its world, gives
him grounds for hope, this recovery is not yet secure, as is hinted in the
adversative clause, the "but," with which the passage takes a new turn:

> . . . ma non sì che paura non mi desse
> la vista che m'apparve d'un leone.
>
> (I. 44–45)

(. . . but not so much as to keep me from fearing
the sight which appeared to me of a lion.)

An event in his visual field, the sight of a lion, can upset the equanim-
ity induced by the momentary openness to primal time and throw the
protagonist back into a state of fear. That the fear issues directly from the
sight of an object is stressed again in the immediately pursuant descrip-

tion of the she-wolf that causes Dante to completely lose hope of gaining the summit, by the words "la paura ch'uscia *di sua vista*" ("the fear that issued *from the sight* of it"—I. 54). This peculiar diction may intimate an awareness that the mode of perceiving itself, the sight of outward things, is the root cause of fear. A similar phenomenological hint of the correlativity of mental structure and world inflects the description of the advancing leopard, where Dante's own emotion is transferred to the world, so that he perceives the air itself to be trembling:

> Questi parea che contra me venisse
> con la test'alta e con rabbiosa fame,
> sì che parea che l'aere ne tremesse.
>
> (*Inferno* I. 46–48)

> (This one seemed to come against me
> with its head reared and with voracious hunger,
> so that the air seemed to be set atremble.)

Phenomenologically, Dante's fear focuses on an object present at hand perceived as a threat, but at the same time manifests a structure of temporalization, that of anxiety.

The falling away from primordial time as figured by the Creation to a fallen time of loss, where time is essentially a losing of all that is (as in Augustine's analysis of the nothingness of the pure present in *Confessions* 11), is captured perfectly in a commercial simile otherwise rather out of place in the wild and wooded scenery of Canto I:

> E qual e quei che volontieri acquista,
> e giugne 'l *tempo* che perder lo face,
> che 'n tutti suoi pensier piange e s'attrista. . . .
>
> (I. 55–57)

> (And like the man who greedily accumulates,
> and the *time* comes that makes him lose all,
> who in all his thoughts weeps and saddens. . . .)

All who exist in a temporality based on things present at hand are misers in the sense of counting out their most precious possession, their time, as if it were equatable with discrete objects like coins, subject to loss. This is the temporality into which Dante falls in his failure to make it directly up the mountain. And this temporality constricts Dante within a space where the light is silent ("là dove il sol tace"—I. 60), a place of undisclosedness, where the synaesthetic image seems to include poetry in what is silenced by the impediment to lighting up the world.

This suggests an antithesis between an authentic creative temporality inducing serenity and hope for wholeness and a time in which one is prey to what happens to be present ("le presenti cose," as Dante will later say, in *Purgatorio* XXXI). There is an irony in that the immediate and fearsome presences of the episode, the three beasts, are obviously allegorical. At least formally, we may wish to take their allegorical significance to be that of fallen time and its constrictive immediacy: its three-fold of separate tenses splits off past and future from the present so that annihilating threats can be confronted only *ad seriatim*.[15] But even apart from what they stand for allegorically, which seems not all that clear after centuries of scholarly debate, the fact that they are allegories is itself highly significant. While Dante represents himself as frightened protagonist absorbed in the time of a one-dimensional present, as poet he employs a figural technique that in its essence concerns temporality of a searching sort, which is recuperative of origins and pregnant with destiny, the very opposite of the flat temporality of everydayness and of the merely outward perception of objects.

Dante's allegory, by its own intrinsic call for elucidation, sets up a dynamic interplay between the experience of the protagonist within the fiction and the experience of the reader and writer in relation to it. The emotion of fear is especially apt for eliciting the participation of the reader and author in the journey experience. We have seen (in chapter 2) that Dante also in some ways inverts this relation, so that the "real" experience can equally be the experience of interpreting the poem, in relation to which the protagonist's adventures become instrumental and aleatory. The "repetition" of the protagonist's journey in the reader's— a journey in reading but also in life, which the reading is a constitutive part of—takes precedence for such purposes over that of which it is a repetition, even while following after as its continuation.

Only at this stage of reflection can reading fully register certain subtle intimations in which Dante suggests from the first that his journey coincides with an act of interpretation—though not in any way so as to diminish the reality of the journey, but simply in order to construct the temporality of its happening as determined from a present and out of a future—those of the interpreter—as the preconditions and modalities of having the past that the poem narrates. The process of recounting his journey through Hell, or, in other words, the process of the poem, which

15. The sort of interpretation of the first canto I am offering here is in certain ways reminiscent of Neoplatonic readings, for example, that of the *Aeneid* by Bernard Sylvestris, that were likely an important influence on Dante's poem (see, e.g., Thompson, *Dante's Epic Journey*). Such interpretation is not the fashion today, yet in our determination to define what is valid (that is, modern) critical method we do well not to lose touch with what might have been compelling to our ancestors even about styles of criticism largely relinquished for superficially coercive reasons of "progress." It is not so much Neoplatonic as existentialist religious philosophies, such as those of Gabriel Marcel, Karl Jaspers, and Jacques Maritain, that inform the contemporary relevance of such a reading.

is the hermeneutic process itself, is first proposed as a renewing in thought of the fear attendant upon the original experience. In the second tercet of the first canto of the whole work, following immediately upon his initial exposition of the situation of being lost ("smarrita"), from which the character in the narrative sets off, Dante reflects upon his poetic interpretation of this situation, indicating that the past that his poem re-creates is active upon the present in which he as author re-creates it:

> Ahi quanto a dir qual era è cosa dura
>   esta selva selvaggia e aspra e forte
>   che nel pensier rinova la paura!
>
> (I. 4–6)
>
> (Ah, how hard it is to say what it was like,
>   this wild and bitter and intractable forest,
>   which in thought renews the fear!)

The structure of retroactive involvement is reinforced by the prefix "ri," which recurs three times in the first ten verses, describing the movement of doubling back upon itself intrinsic to the interpretive act, at the levels both of consciousness ("mi *ri*trovai per una selva oscura") and of discourse ("Io non so ben *ri*dir com' i' v'entrai").

Indeed, the retelling of fear is its own tribulation. It seems fair even to infer that the event realizes itself in all its fearfulness only in being recapitulated. That is the further sense in which the saying is hard ("Ahi quanto a dir qual era è cosa dura")—because it participates in, repeating and completing, the arduous event itself. In this way the impinging of the protagonist's past on the poet's present is revealed as reciprocal. Not only is writing continuous with the experience being written about; the writing itself becomes in some sense an origin for this experience as it comes to light in the poem. The past experience is recuperable only in and as (at least in part) the present act of articulating it.

Although it lies near the source springs of the poem's "originality," the phenomenon of re-experiencing events through narration is presented by Dante through a subtle evocation of the time-honored topos of sadness brought on by thinking back over sorrows as one recounts them (*Inferno* I. 4–6), reminiscent of Odysseus's introduction to the story of his pains told to the Phaeacians (*Odyssey* IX. 12–13). This incipit was taken as model by Aeneas at the outset of his tale to Dido ("infandum, regina, iubes renovare dolorem"—*Aeneid* II. 3), and it is echoed once again, with whatever ironies, by Francesca (*Inferno* V. 121–26) and Ugolino (*Inferno* XXXIII. 4–9). Most significantly of all, the line from the *Aeneid* expressly embodying the narrator's emotional involvement with the past from which he recoils ("quamquam animus meminisse horret luctuque refugit, / incipiam"—II. 12) is verbally incorporated into Dante's prologue ("così l'animo mio ch'ancor fugiva"—I. 25). Hence the power of origination inherent in the poem itself, in its telling or writing as an experience in its own right with a potential to generate retroactively by reliving, the past as it is recounted, is paradoxically discovered as belonging to poetic tradition all along, now re-enacted in an especially intense, self-reflective way by Dante. In comparison, the usual and narrower conception of originality as defined *against* tradition, that is, as what has never yet been thought or said, leads to contests in triviality.

From these earliest moments, then, the poem enacts a pattern of participation whereby the author, and by extension the reader, is made to share in the experiences of the protagonist. The reliving of emotions in the writing down of the experiences that originally caused them is constantly stressed throughout the poem, again, for example, at the other extreme of the *Inferno,* in Canto XXXIV. 10: "Già era, e con paura il metto in metro" ("Already I was—and with fear I put it into verse"). As little as an adverb can often suffice to transfer the emotion of fear or of another closely related affective state from the protagonist to the one who interprets his experience:

> Finito questo, la buia campagna
> tremò sì forte, che dello spavento
> la mente di sudore *ancor* mi bagna.
> *(Inferno* III. 130–32)

> (Once this was over, the dark plain
> trembled so violently that the memory
> of the terror bathes me in sweat *again.)*

> Ahimè che piaghe vidi ne' lor membri,
> ricenti e vecchie, da le fiamme incese!
> *Ancor men duol pur ch'i' me ne rimembri.*
> *(Inferno* XVI. 10–12)

> (Alas, what wounds I saw in their members,
> recent and old, ignited by the flames!
> *Still I am pained only by remembering it.)*

> I' vidi, e *anco* il cor me n'accapriccia. . . .
> *(Inferno* XXII. 31; cf. also XXIV. 82–84)

> (I saw, and *still* my heart recoils. . . .)

The emotion of fear felt *then* regularly induces Dante, as if inadvertently, to shift into the present tense; this tends to erase the boundary between the action represented in the narrative as completed in the past and the present act of representing it:

Allor fu' io timido a lo stoscio,
    ch'i' vidi fuochi e senti' pianti;
    ond' io tremando tutto *mi raccoscio.*
    (*Inferno* XVII. 121–23; cf. also XXVIII. 112–14)

(*Then* I became more frightened at the descent,
    for I saw fires and heard plaints;
    at which all atremble *I cling* tighter.)

This participatory intensity induces in Dante even an anticipated experience of the future with its ineluctable repetitions of the fear in times to come:

Poscia vid' io mille visi cagnazzi
    fatti per freddo; onde *mi vien riprezzo,*
    e verrà sempre, de' gelati guazzi.
                              (*Inferno* XXXII. 70–72)

(Then I saw a thousand faces made
    canine by the cold; *whence a shiver comes over me,*
    and will always come, at frozen-over fords.)

By these inflections of tense, Dante reveals the time dimension of retelling and interpretation in which the journey his poem recounts transpires. Accordingly, it is not only as a particular, intermittent topos, but as a constant factor operative throughout the whole work, that a reader is involved as an interpreter whose very existence is called upon in structuring the event of the poem. This is particularly revealed in the experience of fear/anxiety that marks the journey and its telling from their inception in *Inferno* I, and repeatedly.

The hints that the images in the first canto are allegorical prepare for the hermeneutic injunction of *Inferno* IX, where the author will demand interpretation of the allegory on the part of the reader in an act necessarily reinscribing meanings within the temporality of the reader's own existence. Thus the arrest to progress later in *Inferno* IX, where narration seems to be pierced by interpretation from outside, is not just one tough juncture along the way. The entire thrust and torque of the journey as directed to a final goal (though this is only to be repeated) and as leveraged from beyond itself come into question and create tension at this nodal point, from which the shock reverberates up and down the poem to its furthest extremes.[16]

16. From early on in criticism of the *Commedia,* cantos I and IX were singled out as problematic and, according to the usual consensus, inferior on account of their explicitly allegorical nature, considered retrograde relative to the thoroughly historical character of representation in which the poem's originality was recognized. The present assessment privileges these junctures, showing their pivotal importance for defining precisely the historicity of the poem as not excluding but rather as intrinsically bound up with interpretation even in the form of allegory.

4. DANTESQUE ALLEGORY AND THE ACT OF UNDERSTANDING

> A descriver lor forme più non spargo
>   rime, lettor; ch'altra spesa mi strigne,
>   tanto che a questa non posso esser largo;
> ma leggi Ezechiel, che li dipigne,
>   come li vide da la fredda parte
>   venir con vento e con nube e con igne;
> e quali i troverai ne le sue carte,
>   tali eran quivi, salvo ch'a le penne
>   Giovanni è meco e da lui si diparte.
>
>   (*Purgatorio* XXIX. 98–106)

In the perspective the history of interpretation affords, what Dante does in expressly calling on his reader to discover or construct the allegorical meaning of his narrative can be seen in its full significance. It can be usefully compared with Schleiermacher's shifting of the ground of hermeneutics from the hierarchically architected senses of a text, such as the multiple senses built into Scripture according to the principles of medieval exegesis, to the act of understanding. Schleiermacher denies even that metaphorical expressions in general, such as "coma arborum" or "tela solis," used in classical poetry, contain intrinsically multiple senses. They have but one proper sense, to be determined by "grammatical," or, equivalently, "historical," interpretation, while their figurative sense calls for an entirely distinct category of interpretation, the "psychological." For the figurative sense has to do only with how the words are used and understood, not with what they properly mean. Precisely the *use* in combination with one another of the words "sol" (sun) and "tellum" (spear), not any double meaning dwelling in the respective semantic paradigms of the words themselves, creates a metaphorical meaning, a meaning carried away from what the words as such mean.[17]

Schleiermacher's championing in this way of the "perfect unity of the word," and ipso facto his mounting of a polemic against the tiered, spiritual senses of medieval exegesis, adheres to and follows the Reformers' doctrine of the "one sense" of any given scriptural passage.[18] The Re-

---

17. I am here drawing on a sophistication of Schleiermacher's view based on contemporary structural linguistics and the Jakobsonian concept of axes of combination (= syntagmatic) and selection (= paradigmatic) proposed by Peter Szondi in "L'herméneutique de Schleiermacher" *Poétique* 2 (1970): 141–55. For metaphor as a specific use, rather than extra senses, of language, see also P. Ricoeur, "La métaphor et le problème central de l'herméneutique," *Revue philosophique de Louvain* 70 (1972): 95–112, and Donald Davidson, "What Metaphors Mean," *Critical Inquiry* 5 (1978): 31–47.

18. A long tradition of Protestant hermeneutics from Luther through Flacius, Ernesti, and Meier prepared the way for Schleiermacher's theoretical innovations. See Dilthey's classic 1900

formers too, of course, had to admit that Scripture has spiritual meaning, but this was viewed as a matter of its being *understood* spiritually, which understanding was still based on the one proper, literal meaning that they allowed. Hence one true sense, "Though not but by the Spirit understood," as Milton echoes in *Paradise Lost* (XII. 512–14).

In Schleiermacher's theory of two distinct types of hermeneutics, grammatical and psychological, what needs to be interpreted is not only a text, with its historically determinable grammar, but also an intention or a mental act (to use Dilthey's terminology). Specifically, psychological interpretation aims to grasp the *genesis* of an utterance or of a text in the life and mind of an author, itself embedded in a linguistic and cultural world. Meaning is no longer confined within the objectively fixed senses, however many, contained in the text. For Schleiermacher, the act of interpretation is exactly the reverse of the act of creation and expression: "Hermeneutics and rhetoric are intimately related in that every act of understanding is the reverse side of an act of speaking, and one must grasp the thinking that underlies a given statement."[19] In like manner, the reader of the *Commedia* is called upon to repeat the protagonist's (which also means the author's) experience in interpreting Dante's verses. This becomes explicit and insistent in direct addresses to the reader such as the following:

> Se Dio ti lasci, lettor, prender frutto
> di tua lezione, or pensa per te stesso
> com'io potea tener lo viso asciutto,
> quando la nostra imagine da presso
> vidi sì storta che il pianto degli occhi
> le natiche bagnava per lo fesso.
>
> (*Inferno* XX. 19–25)

> (May God grant you, reader, to reap fruit
> from your reading: now think for yourself
> how I could keep my face dry,
> when I saw our image up close
> so twisted that the weeping of the eyes
> bathed the buttocks through the crack.)

> Com'io divenni allor gelato e fioco,
> nol domandar, lettor, ch'io non lo scrivo,
> però che ogni parlar sarebbe poco.
> Io non morì, e non rimasi vivo;

---

essay "Die Entstehung der Hermeneutik," in *Gesammelte Schriften,* vol. 5 (Leipzig: Teubner, 1924), sec. 3.

19. Schleiermacher, "Hermeneutics: The Compendium of 1819 and the Marginal Notes of 1828," in *Hermeneutics: The Handwritten Manuscripts,* p. 97.

pensa oramai per te, s'hai fior d'ingegno,
qual io divenni, d'uno e d'altro privo.

(Inferno XXXIV. 22–28)

(How I then became frozen and faint,
   don't ask, reader, for I will not write it,
   because every speech would be too little.
I did not die, nor did I remain alive;
   think now for yourself, if you have any wit [or "genius"],
   what I became, deprived of one and the other.)

The reader is assimilated to the poet in the exercise of "ingegno," which was invoked at the outset as a principle of creative composition/interpretation: "O Muse, o alto ingegno, or m'aiutate" ("O Muses, o high genius, help me now"—*Inferno* II. 1). The situation of being in suspense between life and death, experienced as negation of both the one and the other, is what arouses the anxiety beyond words referred to in this as in every other transitional passage where the meaning of experience per se is approached and its hermeneutic infrastructure brought into view. In response to such fervid invitations to participation, the meaning of the poem is to be grasped through understanding what the experience represented therein felt like, and so by attributing a meaning personally experienced to the utterances of the poem.

The significance of Dante's address to the reader in conjunction with the allegory of the Medusa in *Inferno* IX can perhaps be understood more profoundly following the suggestion of Schleiermacher's theory as that of displacing allegory from the ground of the senses purportedly inherent in a text to that of the reader's understanding of the text. Although the two may perfectly well operate together, the sorts of personal identification and participatory understanding that are called for by the reader's interpretive act cannot but induce modifications and appropriations of any meanings inherent in the text as such. The senses of the narrative that result are inevitably products of understanding and correlative to it.

Thus, when allegory is expressly linked to the address function, as in *Inferno* IX, Dante discovers the dynamism of allegory that reads the reader, exposing the reader's own structure of understanding. Of course, he really only rediscovers it, since this sort of existentially involved interpretation was in fact dominant in ancient Christian hermeneutics. He could not but have taken to heart Augustine's "Tolle legge" story, to mention just the most famous model, in which the saint's conversion to Christianity is provoked by his reading himself into a text and receiving it as addressed to him personally ("nihil aliud interpretans divinitus mihi iuberi"—*Confessions* 8. xii).

Pier Cesare Bori, in *L'interpretazione infinita: L'ermeneutica cristiana*

antica e le sue trasformazioni, follows through the patristic period the widely
diffused notion that the text of Scripture grows along with the mind and
spirit of the one who interprets it. This entailed that the text was taken
not as objective and static, containing within itself preconstituted mean-
ings, but rather as rooted in the existence of the reader; it was intrinsically
addressed to, and part of, him. The wheels of Ezekiel's chariot, which
followed wherever the chariot went on account of the spirit that was
within the wheels, were the emblem, as read by fathers up to and includ-
ing Gregory the Great, for a mystery that alters its shape and size in
proportion to the capacity of the interpreter to understand.[20]

The freedom and flexibility of patristic exegesis was deliberately
checked by Scholasticism, which insisted on the literal-historical sense as
the only legitimate basis upon which the three allegorical senses could be
built.[21] Influentially, Thomas Aquinas attempted to rein in the arbitrary
proliferation of the senses by maintaining that any allegorical or spiritual
senses were necessarily founded upon a literal sense that coincided with
the Author's intention.[22] On this basis, the four-fold senses tended to be-
come hypostatized into an objective form as mental contents that had
been meant once and for all. Ways of understanding the text that would
be pragmatically engaged with the reader's individual existence, not to
mention historical situatedness and cultural context, were no longer in
theory supposed to have any positive contribution to make to the mean-
ing proper of the sacred text. It became fixed and, strictly speaking, inca-
pable of being "appropriated."

Dante makes the reverse move back from allegory based on tiered
senses contained in a text considered in isolation from the reader, that is,
as simply the meanings planted there and "authorized" by God, to derive
allegorical meaning rather from the reading of the text, or from the act
of understanding, in his address to the reader soliciting participation in
determining and actualizing meaning. We have seen how this involves
the reader's own existence and its temporality in constituting the text's

20. Bori takes as his touchstone the formulation by Gregory the Great, in his commentary
on Ezekiel, of this principle that Scripture itself progresses along with the progress of whoever
learns from it: "Et quia unusquisque sanctorum quanto ipse in Scriptura sacra profecerit, tanto
eadem Scriptura sacra proficit apud ipsum" (*In Hiez* 1, iii, cited in Bori, p. 44).

21. This story is told, memorably, by Beryl Smalley in *The Study of the Bible in the Middle
Ages* (Oxford: Clarendon Press, 1952). Compare the much compacter account by Friedrich
Ohly in *Vom geistigen Sinn des Wortes im Mittelalter* (Darmstadt: Wissenschaftliche Buchge-
sellschaft, 1966).

22. *Summa theologica* 1, q. 1, art. 10: "[S]ensus spiritualis; qui super litteralem fundatur, et
eum supponit. . . . [S]ensus litteralis est, quem auctor intendit." Aquinas was following Hugh of
St. Victor and Alexander of Hales, and was to be followed by Nicholas of Lyre in this emphasis.
See A. J. Minnis and A. B. Scott, *Medieval Literary Theory and Criticism c. 1100–c. 1375: The
Commentary-Tradition* (Oxford: Clarendon Press, 1988), p. 197 ff.

meaning. Without any of the deliberateness of a new manifesto on allegorical meaning, Dante in his craft as poet, specifically as narratologist, has in fact felt his way to the creation, or rather revival, of a radically different kind of allegory. In practice, he departs momentously from the Scholastic exegetical models he himself rehearses in the *Convivio* and, if he wrote it, in the Letter to Can Grande.

The question whether Dante's allegory is an allegory of poets or of theologians, which has been made so much of in the criticism[23] and which has proved so insoluble, can be displaced by recognizing how, fundamentally, Dante's allegory is an allegory of reading. Dante involves the reader "irrevocably" in the constructing of his allegory. The meaning of his narrative, whether it is one or many, and even whether it is divinely or fictively created, must be reckoned not as an ideal meaning-in-itself external to the reader and the temporality of existence: it only realizes itself in reading and in the life of the reader. This has in effect been clearly seen and demonstrated by A. C. Charity in his analysis of "applied typology" in the *Commedia*.[24]

Dante manifests keen insight into the act of interpretation as intrinsically constituting the meaning of what is being interpreted, an outlook that began to grow self-conscious and programmatic in romantic hermeneutics but that a broad hermeneutic outlook can teach us to appreciate as perennial. Reading him from a vantage point gained centuries later, we can formulate the insight at work in his interpretive practice in more evolved, or at least more modern, theoretical terms. It is by a full disclosure of the act of interpretation, which his poem is not only about, but first and foremost *is,* that Dante discloses a truth about human existence, its constitutive temporality and its potential for salvation. He lays bare a specific, complex act of temporalization, that which creates and realizes the poem. And in so doing he shows the essential structure of human being as historical.

It is important to attend to the effectual working of the addresses

---

23. See Hollander, Barolini, and Singleton, cited in chap. 1, sec. 2.

24. A. C. Charity, *Events and Their Afterlife: The Dialectics of Christian Typology in the Bible and Dante.* Having defined Christian typology as "the science of history's relations to its fulfillment in Christ" (p. 1), Charity concentrates on explicating "the 'scope' of typology, and the 'point' of its argument," (p. 101) in order to bring out the existential bearing and the call to transform existence expressed in the analogical relations among historical events in which typology consists. He writes, "In the *Comedy,* as in the Bible, the existentiality of its address to the readers, the poem's whole urgency and its seriousness, provide the context in which its use of typology should be seen" (p. 212). Charity even recognizes that "For such a claim [that poetry could be a means of grace] to come into existence a new kind of poetry would be needed—and, perhaps, a new kind of reader" (p. 212), although without exploring Dante's exploitation of the specifically literary resources of the address to the reader in making his poem "a possible means of grace."

beyond their express intent. The activity of interpretation to which the reader is summoned may, of course, be taken as conforming to the model of the multiple allegorical senses inherent in the text. We may—and certainly at one level should—understand Dante to be adjuring the reader to find a definite sense or doctrine already planted there, in the text. But, in effect, readers responding to this directive begin generating meanings that also and inevitably stem from themselves, from their own perspectives and preoccupations. The meanings found beneath the veil turn out to be various and personal, as the history of the criticism of Dante's poem massively demonstrates.[25] Dante himself in his journey of interpretation continually privileges the kinds of interpretations that can only be personal; what more intensively personal interpretation of the Middle Ages than Dante's? As a result, whether or not by design, the engendering of meaning through engagement with the poetry in individual acts of understanding belongs quintessentially to Dante's poem.

Nevertheless, such a license for personal and appropriative reading incurs liabilities of which Dante is far from unsuspecting. In fact, the risk of misreading through individual bias or aberration would be the central preoccupation of the Medusa passage according to a long tradition of reading it as an allegory of heresy, the sin that will be punished in the zone of Hell entered into at the end of *Inferno* IX. Such a reading begins with Iacopo della Lana and is reproposed more recently by Giuseppe Mazzotta in *Dante: Poet of the Desert*. Drawing on Henri de Lubac,[26] Mazzotta fills in the exegetical background for the phrase "sano intelletto," adopted in the address to the reader. It was commonly employed with reference to the advocate of an orthodox understanding of scriptural passages, and so to condemn those who interpreted Scripture arbitrarily or "subjectively," not according to the Catholic faith and the Holy Spirit, by which alone interpretation arrives at "quello che le cose sono," as the *Convivio* (IV. xv, 11) puts it.

Interpreted along these lines, the allegorical meaning of the Medusa would be madness, the association of which with heresy is amply docu-

---

25. This is made strikingly apparent by the diverse interpretations of the passage in *Inferno* IX inventoried by Amilcare Iannucci in "Dottrina e allegoria in Inferno VIII. 67–IX. 105," in Michelangelo Picone, ed., *Dante e le forme dell'allegoresi*, pp. 99–124. What else could be expected, since as Giovanni Pascoli, notes in *Minerva oscura: La costruzione morale del poema di Dante* (Leghorn: Giusti, 1898), "[D]opo aver detto, MIRATE, egli lascia i nostri occhi in mezzo alla caligine" ("After having said, LOOK, he leaves our eyes in the fog"—p. 1)? Precisely "qui, più che in ogni altro luogo e momento, è dubbio e oscurità" (p. 3). Pascoli further points to a necessarily temporal, developmental or interpretive, dimension to the disclosure of the meaning of Dante's text: "è naturale che derivi non piccola oscurità perchè l'autore, fingendo che l'attore sia ammaestrato nella verità via via, non può dire la verità, quale è, d'un tratto" (p. 9).

26. Henri de Lubac, "Subjectivisme et intelligence spirituelle," in *Exégèse médiévale*, vol. 2.

mented in mythological traditions available to Dante; it is specifically the madness of *insania intellecti* that designates, in the exegetical tradition, the mental disposition of the heretic. In this view, the address to "sane intellects" would bid readers to avoid what Mazzotta calls the heresy of reading, that is, "the doctrinal error of extrapolating, unaided, one's own truth from the poem" (Mazzotta, *Dante. Poet of the Desert,* p. 276). We are left to infer that Dante symbolically, and as an example to be followed, avoids precisely this heresy of subjective reading by turning away from the Medusa in conjunction with the address.

This may be a compelling reading of the hermeneutic injunction, even though della Lana buries it under several pages of codex devoted to an exhaustive typology of heresy.[27] But if it is correct, Dante appears to be making two rather contradictory, though both very provocative and persuasive, statements, and in effect to be setting up mutually contrary norms, in the same passage. The struggle between interpretation in a conservative, church- and tradition-bound mode and a much looser, freer interpretive practice that in crucial respects relativizes meaning to the reader may lie behind the extraordinary tension and drama of this scene. Dante certainly presents it as supremely tense and dramatic, but perhaps the underlying source of the tremendous anxious energy has been more disguised than disclosed by the various thematic leads that have been taken up by one critical approach after the other in order to elucidate the allegory. Perhaps the conflict is fueled by what does not appear thematically in the text at all, namely, Dante's divided convictions concerning, on the one hand, an authoritative, exclusive, certifiably nonheretical approach to interpretation and, on the other, a more free-spirited opening of interpretation to the living participation of the individual reader, who alone can be converted.

The two tendencies of the text are explicitly brought out by the two competing ways of interpreting *Inferno* IX that they have fostered. One way makes it a manifesto of interpretive relativism and of the (alleged) fact that one is always reading oneself and, even more self-referentially, one's own act of reading, in whatever text one reads. Thus Freccero accounts for petrification and impasse as images of interpretive failure specifically referred to Dante's own reading of his personal history, proposed as an example for readers, who are equally at risk of falling prey to petrified understanding. And unless the readers, like Dante, succeed in interpreting myths like the Medusa in terms of their own existence, and in this way apply the allegory to themselves, they will remain blocked at the surface of the letter, which is fatal. The other way—Mazzotta's—

---

27. Iacopo della Lana, *Comedia di Dante degli Allagherii col commento di Jacopo della Lana bolognese,* vol. 1, ed. Luciano Scarabelli (Bologna: Tipografia regia, 1866).

gathers a contrary lesson out of the same passage, a warning against the heresy of reading one's own passion or bias, one's own personal religious conviction or conversion, into the text, rather than staying within the limits of an objective doctrinal meaning, which the Church can establish for all. The Medusa counts as a symbol for "insane" intellect, and so for heresy as defined in the exegetical tradition, and not for the special significance she may have had for Dante in his personal career, specifically at the stage of his stony ("petrose") rhymes.

The desire to caution the reader against unauthorized interpretation and the exigency of passing beyond the letter by reading one's own life story in the text—expressed by Mazzotta's and Freccero's readings respectively—comprise poles that may simultaneously be exerting pressure on the strenuously wrought, madcap imagery of the episode. Dante may not have known how to resolve this conflict, nor even have been conscious of it in terms like the ones in which it has presented itself to us. Nevertheless, the text he produced evidently manifests both fundamental, and fundamentally contradictory, attitudes towards interpretation. As such, this ineluctable crux becomes another instance of Dante's vexed, obsessive, and perhaps, in the end, "insane" relation to authority.

FOUR

The Making of History

1. RELOCATING TRUTH: FROM HISTORICAL
SENSE TO READER'S HISTORICITY

*T*he question of truth has riddled the reception of Dante's poem from the beginning of a tradition of commentary as old as the poem itself. How are the truth claims made by the poem to be taken? For a numerous company of critics stretching from Dante's contemporaries to our own, they are typically poetic posturings, one more fine example of the art of self-staging, which Dante masters to perfection. For no less imposing a constituency of interpreters, however, everything depends on recognizing that some kind of claim beyond the scope of poetic art is being made: a claim that actual historical experience or true religious vision is being reported.

Even that such issues should be raised, insistently across seven centuries of interpretation, marks the *Commedia* as an exceptional case among the works we study as literature in our academic curriculum. Like perhaps no other literary work, Dante's poem imposes itself as somehow more than imaginative literature according to the usual conception, as in some way religious truth, divine revelation. Dante's poem is not content simply to be a poem without expressly and clamorously raising the whole question of poetry and its potential for truth and even for true religious revelation. We need to ask how on earth it does this. We are guided in this inquiry by the premise that insight into interpretation gained through contemporary hermeneutic philosophy and theology may enable us to understand some things about Dante's poetic and interpretive procedures perhaps even better than he understood them himself.[1]

Understood hermeneutically, in terms of a dialogue between past and present, the question of the truth of the *Commedia* does not concern merely a textual artifact; it interrogates the questioner and places moder-

---

1. The saying that a latter-day interpreter may understand a text better than its own author became a slogan of modern hermeneutic tradition through its adoption by Friedrich D. E. Schleiermacher.

nity *en face* of a claim out of its past. Of course, it is perfectly possible to accept that a *claim* is being made to authentic religious revelation and nevertheless to view this as all part of a poetic pretending, a rhetorical hypothesis or hyperbole. Yet such a neutralization of the claim already entails a *decision* as to what is at stake and as to what kind of interest it is possible, or at least preferable, for the poetry of the *Commedia* to hold for us. It refuses to face frontally the question of truth, which the poem has posed so forcefully to its readers, provoking decisions and divisions, pretending rather to analyze it neutrally from the outside. It manifests a refusal to allow oneself to be *claimed by* this truth and so to enter into the event of the poem.

Can we be sure that the poem, with its Christian medieval ethos, can no longer make any claim upon us as moderns? This is often simply assumed in the scholarship, but must rather be responsibly assumed as an interpretive decision, not just a given, as if "modernity" were an orthodoxy itself impenetrable to beliefs arriving from "elsewhere." This would obviously be an egregious misreading of modernity, which has in fact been the scene of numerous religious revivals, some of them Christian. A past we simply assume we are liberated from may only have been forgotten and thereby bind us the more insidiously. Although in general we have long ceased to consider the question of truth as relevant to the understanding and appreciation of poetry, in Dante criticism even presently it can still be described as "the one fundamental question for all readers of Dante's poem." Teodolinda Barolini reviews recent Italian and American criticism in order to show that both in different ways have come to an impasse over "the one central issue of the poet's truth claims." [2] Why should the question of truth be so peculiarly important and so vexed in the case of the *Commedia*? [3]

2. Teodolinda Barolini, "Detheologizing Dante. For a 'New Formalism' in Dante Studies," *Quaderni d'italianistica* 10 (1989): 35; later published as "Detheologizing Dante: Realism Reception, and the Resources of Narrative," in *The Undivine Comedy: Detheologizing Dante*. Robert Hollander, in "Dante *Theologus-Poeta*," also considers that the debate over the allegory of the theologians versus the allegory of the poets, which means over the literal and historical truth of the narrative, is "what can fairly be considered the central problem in the interpretation of the *Commedia*" (p. 61).

3. Actually, the *Commedia* represents only an outstanding case of the sort of question that is raised by texts in general on being approached "hermeneutically." Gadamer, in criticizing the opposite approach, namely, "historical objectivism" ("Der historische Objektivismus"), concentrates on just its tendency to suspend the claim of traditionary texts to say something true: "The text that is understood historically is forced to abandon its claim to be saying something true. We think we understand when we see the historical situation and try to reconstruct the historical horizon. In fact, however, we have given up the claim to find in the past any truth that is valid and intelligible for ourselves. Acknowledging the otherness of the other in this way, making him the object of objective knowledge, involves the fundamental suspension of his claim to truth" (Gadamer, *Truth and Method*, pp. 303–4).

For a start, it is observed on all sides that Dante's poem makes excep-
tional and exceptionally insistent claims for its status as revelation, vision,
or experiential record. Can these claims be comprehended as simply part
of the pretending that we grant as a charter right to poetry? Or do they
rather outstrip the poetry as assertions of truth of a theological order to
which poetic inventions can but serve as handmaiden? Even the appar-
ently straightforward claim to be faithfully reporting a first-person expe-
rience—where the speaker actually was ("fu' io") and what he really saw
("vidi")—sunders into the two seemingly incompatible possibilities of
either the fictive discourse of poetry or (allegedly) true religious witness.[4]
Formulated naively, the question is easily dismissed as a natural response
of wonderment such as might be expected of children—"Did it really
happen?"—and not the sort of thing the literary critic need be seriously
concerned about. But the peculiarly affecting power of Dante's poem is
inseparable from these claims, in such a way that they have proved un-
avoidable even in evaluating his poetry and its effectiveness as such.

Of course, the poem itself cannot answer the question whether its
truth claims are within it or beside it, whether they are just poetic pos-
tures or "serious" in a sense exceeding poetry as a rhetorical form alto-
gether. This is an interpretive choice, and on it depends what the poem
is for us. Suffice it to say that Dante creates this choice for us. Although
there is always the possibility that "believing" readings err in taking seri-
ously what was intended only as a literary fiction, the invitations within
the poem make this an option that simply cannot be ignored. It has en-
tailed undeniable consequences in the history of reading, which, in-
tended or not, belong to the poem and its life down through the ages.
Discussion of the *Divine Comedy* has since its origins been haunted by
the supposition or the claim, whether it is affirmed or denied, that this
poem is somehow more than a poem, more than an imaginative fiction;
readers of all persuasions have had to reckon with the insinuation that it
is a true account of an actual historical journey, an *elevatio ad coelum*,
whether in the body or out of the body one knows not, God knows, to
echo the passage from 2 Corinthians 12:2–4 about Paul's being rapt to
the third heaven that Dante himself echoes in the proem to the *Paradiso*.

The question of the truth of the *Commedia* actually comprises many
questions. Is it a true story? Does the narrative relating Dante's journey
through the three realms of the world to come purport to be literally
true and so to be a historical account? Was Dante a prophet? Is his poem
inspired? Is it supposed to be a true revelation of a metaphysical order of

---

4. The citations, from the opening verses of *Paradiso* I, have become a crux for these ques-
tions, thanks to commentaries on them by Pietro di Dante and perhaps by Dante himself in the
Letter to Can Grande. See Giorgio Padoan, "La 'mirabile visione' di Dante e l'Epistola a Can-
grande," in *Il pio Ennea, l'empio Ulisse* (Ravenna: Longo, 1977).

being or of an eschatological dimension of existence? And these formulations cover only what might be termed "religious truth," whereas the poem certainly has no less pretensions to disclosing philosophical, psychological, social, existential, and so on, truth and truths, although a powerful compulsion to unity in Dante's Christian, semiologically centered universe would make all these appear as facets of the poem's Truth.

The question specifically of the truth or "historicity" of its narrative—the question whether and in what sense it may be, or at least be given out as, a true story—has insistently asserted itself as the central question concerning its truth throughout the history of the interpretation of the poem. It was already an issue for the first generation of commentators, including Dante's own son, Pietro. Evidently concerned with warding off the accusations of heterodoxy and madness that seem to have dogged Dante to his grave, Pietro explains that his father only poetically feigns ("poetando fingit") to have gone on the journey through the other world to the empyrean narrated in the *Commedia*. Pietro is joined by other fourteenth-century commentators, such as Benvenuto da Imola and Francesco da Buti, in their somewhat nervous and hedging explanations that Dante visited Paradise "mentaliter et non corporaliter," ("mentally but not bodily"), that he was there "intellettualmente, ma non corporalmente, ma finge secondo la lettera ch'elli vi fusse corporalmente."[5]

Today, critical reflection on this issue is largely beholden to the accounts of Dante's poetics produced around midcentury by Erich Auerbach and Charles Singleton. Both critics strongly maintained that the *Commedia* is fundamentally different from other poems in that the story it relates is presented not as poetic fiction but as true history; as in the case of Scripture, the narrative of the *Commedia* must be taken to be literally and therefore historically true. Both critics stressed the primacy of the literal, historical sense of the narrative as the basis for all the others (its allegorical senses). For both critics, the poem's claim to being true was founded upon the claim that its narrative is a true story, or, in other words, that it is history.[6]

5. On these early commentators and for references to their works, as well as for the attack by the Dominican Guido Vernani upon Dante for his fraudulent "poetics fantasmatibus et figmentis," see Giorgio Padoan, "La 'mirabile visione,'" pp. 41–42. Michael Caesar concurs that "In practice, the fourteenth-century commentators are unanimous in rejecting or circumventing this claim [that the journey is historically true], if such it is, and in insisting to various degrees on the fictionality of Dante's invention, not least, it seems, in order to protect the poem from suspicions of heterodoxy or worse" (Caesar, *Dante: The Critical Heritage*, p. 8).

6. It should, of course, be remembered that Auerbach and Singleton were not working out a common program of interpretation, but rather were both working in highly original ways; in practice their approaches became even more differentiated than in their theoretical paradigms. As Barański notes "[L]o spazio fra il figuralismo di Auerbach e l'esegesi morale di Singleton è notevole, malgrado la loro comune ascendenza biblica" ("Allegoria," p. 83).

The synonymy of the literal and historical senses of a narrative, thitherto in Christian exegetical tradition reserved for Scripture, as the writing of the author who can write with things in the language of real events rather than just with words, was thereby extended to a poem of human authorship but unique, therefore, among subcanonical Christian writings. Auerbach's seminal study of Dante's figural realism established that the *Divine Comedy*'s mode of signifying was like that of the Bible, known in exegetical hermeneutics as "typology," in that the literal sense of the narrative was given as true and historical, in such a way that the supposedly real persons and events literally designated by the narrative were used in turn, to prefigure other realities to come in the historical, moral, and eschatological orders: "[I]n a figural relation both the signifying and the signified facts are real and concrete historical events. . . . [N]either the prefiguring nor the prefigured event lose their literal and historical reality by their figurative meaning and inter-relation."[7]

The emphasis upon "reality" of a historical nature, so strong in both Singleton and Auerbach, was promoted by Dante's significance for them as the quintessentially Christian poet. For Judeo-Christianity is distinguished as a historical religion, and Dante's poetics are conceived within and in order to mediate a world-historical dispensation opened by the incarnation of Christ. The Word made flesh or the truth become substantially manifest in visible, palpable form is the master model of revelation by which any claim to reveal truth in poetry must inevitably be measured.

Singleton framed the question in terms, going back to Dante himself, of the contrast between poetic and theological allegory.[8] Construed according to the allegory of the poets, the literal sense of the poem, the story it tells, is no more than a fictional construct. Beneath this "beautiful lie" ("bella menzogna") are hidden realities or concepts only obliquely referred to, that is, allegorically signified, as opposed to being mimetically represented or presenced in the narrative. For example, Orpheus's taming the beasts with his music is treated by Dante in *Convivio* II. i as a myth whose true intention is to represent the real power music has to subdue the brutishness in men's souls. The story about Orpheus and the animals has no truth except indirectly as a sign of a condition that does really obtain in the human race.

The allegory of the theologians, on the other hand, postulates, specifically on the model of the Bible, held to be historically inerrant, the

---

7. Auerbach, "Figura," *Neue Dante-studien,* pp. 11–76. The citation is actually from a brief restatement by Auerbach of his views in *American Critical Essays on the "Divine Comedy,"* ed. R. J. Clements (New York: New York University Press, 1967), p. 108.

8. Singleton's interpretation is expounded in *Dante Studies I: Elements of Structure.*

literal and historical truth of the narrative. For instance, when Psalm 113 states, "When Israel went out from Egypt, the house of Aaron from a barbarous people," this describes a historical event, the Exodus. This event is further laden with allegorical significances having to do with the prefiguration of Christ's rising up out of death's kingdom, the moral agent's being liberated from the bondage of sin, and the soul's exit from this ephemeral world into eternity, but the Exodus story signifies all of these on the basis of first being itself given as a real historical event. The letter of the narrative describes *in verbis* an actual happening that then signifies *in factis* these allegorical meanings. Thus the autobiographical event verbally described by Dante's poem would in fact stand for theologically conceived events at each of the three levels of allegorical meaning.

Singleton devoted himself to the cause of establishing as a fact beyond dispute that Dante had adopted the allegory of the theologians as his mode of signifying in the *Commedia*. Accordingly, the narrative of Dante's journey to the other world was asserted as literally true, and valid interpretation of the poem depended above all on first recognizing this fact. Still, Singleton allowed that this very assertion of truth belonged to the poem as a fiction, so that the convention of theological allegory and its literal/historical truth claim was itself operative within the jurisdiction of another convention, namely, that of poetry or fiction, which can make-believe whatever it pleases. It is possible for poetry to pretend even that it is not pretense but rather truth, and this is exactly what happens in the peculiar allegorical mode of the *Commedia*. Hence, in Singleton's famous and paradoxical formula, "the fiction of the *Divine Comedy* is that it is not a fiction" (Singleton, *Elements of Structure*, p. 62).

To the extent that we keep in focus this outer frame in which the claiming of historicity for the literal sense of the narrative according to the allegory of the theologians amounts to a poetic posturing, however serious and sincere it may be conceded to be, the mode of the narrative must be qualified as "realism" rather than as the literal signification of reality. Both Auerbach and Singleton exalted Dante's art of realism as something of an original departure in the history of culture. They saw the expression and manifestation of the poem's assertion of literal, historical truth in the realism that they recognized as distinguishing Dante's art from that of his contemporaries and predecessors, indeed, as the outstanding breakthrough of his genius, both in the history of literature and in the pursuit of his theological ends. The mimetic lifelikeness of Dante's representations seemed implicitly to assert that they were real and true, and so realism seemed to be of a piece with the poem's claim to truth and historicity. Indeed, it might be inferred that this claim was actually made principally only in and through the realism itself. Nowhere does the poem make any *un*rhetorical statement that it is a true account. Indeed, how could it do any such thing, being a poem?

Furthermore, realism seemed uniquely appropriate as a style of art for representing an empathically Christian truth. Christianity proclaimed that truth had been revealed in a historically incarnate form. The man from Nazareth, of the lineage of David, had declared that he *was* the Way, the Truth, and the Life. And how could a historically embodied truth be represented, if not in realistic terms? Dante's realism was so important to Auerbach and Singleton because it seemed to respond to the exigency of revealing a Christian truth in a Christian way, that is, as incarnate in concrete, historical form. The abstract, rational truths of Platonism could well be expressed in a symbolic language and allegorical code that did not try to imitate the world as we know it but rather gestured beyond it toward an ideal world of pure forms. But the incarnate truth of the Christian religion demanded to be represented in the full historical concreteness that only realism was capable of achieving.

This association of realism as Dante's style of representation with the poem's claim of representing a historical reality has often proved to patent to be resisted. The characteristics that make the narrative of the *Commedia* "realistic" were at the same time supposed to be those that certified it as being true; thus realism was taken as a warrant for literal or historical truth. Although both Singleton and Auerbach underscore the "margin" between them,[9] refusing to forget that for Dante poetry is, in any case, following the definition of *De vulgari eloquentia,* a "fictio rhetorica musicaque poita," it became all too tempting for criticism under their sway to take this connection between realism and historicity as necessary and inevitable: why else would Dante make his creations so lifelike if not to have them taken as actual, real-life, historical agents and events, since it is just this historicity of the literal meaning of his poem that is demanded by the allegory of the theologians or the figural realism which Singleton and Auerbach, respectively, were convinced was the poem's mode of signifying?

In her review of critical viewpoints on the truth claims of the *Commedia,* Teodolinda Barolini concentrates on realism as "the consequence" of the poem's claim to being true. Yet realism is only one of many techniques—including some with tendencies toward the fantastic—that Dante uses in presenting his poem as true. The poem's truth claim is not to be narrowly identified with the presumed historicity

---

9. Singleton sagely remarks, "The poem is distinguishable from Scripture and from reality and from history in its being a fiction. Its distance from its three models (and, that is, the distance from existence) is the very condition by which it can be true" (Singleton, *Elements of Structure,* p. 62).

of its literal sense but more broadly embraces its prophetic truth, which
for one like Bruno Nardi, whom Barolini cites, can consist in its being
true vision ("visione verace"), which it is even harder to understand
should necessarily have to be conveyed through realistic representation.
We might rather expect the opposite of a realistic style for the represen-
tation of an extraordinary visionary experience, in religious terms, a mi-
racle granted by exceptional grace.

In the interest of maintaining the literal truth claim, the consensus
about Dante's realism sometimes tended to overlook or play down, or
else ingeniously reinterpret as "preemptive psychology," all the disclaim-
ers that punctuate the narrative with deliberate exposures of its artificial-
ity, of the fact that it is not real however much it may seem so; the
continual reminders that it is only a verbal construct, grossly inadequate
to the task at that (see, e.g., *Inferno* IV.145–47, *Purgatorio* IX.70–72, *Para-
diso* XXIII.55–69); and those junctures where the narrative becomes
frankly fantastic, the very opposite of realistic. The poem is instinct with
warnings, both subtle and blatant, against mistaking realism for reality.
One of the most conspicuous is the episode concerning the monster
Geryon, who rises out of the depths and out of many texts, a sort of
literary collage, to ferry Dante and Virgil down to the eighth circle of
Hell. Aware that he is severely straining credibility, Dante reminds his
reader that truth often has the face of a lie and ironically swears by the
notes of his "comedía" that he actually saw the marvelous monster, just
as he describes it, come swimming up from the infernal ditch. There are
no limits to how far a fiction can go in vouching for its own truth. Not
only what is said in the story but even the poet's own affirmations *in
propria persona* are within the poem and participate in its condition as
fiction, so that the narrator can swear an oath and have this, too, belong
to the playful pretending of a fictive mode. He exploits the fact that the
most realistic narration and the most solemn profession alike are none-
theless wholly fictive in the discourse of a poem.

This need not be taken to mean that the literal sense of the narrative
is definitely not historical and purely a fiction. The narrative oscillates
between these two possibilities of interpretation, and finds its true sense
only in its appropriation by the reader in an act of interpretation and
decision. Only so can it become truly revelatory. There is a suggestion
that Dante may really have gone to the other world, a possibility of taking
this in the most direct, literal way, which, however, cannot be definitively
affirmed on the basis of the poem's representations. Belief in this is pos-
sible only on the basis of a kind of faith. But whether it is believed or
not, the narrative opens up for its readers possibilities of existence that
can be taken over and made their own. Such appropriation is the event
in which the poem assumes concrete historical reality, and in this event

the poem can happen as a personally experienced revelation of truth, based on the reenactment of Dante's "essemplo" (*Paradiso* I.70–72).

Singleton and Auerbach made it unmistakably clear that Dante's poetry is in its essence historical and incarnational. This followed directly from its essentially Christian inspiration. But what is truly historical, more than the literal sense of the narrative, which becomes overtly and conspicuously fictive, preposterous, impossible, for example, in the episode involving Geryon, is the historicity of the reader. The main locus of history in the poem is not the literal sense and mimetic surface of the narrative—as if by ever more perfect imitation this might pass out of the realm of fiction into the real—but the existence of a reader who can really and historically appropriate a text, bringing its implications to fruition in life and action. This is what Christian incarnation ultimately entails, as when the Church in the world becomes the embodiment of Christ by its receptivity to and enactment of his word and spirit. Thus the truth of the poem happens only through appropriation, when the narrative and its possibilities for existence are appropriated into the life story and personal history of individuals presumably discovering the authentic historicity of their existence in Christian conversion.

This is to understand the event of the narrative as historical in an existential sense. The historicity in question pertains to the existence of the reader, an individual who exists as a relation between a personal past and a future destiny. Dante-protagonist as literal, historical presence in the narrative is vitally important as an image of the concrete historicity that each reader possesses or can attain.[10] He illustrates how relating one's past tradition and future horizon through a present of decision works to construct the historical reality of an individual life. Hardly any more compelling illustration of this historical character of personal existence could be imagined than Dante's own life story as represented in the *Commedia,* in its trajectory between the dark wood of a past of error and the anticipation of the divine vision for all eternity. But even beyond this image, readers find a model for the historizing (history-making) structure of their existence in Dante's activity as author, interpreting his whole life as directed toward a final destination, synthesizing the narrative from a point beyond it, articulating his own existence into that of a protagonist

10. The vocabulary of "historizing," "historicality" ("Geschichtlichkeit"), etc. comes out of the writings of Martin Heidegger (see especially *Sein und Zeit,* secs. 72–77). Such terms refer, according to their grammatical inflections, to various aspects of history as constructed by interpretation and existentially grounded. I use "historicity" as part of the same family of words, preferred only for grating a little less harshly against the English speaker's ear. It is *not* to be confused with Heidegger's "Historizität," used in connection with scientifically grounded methods of historicizing.

and a distinctly figured authorial *persona* who interprets the protagonist's journey.

I suggest that Dante felt the truth of his poem was fully historical, as he seems to have implied in the Letter to Can Grande, as incredible as that may have seemed even to him, because he devined the existential grounds of the sense and very intelligibility of history. In other words, he felt that he could claim historicity for the experience proposed by his poem on the basis of his sense that, for all its use of fictions, the story of his journey and its making was the very reality of his own life as an interpretive venture. The same would hold, presumably, for the story of any Christian conversion. It is a multidimensional, a polysemous historicity, truer than any one-dimensional narration of facts could be, for it is laden with all the possible ways of construing one's past and relating it to a future one projects in a present one decides. Even the pure fictions have everything to do with Dante's interpretation of his past and his defining for himself his future, and in this sense they have everything to do with his real, personal historicity. This is historicity in a sense ultimately more important than that which may or may not belong to a historical ride on the back of a monster composed out of literary pastiche or the historical fart of a devil called Malacoda.

Historicity in this sense is completed in the application of Dante's adventures in interpretation to the life of the reader, for it is a historicity that comes about always in conjunction with a present act of interpretation, determined by and determining past, present, and future in an event of understanding in which they come to be understood. The claim to historicity, then, cannot be reduced to a claim to know past fact (including the future prophetically disclosed as if it were fact). If the history in question were merely a past event, it could not be experienced as religious truth by anyone, not even by Dante the author. Hermeneutic access to the truth of history as an ultimately religious truth can be secured only through its event in the present. To understand how this is so—and it is something Dante profoundly understood—we are greatly aided by the hermeneutical and existential theology of modern times, which has explored the way religious truth is conditioned by, and is the expression of, the historical-existential structure of human being.

The work especially of Rudolph Bultmann, along with many followers, has opened this direction of thought and inquiry. As read through Bultmann's existentialist hermeneutic, even the historical affirmations of the New Testament need to be understood first as appeals to understand oneself in accordance with what those affirmations disclose about the fundamental structure of human existence, before they can be understood with reference to the past. For everything that can be understood in and as history is conditioned by how one understands oneself presently. Thus Bultmann writes, "And just as little as the proclamation [in preaching Christ] communicates something that happened at a certain place and at a certain time, but rather says what has occurred to the person being addressed, so little is faith the knowledge of some fact within the world or the willingness to hold some remarkable dogma to be true. Rather it is the obedience that obeys God not in general or *in abstracto,* but in the concrete now." [11]

Sometimes Bultmann seems to recommend that faith disembarrass itself altogether of beliefs concerning a historical past, substituting instead understanding of oneself in the present exclusively. This emphasis risks divorcing one time dimension—that of the present—from the others. Dante, for all his keen appreciation of the retroactive shaping power of interpretation and self-understanding, of how interpretation in the present impinges upon the very reality of the past, does not elide the past nor even diminish the effect of its presentation as "fact," but rather holds this always together with its determination by interpretation in the present. Similarly, present interpretation, and, centrally, the interpretive decision of faith (i.e., to understand oneself as God's creation redeemed by Christ), is not for Dante *simply* an arbitrary existentialist leap ex nihilo. Although this aspect of the human situation is certainly to be experienced to the full—indeed, all the way to the bottom of Hell's abyss—it is not to be taken as the ultimate truth about our existence, but rather as a very basic, universal experience out of which it is also possible to participate in a continuation of the past and, particularly, of the act of faith of Christ himself transmitted through gospel and tradition. Belief in the historical facts of the gospel is certainly not irrelevant to the articulation of this faith, but neither can it be divorced from the act of understanding oneself in the present in relation to the Savior. The historical veracity of the gospel story, as of Dante's miracle story, to be neither proved nor dismissed, makes for the tension of faith, and Dante exploits and explicitates such tension poetically.

Read in the perspective of existentialist theology, the New Testament, mythology and all, manifests an interpretive understanding of human existence. The mythology represents otherworldly realities as objective, historical events and entities of the world. Existential interpretation uncovers these representations as embodying an implicit interpretation of human existence in its character, for example, of openness to the future (or hopefulness), full acceptance of one's being as contingent and as given together and shared with that of one's fellows (or love), and resolute

<hr>

11. Rudolph Bultmann, *Existence and Faith: Shorter Writings of Rudolph Bultmann,* ed. S. M. Ogden (Cleveland: World Publishing, 1960), p. 87.

commitment to assume one's destiny freely (or faith). It is primarily in their existential import, then, that the affirmations of the New Testament would have their religious truth. But this does not mean that their supposed historical truth is null and void. It means, rather, that the positivist myth of history is exploded and that the historicity of faith belongs in the first instance to the interpretive acts that constitute the historical being of one who believes. History can never be reached except through a present act of interpretation reactivating the past as it is presently meaningful in human existence.

This insight reflects broadly on phenomena of religious understanding, for example, upon why Jesus' miracles, as recounted in the gospel, are generally not discernible except to the eyes of faith. That Jesus is Lord of my life now, as witnessed by faith, not documentary historical evidence, is the basis for affirmations about his miracles and resurrection. In this sense, all the statements of the Bible are to be read fundamentally as interpellations, appeals not to accept objective facts but to define oneself in such a way as opens a whole new field of objectivity from a perspective of faith: "Therefore, *faith* also, like the word, is revelation because it is only real in this occurrence and otherwise is nothing." It is "no disposition of the human soul, no being convinced, but rather the answer to an address" (Bultmann, *Existence and Faith,* p. 87).

Precisely this emphasis on address in Bultmann's thought has been pursued further by Gerhard Ebeling, who writes, "[T]he content of what God says always unconditionally concerns the person of the hearer. . . . God's Word rightly understood is never statement but always address."[12] The same needs to be said in some sense of the *Divine Comedy,* if it is to be understood in a manner commensurate with modern hermeneutical insight, itself a recovery, I would suggest, of a sense of interpretation as intrinsic to history and its truth that was second nature to Dante. Particularly, the addresses to the reader make evident the extent to which Dante himself was conscious of this dimension of address in which, necessarily, the significance of his discourse is realized. It is especially in the addresses to the reader that Dante shows how the historical sense and meaning of the whole poem become actual precisely at the locus of the individual whose existence in the past, present, and future is engaged by the event of the poem.

Dante as poet understands that history can never be attained as an achieved fact, over and done with in the past. History always reaches us out of the past through the mediation of an interpretation in the present, an appropriation determined by what is meaningful in a new situation. Dante refuses to overlook this dynamic factor of interpretive activation

---

12. Ebeling cited in Funk, *Language: Hermeneutic, and the Word of God,* p. 25.

of the past, the historizing in the present and with a view to the future that alone gives a meaning to history and lets "facts," because significant in these relations, emerge as what they are. He compellingly illustrates this by the way he and Statius appropriate Virgil, discovering latent Christian meanings in Virgil's ostensibly pagan text. The basis for this appropriation even by misprision is a present context of interpretation. In *Purgatorio* XXII.76–81, Statius explains how the whole world was pregnant with the true faith sown by the gospel message with which Virgil's words "consounded" ("consonava"). This episode, to be examined in detail in the next chapter, illustrates how what shows up as history always radically depends on an act of reading, in this case Dante's reading of how Statius might have read Virgil. Dante's poem consistently presents history as a series of just such acts of reading.[13] It foregrounds how histories happen the way they do precisely because the reader is in their midst.

One of Dante's most famous figures, Francesca, famous as a lover, even more fundamentally owes her fate to her actions as a reader. A contrast between her and Statius as reader is hinted at when he echoes but corrects her amorous rhetoric, which had exalted love as a sort of spontaneous combustion ("Amor ch'al cor gentil ratto s'apprende"), by an ethical rhetoric transfiguring the motif of amorous inspiration:

> "Amore, / acceso di virtù, sempre altro accese. . . ."
> (*Purgatorio* XXII. 10–11)

> ("Love, / ignited by virtue, always ignites another. . . .")

The courtly language of Francesca in *Inferno* V distorts her sin of lust, the subjection of reason to impulse by carnal sinners ("i peccatori carnali, / che la ragion sommettono al talento"—V. 39), through the lens of *dolce stil novo* lyric, with its supposedly ennobling ideal of love and sublimating of passion. She is "reading" even as she speaks, inasmuch as she quotes from Guido Guinizelli ("Al cor gentil rempaira sempre Amore") and from Dante's own love poetry (*Vita nuova* XX), and it is thus exquisitely appropriate that her sin should be represented as having been abetted by a book, in which a text and its author are conflated, sharing the role of literary intermediary as pander: "Galeotto fu 'l libro e chi lo scrisse" ("Gallehault was the author and the one that wrote it"—*Inferno* V. 137).

Francesca indeed rightly indicates how literary mediation lies at the root of her sin. She implies that it is by identifying herself with Guinevere that she falls into the forbidden embrace. What she does not seem to

---

13. A plethora of compelling exegetical instances of this can be found, for example, in Mazzotta, *Dante. Poet of the Desert.*

realize is that this shows it to be a sin not of love or lust so radically as of self-misunderstanding and misrepresentation. The story she tells reveals in indirect ways a meaning of its own, realized in the very act of its being told by Francesca, that undermines her interpretation of her lapse as inspired by essentially noble love. Renato Poggioli has effectively explored how Francesca's failure to recognize the ineradicable difference between herself a member of the corrupt world of the petty bourgeoisie, and her courtly models is unwittingly betrayed by the cruder language, the "questi" for her beloved and the anatomical terms like "bocca," that unmasks the ugly lust behind her high, refined citations.[14] Moreover, she begins the story with a description of her place of origin—"su la marina dove 'l Po discende / per aver pace co' seguaci sui" (*Inferno* V. 97–98)—using an idyllic image of peace and amity that is belied by the tempestuous languishing to which she is perpetually condemned in her end. To the extent that the distortions in question are achieved in the present moment of her appearing to and conversing with Dante, her essential sin of self-misinterpretation, willful or unconscious as it may be, is textually embodied, and in this sense "carnally" enacted, by her own words in this very text.

This sort of textually achieved sin propagates itself. Francesca's seductive self-presentation, dressed in attractive rhetoric, unmans Dante. Already self-deceived by a romantic perception of the rout of the lustful, whom he describes as "le donne antiche e' cavalieri" ("the ancient ladies and the knights"—V. 71), he completely falls for Francesca's mendacious narrative in what is marked in the final stroke of the canto as a moral falling into mortal sin, a symbolic death associated with the body and hence with sensuality:

> E caddi come corpo morto cade.
> (*Inferno* V. 142)

> (And I fell as a dead body falls.)

Thus Dante, too, as character in this text, misinterprets himself, characterizing his sympathy for Francesca as motivated by "piety": "Francesca, i tuoi martìri / a lagrimar mi fanno tristo e pio" (V. 116–17). For the libidinous interest aroused in him is unmistakably betrayed by the eager accents with which he asks for details, the how and when, evidently anticipating something spicy:

14. Renato Poggioli, "Paolo e Francesca," in *Dante: A Collection of Critical Essays,* ed. J. Freccero (Englewood Cliffs, N.J.: Prentice-Hall, 1965). A penetrating reading of the "interpretive poetics" of Canto V of the *Inferno* is also offered by Jesse Gellrich, *The Idea of the Book in the Middle Ages* (Ithaca: Cornell University Press, 1985), chap. 4.

"Ma dimmi: al tempo d'i dolci sospiri,
a che e come concedette amore
che conosceste i dubbiosi disiri?"
                              (*Inferno* V. 118–21)

("But tell me: at the time of the sweet suspirations,
with what and in what way did love concede
that you 'realized' your dubious desires?")

The sin of lust here represented as mediated by reading ("Per più fiate
li occhi ci sospinse / quella lettura"—V. 130) is thus actually reenacted
in the readings that Francesca and, following her, Dante perform in the
canto—and potentially also in the reading that we, its readers, perform
upon it. At each of these levels, the sensuality that perverts rational un-
derstanding and motivates misinterpretation is made manifest in an act
of reading and in fact coincides with it. This transfer of the happening of
the sin from a past that can only be represented (and whether truly or
not cannot but remain moot) into the immanent event of reading and
interpretation constitutes one of the compelling ways in which Dante
apprehends history as interpretation and as therefore accessible to the
present. This is not to deny the reality of the historical past, but only to
shift the point of focus to our present endeavor of interpretation in prog-
ress whenever we are engaged in representing the past, and so to the way
that all history and its truth is leveraged from this pivot point.

In these ways, then, Dante's text contrives to lay open an extensive
background of interpretation, and of interpretations of interpretations, at
work in the story Francesca tells, and succeeds by linguistic nuances in
implying a whole history contrary in meaning and moral significance
to the one Francesca self-consciously relates. The truer history, the one
resulting in visible punishment, is made manifest, not so crucially in any
facts or events represented by Francesca as in the interpretations per-
formed in and by the text, and in turn by the reader upon the text, in
the first instance by Dante himself and behind him by the rest of us,
vulnerable to the seductions of the story Francesca is nevertheless ex-
posed as fabricating. We may admit that there is also something immedi-
ately compelling about the image of Francesca and Paolo enveloped in
turbulence—but that is not where we touch history fundamentally in
this canto. It is rather in the interpretations by which Francesca makes
up her own story, dissembling her sin with lovely language, together with
Dante's interpretive unveiling of this history of deception by the subtle sug-
gestions of his poetry, that the historical character of the poem is achieved.
And here reading is directly involved in determining the dynamic force of
all such facts as can be represented. The poem as an event of reading

gives us direct access to human historicity being constituted by interpretation, rather than just to history as represented by realistic mimesis.

In episode after episode, Dante presents the true sense of his characters' histories in and through their modes of interpreting themselves presently in the text. It is no exaggeration to say that the destinies of the characters throughout all three realms of the afterlife—which destinies reveal in full, as in the sight of God, the final truth about each character's earthly existence—coincide with their own readings or misreadings of themselves and of their places in God's plan. Everything in Dante's poem and its implicit ontology is interpretation, and is revealed as such. The characters' self-interpretations are the rationale for their being just where they are in eternity. From Francesca to Brunetto, from Capaneo to Ulysses, the denizens of Hell are shown as sinning fundamentally by obstinate, irreversible misunderstandings of themselves and what they really are. The judgments manifest in them show how God sees them, but they generally do not see themselves that way; all have trapped themselves in an eternal struggle against the truth, their truth.

Of course, the sinners are punished for what they have *done,* yet this is consistently presented in its extricable relation to how they understand themselves and the significance of what they *do.* Fundamentally, understanding oneself as separate from God is what makes certain ways of behaving sinful. By exposing the act of self-interpretation that is bound up with the external act in which sin is manifest, Dante reveals how an ongoing reality of constituting oneself as historical through self-interpretation in a certain freely chosen way, rather than just some nefarious deed that might simply be forgiven and let rest in peace as "history," is the direct cause of unending suffering for damned souls.

History is disclosed as a hermeneutically constructed historicality at the level not only of personal histories but also of universal history, particularly that of the Roman Empire. Dante "makes" Roman history into a secular parallel to the sacred history of the Old Testament. Reading St. Augustine's version of Roman history as a bloodbath in the city of men together with Virgil's story of the providential election of Aeneas's descendants to rule the earth's peoples, Dante brings an entirely new sense out of both. The lust and violence of Roman history are not in the least attenuated in Justianian's recapitulation of this history as symbolized by the vicissitudes of the providential sign of the eagle in *Paradiso* VI, in which "by telling the history of the empire through its emblem, Dante implies that history is a representation and a purely symbolic construct" (Mazzotta, *Dante. Poet of the Desert,* p. 180). Rather, the apparently senseless violence takes on typological significance in terms of the Exodus of the Hebrews from Egypt, echoed by Augustus's defeat of Antony and

Cleopatra, and of Christ's violent sacrificial death, turning the unedifying saga into a species of sacred history, a *Heilsgeschichte.*

This broader sort of history, too, shows how the realism paradigm oversimplifies in restricting the locus of incarnation in history to the literal sense of the narrative, rather than finding it in the sense-making process set in motion by the interpretations of the poem, both those of the characters and their histories within it and those of the author and finally the reader, expressly invoked in the addresses, as a historical site for the interpretation process. Not the presumed historical sense of the narrative but the historicity of the reader is the key to Dante's truth's becoming fully historical and so a conformable sequel to the Christian revelation founded on the Incarnation. The true understanding occasioned by the narrative can be described most generally as understanding of the interpretive structure of our human, historical reality, of the fact that we are implicated in the real that discloses itself to us in and as the understanding we come to of ourselves. We have examined some modes of this implication of a reader's existence in the poem and its discourse of address, on the basis of a Christian understanding of the temporality of existence, in the preceding chapters.

The most serious problem, then, with the view that situates the poem's claim to historical reality primarily in its mimetic realism is that it shallows out history into a narrative surface, the so-called "first sense." Equating historicity as the ground and anchor for Dante's truth claims with mimesis in this way defrauds Dante's richly hermeneutic understanding of history by a narrow, positivistic conception of it as what manifestly happens on the scene of history, like a sequence of images across a movie screen. For Dante, it is no longer necessary to take history as something flatly given, like a spectacle on a screen. Dante's poetry's greatness resides perhaps principally in its opening to view the interpretive depths out of which historicity emerges as a complex product, a *poiēsis,* that is, a "making," in the etymological sense of the word Dante himself seems to have had in mind in *De vulgari eloquentia,* where he refers to the "true sense of 'poetry'" ("si poesim recte consideremus"—II. iv).

Singleton's final statement on the poetics of the *Commedia* was entitled "The Irreducible Dove." The title alludes to St. Thomas Aquinas's famous *quaestio* whether the dove that descended upon Jesus at the moment of his baptism, according to the Gospels, was a real dove. Singleton echoes Thomas's resounding affirmative that the literal sense of the Scripture designates an unequivocally real and historical event, and maintains that the same must hold for the *Commedia,* if we accept its special, quasi-scriptural mode of signifying. What is irreducible, then, for Singleton is history. As Singleton construes it for Dante, history is the writing of God, which Dante imitates, so that his journey through the other worlds is taken as historically real and the narrative that recounts it as literally true, all within the convention of the poem as a fiction.

We should certainly agree that history is what makes the difference between Dante's prophetic poetics and the Platonic poetics of his predecessors together with all other forms of poetic allegory. But history in the *Commedia* is anything but irreducible. Where Singleton treats history and the real as something given, "irreducible," concrete, Dante dramatically and compellingly illustrates the nature of the historically real as hermeneutically constructed. The history that Singleton assumes as an extrapoetical given, an irreducible ground of truth in the poem, is opaque fact, but Dante opens up history to view in its making; and where Singleton's theory shallows out the historical sense of the poem to the literal, mimetic surface of its narrative, Dante reveals its hermeneutical depths. The poem does not hypostatize history, as Singleton's (and perhaps Dante's own) theory of allegory does; it interprets history dramatically through investment in the movements of meaning in language of which history, in specific case after specific case, is shown to be an effect. Dante suggests beneath the visible spectacle of the narrative the conflict of interpretations, the complications and continuities as well as the exclusions and mutations and misprisions of tradition, which show through the mimetic action at every point in the poem's making of "history."

Both verbally and visually Dante's mimesis is full of depths of allusion and a referentiality reaching way beyond the immediate literal sense of the narrative, revealing and concealing far more than is present in the here, now of the narrative action. Indeed, the locus of the making of history is not the plot of the poem so much as the act of reading. The more significant implications of the poem's claim to truth and historicity concern not the historical sense of the narrative so much as the existential historicity of the reader as the basis for the interpreting that makes history and discloses truth. This is pointed up in instance after instance within the poetic fiction, as well as being embodied by Dante's poem itself as a monumental work of interpretation.

Generally, it is only at the theoretical level that the constriction of the sense of history to the literal sense of the narrative has been operative. Singleton and Auerbach have led the way in discovering the interpretive constructions of history that are so powerfully manifest in Dante's poem. Singleton's championing of the Augustinian principle of retrospective comprehension of the meaning of a historical, as of any syntactical, sequence, the meaning of the whole becoming comprehensible from the end point that completes its sense,[15] belongs to the appreciation of history

---

15. "The Vistas in Retrospect," *Atti del congresso internazionale di studi danteschi* (April 1965): 20–27; later published in *Modern Language Notes* 81 (1966): 55–80.

as a structure of meaning rather than as an empirical given. And to Auerbach we owe the understanding of history in the *Commedia* as "figura."

Moreover, Singleton is profoundly right and virtually visionary in his perception that Dante's hermeneutic—call it the allegory of the theologians (or perhaps theological poetics)—aims to reach a truth that transcends history (projected, we must add, from within the very historical conditionedness of all understanding in language). This is of capital importance, and it is worth quoting Singleton at some length: "[O]ur faith in the ability of the word to contain a changeless truth continues to diminish until we find it hard and some of us find it intolerable to see things timelessly. When we shall have completely lost the belief in the possibility of transcending the world of change which is the world of history, then we shall have lost a space, a dimension, which is needed not only by religion and metaphysics but by myth and poetry as well. When there is no transcendence of change, no escape from the flux of things, how can we have anything but history? (I will not press the question, that being true, how we can have history either!) How, in short, can the word any longer hold truth as it did for Plato and for Dante?" (Singleton, *Elements of Structure,* p. 78)

This gestures toward what has largely been lost from the contemporary hermeneutical horizon. It is fairly typical of contemporary philosophers and critics to embrace hermeneutics as the good news of a radical and irreparable breaking away from "any transcendental standpoint beyond historical consciousness."[16] Dante well understood, at least in poetic practice, what has been rediscovered and elaborated theoretically by the modern hermeneutic revolution, namely, how history is constructed through retrospective projections of significance, with all the contingencies of language and interpretation this entails. The interpretive dynamics of his text can be more sharply focused today than ever before on the basis of what is in some respects a more finely articulated theoretical understanding of the hermeneutic principles of historical interpretation. But Dante also understood something about truth and history that has become almost impossible for us to think today, in our conceit of being disabused of illusions in having achieved a "postmetaphysical" standpoint. We stand to understand our own interpretive reality much better by heeding the phenomenon of interpretation revealed with a certain primordial wholeness in Dante's poem. His belief in eternal truth lies beyond, not before, the "revelation" of historical contingency, and, specifically, of the historicity of truth, which has had so great an impact on

---

16. Donald Marshall, "Truth, Tradition, and Understanding," *diacritics* 7 (1977): 73. This issue will be discussed in section 2 of chapter 5.

the present age that no recovery from this insight—blinding like all insight—seems yet to be in sight.

2. REALITY AND REALISM IN *PURGATORIO* X

Mimetic realism, beyond serving as a compositional technique throughout the poem, though perhaps not always in the same way,[17] becomes the specific thematic focus of Canto X of the *Purgatorio*. Realism here is seen as God's own style of art in the bas-reliefs that adorn the marble wall of the mountain of Purgatory along its first ledge, where the proud are punished. These sculptures ("intagli") appear so true to life that they put to scorn not only the consummate artist Polyclitus, but even nature herself. In the first image, the angel Gabriel of the Annunciation seems so real ("sì verace"—X. 37) that one would swear he was actually saying "Ave." The representations do not however serve merely to achieve supreme mimesis in forms paradoxically more natural than nature. They are placed along the way of the pilgrim to be seen as he passes, for his instruction and edification. They depict exempla of humility, beginning with that of the Virgin Mary, to be emulated by souls seeking to expiate sins of pride.

What we have, then, is mimetic art geared to a didactic purpose. And this being the case, their more than perfect simulation of reality works not to gain these representations' acceptance as really being what they represent. Mimesis here carried to a perfection that only God is capable of ultimately functions not to capture the real and render it immanently present in an artistic representation. Rather, reality is achieved, even by this superlative degree of mimesis, through the application of the moral and religious lessons it enshrines to the lives of existing individuals, here the penitent proud. The apparent incarnation of reality in the image gives way to a true incarnation of real humility in the lives of those who see and act so as to incorporate the example depicted into their personal existence.

The first scene, that of the Annunciation to Mary, is succeeded by two others, one drawn from the Old Testament and the other from pagan antiquity. Both are in some ways prefigurations of the Christ event announced in the first, for they are, respectively, the stories of King David and of the emperor Trajan, each of whom anticipates in part *Christus rex,* the Salvator Mundi. Moreover, all three are pictorial *narratives.* This, too, gives the images a historical dimension reaching beyond their imme-

---

17. Cf. Barolini, "Detheologizing Dante," p. 5, taking issue with Freccero as to whether mimesis is peculiarly the technique of the *Inferno.*

diately visible presence and appearance. This historical dimension is verbally intimated when Dante describes how his attention moves from the first to "un'altra storia" (literally, another story or history), and again to the third scene "storiata"—that is, chased or engraved, but with the same intimation of "history" once again—in the mountain wall.[18]

David is pictured, following the story in 2 Sam. 6.12–23, dancing triumphantly before the ark of the covenant brought to Jerusalem, while his wife, Michal, looking through a window, despises him in her heart for what she perceives as his unregal comportment. The narrator, however, lauds the dancing David as "l'umile psalmista" ("the humble psalmist"), both more and less than a king, and notes furthermore that Michal, evidently as punishment for her proud scorn, bore no child to the day of her death. As in the first scene, the verisimilitude of the image works not to gain it simple acceptance as being what it represents, but rather to solicit interpretation. This occurs precisely when the perfect simulation of reality causes Dante's senses to disagree with one another. For sight tells him, yes, David sings, but hearing says, no. Similarly, his eyes see the smoke of what must be burning incense, but his nose avers the contrary. The image as such is thus exposed as mere appearance, as results also from the narrative's intensive employment of a rhetoric of appearing ("pareva," *Purgatorio* X. 37; "parea, *Purgatorio* X. 58, 79). The reality or truth of the image, then, must in the end be sought rather in its moral and typological meaning.

The story featuring Trajan in the third bas-relief depicts his being persuaded to postpone his proud military campaign for the time necessary to render justice to a widow for her murdered son. As one more fold in the way that the image, despite the immediacy of its appearance, actually mediates layers of history, the emperor is first referred to under the form of a circumlocution that alludes to another popular legend about Trajan's having been saved by the intervention through prayer of Gregory the Great. Indeed, Gregory was supposed to have prayed for Trajan upon seeing, while passing through Trajan's forum, this story of his mercy and justice toward the widow sculpted in a series of scenes on a column, "Trajan's column."[19] In this way, we are incidentally reminded that such are the consequences the image may have for life, even eternal life.

None of the images simply is what it is, like a thing. All function as signs. Even beyond their thematic function as signs of humility, by their

---

18. This point and a number of others occurring ad hoc in this section are made (or relayed) by Mazzotta, *Dante. Poet of the Desert,* pp. 237–54.

19. On this, see Nancy Vickers, "Seeing is Believing: Gregory, Trajan and Dante's Art," *Dante Studies* 101 (1983): 67–85.

very existence they are signs of God their Artificer, and are indeed said to be valued because he made them: "per lo fabbro lor a veder care" (*Purgatorio* X. 99). Although flawless mimetic art is capable of making us accept a representation as a thing rather than as a sign, that is exactly what in the end does not happen with these didactic images. And in this sense they can be referred to as "visibile parlare" ("visible speech"). We must understand this phrase to mean not only that dialogue is rendered in visible form, which would be just another affirmation of their perfection as imitative art. More importantly, "visibile parlare" indicates that the image is used as a kind of speech, that it exists not just in reified form as an object, but as language.[20] Not what it is in its visible appearance, but what it signifies within the relations established by history and interpretation constitutes the vital reality of these visual images, what they really say, and to this extent they are language.[21]

We noted at the outset that the scenes are viewed in step with a rhythm deriving from Dante's trajectory along this first cornice of Purgatory. Dante-protagonist actually has to displace himself in order to see close up the third panel in the triptych—"I' mossi i piè del loco dov'io stava, / per avvisar da presso un'altra storia" (*Purgatorio* X. 70–71)—thus introducing a dimension of time and movement, pivoting on Dante himself as viewer. Virgil's prompting him not to arrest his gaze ("non tener pur fisso ad un loco la mente") renders imperative this principle of movement. It is precisely this forward impetus that sharply distinguishes the scene from its model in the first book of the *Aeneid*. Aeneas nostalgically views scenes from his own past, representing the battles of proud Troy

20. For a contrasting view linking this phrase to the writing over the Gate of Hell and in the sky of the heaven of Jupiter by the eagle ("Diligite iustitiam") as instances where speech is visible, instead of emphasizing that here the visual is linguistic, see Robert Hollander, "God's 'Visible Speech,'" *Allegory in Dante's Commedia* (Princeton: Princeton University Press, 1969), pp. 297–300.

For a strongly corroborative interpretation of the images of *Purgatorio* X as not only language but also a form of dialogue, and the argument that "reading cannot be regarded as a mere coming into possession of a textual object but the subjectification of that object into a dialogue partner," see Domenico Pietropaolo, "Dante's Paradigms of Humility and the Structure of Reading," *Quaderni d'italianistica* 10 (1989): 199–211. For a technically sophisticated analysis of Dante's "translinguistic perception" in this canto, see Gino Casagrande, "'Esto Visibile Parlare': A Synaesthetic Approach to Purgatorio 10.55–63," in *Lectura Dantis Newberryana* II (Evanston: Northwestern University Press, 1990).

21. The text further states that this visible speech was produced by God; it is a logos preexistent in its meaning and presence to God, the one who never saw anything new: "Colui che mai non vide cosa nova / produsse esto visibile parlare, / novello a noi perchè qui non si trova"—X. 94–96). Here we touch on a metaphysical dimension of significance that runs throughout the entire poem, uniting an antecedent totality of meaning that characterizes language as a synchronic system in which every element is presupposed for the intelligibility of all the others, with the appropriative event of speech.

("superbo Ilion," as *Inferno* II has it) pictured on the walls of the temple of Juno at Carthage. Carthage as a whole in the *Aeneid* symbolizes delay and truancy from historical destiny, and there Aeneas is discovered feeding on an empty image (animum pictura pascit inani"), sighing and weeping unmanfully. Worst of all, he is provoked to vaunt proudly (and foolishly) the saving value of earthly fame: "ferret haec aliquam tibi fama salutem" (*Aeneid* I. 963). The word "salus" for Dante in Italian, of course, takes on the connotation of Christian salvation, which, ironically, is just what is lost through this kind of inane image gazing, an antimodel for Dante's progressive and morally profitable scrutiny of salvific images along the path of Purgatory.

Beyond this physical movement from one to the next, the scenes also have an intrinsic temporal relation to one another determined by their typological significance. The ark of the covenant as a figure for the Church, Christ's body, and the emperor as a figure for *Christus rex*, prefigure the keystone scene that announces the Incarnation. In this sense, they anticipate a historical event that exceeds and fulfills them. Dante sets them up so that we can see the mimetic images typologically, as representing elements in a process of redemption stretching from the past into the future, including that of the interpreter. Thus even these programmatically realistic scenes reveal their meaning not all at once in the presence of an object that simply is what it means, but rather through a temporality of interpretation that involves the reader in their art as event. Just where Dante exalts the static, mimetic art of sculpture as a thing able to rival reality in plastic look, the temporality of the image as an interpretive phenomenon emerges decisively from beneath this surface and pretense. The images' lifelikeness is a miracle not only of mimetic resemblance but perhaps more profoundly, of their life in history and as interpretation.

The canto itself makes this shift from the image as a sort of icon, an attempt to embody the real in the immediacy of its perceptible presence, to its application in the life of an individual capable of incarnating real humility, in its climactic address to the reader. After describing how the proud are punished, doubled over beneath boulders that they bear upward at an indiscernible rate, beating their breasts as they go, the narrator breaks in:

> Non vo' però, lettor, che tu ti smaghi
> di buon proponimento per udire
> come Dio vuol che 'l debito si paghi.
> Non attender la forma del martire;
> pensa la succession; pensa ch'al peggio
> oltre la gran sentenza non può ire.
>
> (*Purgatorio* X. 106–111)

(But I don't want you, reader, to be discouraged
   from good resolution by hearing
   how God wills that the debt be paid.
Do not attend to the form of the suffering:
   think about the sequel; think that at the worst
   it cannot go beyond the great judgment.)

In "Non attender la forma del martire" Dante exhorts his readers not to fix upon the immediately visible horror of this penitential suffering. The imperative "non attender," beyond aiming to turn attention away from this manifest agony, also bears a temporal nuance of not getting stuck dwelling on the form of the appearance of the scene. Instead the reader must temporalize the image by thinking ahead to its sequel, which even in the worst case cannot be further off than the Last Judgment ("la gran sentenza"). What must be grasped is that the spectacle of suffering before Dante's and our eyes has a temporal frame that determines its significance in such a way as makes the sight endurable and even shows its immediately negative valence to be ultimately positive. The meaning is revealed from the end point of the "gran sentenza" of Christian revelation, and that is what Dante and we must keep in "view."

The address makes an appeal for a more dynamic view of the visual image that will see its form as something under way, in process. Indeed, the "forma," which must not be fixed on in its immediacy as *res* or concrete thing, is transformed a few lines later in an imagery of latency and expectancy that captures the essence of Christian existence as ineradicably temporal. The substantive "forma," first used by Dante to designate the immediate appearance of a seemingly unsustainable state of penance and pain, occurs successively in verbal transformations—"formar" and "formazione" (cf. Mazzotta, *Dante. Poet of the Desert*, p. 250)—which bring out the dynamism that Dante insists be seen in the image. They show how the image can be revealing of things to come if it is not taken merely as static form, but rather is viewed out of the inherent temporality of the individual in whom and for whom its truth takes shape in a process of self-forming or -formation:

O superbi cristian, miseri lassi,
   che, de la vista de la mente infermi,
   fidanza avete ne' ritrosi passi,
non v'accorgete voi che noi siam vermi
   nati a *formar* l'angellica farfalla,
   che vola a la giustizia sanza schermi?
Di che l'animo vostro in alto galla,
   poi siete quasi antomata in difetto,
   sì come vermo in cui *formazion* falla?
(*Purgatorio* X. 121–29)

(O proud Christians, miserable and lapsed,
  who, infirm in mental vision
  trust in retrogressive steps,
do you not see that we are worms
  born *to form* the angelic butterfly,
  which flies to justice without impediment?
why do your souls bob on the high sea
  when you are like an unshaped chrysalis,
  even as the worm in which *formation* fails.)

The apostrophe to proud Christians ("superbi cristian") reminds us all that we are worms "born to form the angelic butterfly." The infinitive "formar" designates a dynamic process, an ongoing, progressive forming. It suggests how the maturation of individual Christians from their initial state as chrysalises to become butterflies, succeeds and supersedes the forever fixed images seen in passing along the purgatorial wall. Mimetic forms endeavoring to capture the real in pure presence and actuality give place to the process of formation of the interpreter for whose sake they were made as aids in purging the sin of pride and in learning how to embody real humility. But to the extent that we do not know how to view, or, more exactly, read/interpret, images in this forward-projecting way, and rather take them at face value for their immediate simulation of reality, we remain defective insects ("antomata in difetto"), like a worm in whom formation fails ("vermo in cui formazion falla").

The canto ends with an affirmation of the reality that can be attained through art, not at the level of the image but rather through the process of interpretation, in which the image takes on its life. Art can turn what is not real into reality not by any magic of mimesis, but by the process of interpretation in which projections and possibilities become real determinants of the actual existence of individuals. This lesson is capped off finally in the simile of a caryatid doubled over (like the proud), with knees touching its chest, to sustain a temple eaves. The narrator comments on how, from this unreal, merely represented anguish, a real anguish can be born in the one who views it. And precisely in conjunction with this function the caryatid can be significantly termed a "figura":

Come per sostentar solaio o tetto,
  per mensola talvolta *una figura*
  si vede giugner le ginocchia al petto,
la qual fa del non ver vera rancurra
  nascere 'n chi la vede; così fatti
  vid'io color, quando puosi ben cura.
             (*Purgatorio* X. 130–35)

(As in order to sustain ceiling or roof,
  on a shelf sometimes one sees *a figure*

touch its knees to its breast,
the which makes true from untrue rancor
arise in the one who views; made thus
I saw them, when I looked carefully.)

Once the didactic images of Canto X are viewed not as coinciding with the real through their mimetic perfection, but rather as instigating a process of interpretation aimed at transforming the one who interprets them, their contribution to actually making up reality can again be affirmed. For rather than being real in and for themselves in their iconic immediacy, they participate in the event of appropriation by which Christians become what they truly are. It is out of this process that the morally and spiritually real emerges, to such an extent as to make appear unreal the souls actually present in the banal sense of being on the scene of this cornice. Upon seeing them approaching, Dante remarks that they do not seem to be persons ("non mi sembian persone"). By contrast, the image Dante sees in simile raised to its lofty perch in the temple is a "figura" because it is invested with the future of the one who sees it. It is destined to become a factor in the reality of someone's life journey upward to God in Dante's wake. In this way, the miraculous reality of art, symbolized in the limit-case by its power of perfect simulation, is actually achieved by personal, existential appropriation.

3. SOME HISTORY (AND A REOPENING) OF THE QUESTION OF THE TRUTH OF THE COMMEDIA

In every period of criticism, the ambiguity of the Commedia's discourse as at once philosophical/theological and literary/poetic has variously manifested itself as one, if not the fundamental, problem of interpretation. Critical approaches to the work in general have been determined by the possible ways of negotiating such ambiguity. Among the first generation of readers, Benvenuto da Imola had already noted that "sicut in isto libro est omnis pars philosophiae, ut dictum est, ita est omnis pars poetriae" ("just as in this book every part is philosophy, as was said, so every part is poetry"). Benvenuto further observes how in this case theology can be said to be a divine sort of poetry: "potest namque theologia dici quaedam poetria de Deo."[22] This suggests the audacious proposition that Dante's poem not only contains philosophical and theological knowledge, but is per se gnoseological, or, in other words, that as poetry it is an original and irreducible form of knowledge, knowledge ultimately of God.

The Letter to Can Grande, perhaps Dante's own critical introduction

---

22. Benvenuti de Rambaldis de Imola, Comentum super Dantis Aldigherij Comoediam, 5 vols., ed. J. P. Lacaita (Florence: G. Barbera, 1887), 1: pp. 19, 9.

to the poem, underscores its duplicity as poetical/rhetorical and at the same time theosophical/doctrinal. Having referred to it as a "tractatus"—a technical terminology incorporated into the poem's own initial statement of purpose: "ma per *trattar* del ben ch' io vi trovai" (*Inferno* I. 8)—the letter goes on to give a carefully couched and at the same time provocative definition of the work's "forma tractandi" or mode of discourse: "Forma sive modus tractandi est poeticus, fictivus, descriptivus, digressivus, transumptivus, et cum hoc diffinitivus, divisivus, probativus, improbativus, et exemplorum positivus" ("The form of treatment is poetical, fictive, descriptive, digressive, transumptive [i.e., metaphorical], and at the same time by definition, division, proof, self-evidence, and adducing of examples"—*Epistole* XIII. ix, 27). This definition forges a perfect symmetry between two types of discourse neatly distinguished and balanced by the copulative phrase "et cum hoc." Ernst Robert Curtius details how the second five-term series of "modi" derives from descriptions of theological science such as can be found in Alexander of Hales's and Albert the Great's *Summae theologicae*. The first series of five, by contrast, comprises terms from the rhetorical tradition that was steadily at loggerheads with Scholasticism and its precursor in twelfth-century dialectics.[23] This is perhaps the first and, so to speak, the most "authoritative" statement on the work's hybrid nature.

Furthermore, this statement is symptomatic of another distinguishing feature of Dante's extraordinary work, both of his life's work and his chef d'oeuvre, namely its faculty of auto-exegesis, that is, of continually commenting on itself.[24] From a hermeneutic point of view, of course, all poetry, like language as such, interprets itself. It asks to be taken a certain way, or perhaps in several different ways. This is to say that it is involved in a strategic process of self-presentation and appropriation. What it is depends on how it is interpreted, and this in turn depends on what it gives itself out to be. In this way, poetry's being is borrowed from and reciprocally lends itself to other beings, like authors and readers, in their articulating of their "own" identities. The *Commedia* epitomizes this

23. Ernst Robert Curtis, *European Literature and the Latin Middle Ages*, p. 225.

24. Michael Caesar, *Dante: The Critical Heritage, c. 1314(?)–c. 1870*, in introducing his wide-ranging anthology of criticism on Dante, overviewing its perennial emphases, observes, "If one looks at Dante's writing as a whole, it is striking how much it appears not only to presuppose a dialogue with the reader, but already to constitute a kind of commentary on itself" (p. 1). See, in particular, Gian Roberto Sarolli, "Autoesegesi dantesca e tradizione esegetica medievale," in *Prolegomena alla 'Divina Commedia'* (Florence: Olschki, 1971), pp. 1–39, and more recently Z. G. Barański, "Dante Alighieri. Experimentation and (Self-) Exegesis," in *Cambridge History of Literary Criticism: The Middle Ages*, ed. A. J. Minnis (Cambridge: Cambridge University Press, 1992). See also Gianfranco Contini, "Introduzione alle rime di Dante" (1938), in *Un'idea di Dante* (Turin: Einaudi, 1976), about how "una costante della personalità dantesca è questo perpetuo soppraggiungere della riflessione teorica accanto alla poesia" (p. 4).

hermeneutic process, intensively revealing and exposing the interpretive workings of poetry and language in the necessarily self-reflexive structure essential to any quest for knowledge.

Both the obsessive self-exegesis and the claims to a truth exceeding that normally conceded to mimetic representation are indexes of the overtly and relentlessly hermeneutic character of Dante's poetic art. As such, they can be elucidated, perhaps more perspicuously than ever before, from a hermeneutic perspective that understands both philosophical knowledge and divine revelation as fundamentally forms of interpretation—and so as like, and even as sharing in, the nature of poetry itself.

Beginning even from within the poem, then, with its intensive meta-critical self-commentary, the whole history of reception testifies loquaciously to the deeply significant and problematic gnoseological thrust to Dante's magnum opus.[25] To focus on criticism just in our own century, it has been taken with striking consistency as the point of departure not only for defining what above all distinguishes Dante's from virtually all other poetry but even for denying that it is poetry at all in its integrity, the gnoseological elements being considered an admixture of the nonpoetic. This latter viewpoint is most closely associated with the criticism of Croce, whose approach rests on the "fundamental distinction" between "structure" and "poetry" ("la distinzione di poetico e di non poetico, di poesia e di struttura"), that is, between two terms he poses as mutually exclusive, however much both figure together in the *Commedia*.[26]

Croce cites Vico's censure of the sapiential elements as an impediment to the poetry of the work, grand precisely for its unreflective primitivism, an evaluation carried to the extreme judgment that "if he had known nothing at all of scholasticism and Latin, he would have been a greater poet."[27] Croce hails this rejection of the one aspect of the work in favor of the other as no less than the beginning of "a revolution in Dante criticism" ("una rivoluzione nella critica dantesca"—[Croce, *La poesia di Dante*, p. 173]). Nevertheless, all this reconfirms the doubleness of Dante's work and recognizes in Dante "the double aspect of scientist and poet" ("il doppio aspetto di scienziato e di poeta") that unfailingly recurs throughout the critical tradition, as is brought out in the historical review with which Croce rounds out his book.[28]

25. Aldo Vallone, *Storia della critica dantesca dal XIV al XX secolo*, 2 vols. (Milan: Vallardi, 1981), covers the historical ground that is telescoped here.

26. Benedetto Croce, "Ancora della lettura poetica di Dante," in *Opere* (Bari: Laterza, 1967), p. 5.

27. Croce quotes Vico in *La poesia di Dante*, 2nd ed. (Bari: Laterza, 1921), p. 174: "se egli non avesse saputo affatto né della scolastica né di latino, sarebbe riuscito piú grande poeta."

28. "Intorno alla storia della critica Dantesca," in *La poesia di Dante*, traces this duality through historically significant treatments by such figures as F. W. Schelling and Claude Charles

On the other side, emphasizing the gnoseological aspect rather at the expense of the aesthetic, Bruno Nardi takes a leading role in twentieth-century criticism in asserting the need to recognize the *Commedia's* claim to being not just a poem but an authentic, divinely inspired, visionary experience, a "visione verace." Nardi postulates that as "true vision," a real experience of grace and revelation, not just an artistic simulation of such experience, the *Commedia* is set apart from "literature": "Non artifico letterario, ma vera visione profetica ritenne Dante quella concessa a lui da Dio, per una grazia singolare" ("Not literary artifice, but true prophetic vision, is what Dante held to have been conferred upon him by God through a special grace").[29] Similarly, Giorgio Padoan sharply distinguishes the sense of vision applicable to the *Commedia,* namely, that which refers to the beatific vision, from "vision" in any literary or metaphorical sense.[30]

But is the poem's literary artifice, and again its attempt to disclose philosophical truth, necessarily distinct and separate from its claims to prophetic revelation, as Nardi and Padoan here assume?[31] These clear divisions seem merely to invert the dichotomizing of the early commentators and their anxiousness that the poem be received as fiction, not to be confused with truth (in which case it would be rather heretical falsehood), as exemplified by Guido da Pisa's statement: "Poeta more poetico fingit se istam Comediam, hoc est universa que continentur in ea, in visione vidisse" ("The poet feigns in a poetic vein that he saw the *Commedia,* i.e., the worlds that it contains, in a vision").[32]

Fauriel. The latter counts Dante as exceptional among all great poets for the double inspiration of his poem, "l'une instinctive et passionnée et l'autre studieuse et scolastique" (Croce, *La poesia di Dante,* p. 187).

Étienne Gilson's work on Dante also revolves around this question of Dante's synthesis of the aesthetic values of a rhetorical culture with the philosophical criteria of Scholasticism. See especially "Poésie et théologie dans la *Divine Comédie,*" in *Atti del Congresso Internazionale di Studi Danteschi* (Florence: Sansoni, 1965), where Dante is esteemed as unique in his capacity to unite "l'amour passioné de la beauté littéraire et celui de la vérité sous toutes formes" (p. 264).

29. Bruno Nardi, "Dante profeta," in *Dante e la cultura medievale,* p. 376. The perspective opened by Nardi is worked out with great historical precision and detail in relation to religious-prophetic texts by Niccolò Mineo in *Profetismo e apocalittica in Dante* (Catania: Università di Catania, 1968).

30. Giorgio Padoan, "La 'mirabile visione' di Dante e l'Epistola a Cangrande," in *Il pio Ennea, l'empio Ulisse,* p. 33: "e di visione egli parla esplicitamente anche nella conclusione della terza cantica, e nel significato il più proprio del termine: quello che rinvia alla visione beatifica, non alla 'visione' nell'accezione letteraria."

31. Padoan makes it clear that inspired "visio" also stands in antithesis to any sort of "viaggio filosofico." The work's being an "opera di rivelazione" (Padoan, "La 'mirabile visione,'" p. 48) is defined precisely against its being either "speculazione filosofica" or "finzione poetica" (p. 56).

32. *Guido da Pisa's Expositiones et Glose super Comediam Dantis,* ed. Vincenzo Cioffari (Albany: State University of New York Press, 1974), p. 10.

For Nardi and Padoan, inspired prophecy is not and cannot be poetic fiction or philosophy, but Dante runs all modes of interpretation together in his putatively inspired work. Surely it is misguided to try and separate out the experience itself, prior to its philosophical, poetic elaboration, when the peculiar achievement of the *Commedia* is precisely to mediate revelation and its "facts" or givens by the interpretive processes of poetry, specifically, of a poetry that is intensively philosophical and theological in character. In the cited statements, Nardi and Padoan are still trying to say that the *Commedia* is *not,* in its essence as a revelation, supposed to be a literarily constructed artifice, when Dante seems to include this as part of the very revelatory experience that they do rightly insist Dante insists on.

What often proves difficult for us to understand is how literature and speculative thinking can work hermeneutically as a mediation of true religious experience.[33] The interpretive vehicle—poetry or thought—is not outside the reality of the experience to be conveyed but rather constitutes it intrinsically. No split is assumed between experience and interpretation; the means of understanding participate in what is understood. Philosophico-poetic interpretation is a way of entering into the experience itself, even into Dante's experience of the divine.

What has always been appreciated about Dante's poetry—namely, that its reasoning is passionate and its science indissociable from animating sentiment—shows its full significance in the light shed by existential philosophy on the emotional and conative conditionedness of all cognitive thought, as in the Heideggerian analysis of "Befindlichkeit" (how one finds oneself) as a fundamental determinant of our being-in-the-world, and thus of all our knowledge. This insight into the interpenetration of feeling and forms of cognition (as in faith) has actually been preserved, particularly in Christian tradition, all along. In fact, tradition itself was understood as a kind of tacit knowing by feeling participation in Christian community, and thereby in the life of God through his Spirit, that was always presupposed in any outwardly articulated proclamation of belief or dogma.[34]

Professional Dante criticism sometimes has a tendency to avoid or

33. A growing readiness among contemporary Dantists to recognize the epistemological interdependence of religious vision and poetic art is epitomized by Giuseppe Mazzotta's *Dante's Vision and the Circle of Knowledge* (Princeton: Princeton University Press, 1993).

34. Such insights are mined by Andrew Louth from St. Basil's "De spiritu sancto" and from other Greek, especially Cappadocian, patristic works, in *Discerning the Mystery: An Essay on the Nature of Theology* (Oxford: Clarendon Press, 1983). These are hints of the theological counterpart to "sensus communis" and "Bildung" in the humanist tradition revisited by Gadamer as foundational for hermeneutics in *Truth and Method*. A concept of tacit knowing is developed by Michael Polanyi in *Personal Knowledge* (London: Routledge & Kegan Paul, 1958).

bracket the unanswerable, ultimate, philosophical, and theological ques-
tions that are nevertheless cause for perennial wonderment on the part
of the readers of the poem. Teodolinda Barolini acknowledges that the
interpretation of the *Commedia* has always centered on and still revolves
around the question of truth, but she would have this very recognition
close the question of truth as such, in order that attention might be di-
rected to how the effect of truth is achieved through Dante's artistic tech-
nique, what she terms his "realism": "In sum, I believe we must accept
Dante's insistence that he is telling the truth and move on to the conse-
quences. Therefore, although we must address the text's self-presentation
as true, we must more fundamentally address the critical consequences
of such self-presentation: to wit, the ways in which the text succeeds
in presenting itself as true. In other words, the topic at hand is Dante's
realism."[35]

According to Barolini we must read more "practically" and less "the-
ologically," that is, we must concentrate our analytical powers on ex-
plaining how Dante works to create the illusion of truth, rather than on
actually responding to the claim of the poem to being true. What has
trammeled Dante criticism to date, in Barolini's view, is precisely the
critics' being mesmerized by what the poem says and claims, rather than
analyzing the workings of its forms: "To the extent that we hearken
always to what Dante says rather than take note of what he has done, we
treat him as he would have us treat him—not as a poet, but as an author-
ity, a 'theologian'" (Barolini, "Detheologizing Dante," p. 46). She there-
fore proposes a "new formalism" for the *Commedia* with the goal of "fully
appreciating its achievements as artifact" (p. 46). And hence *her* clarion
call, not just offering formal analysis but making an appeal to Dante stud-
ies to hearken and respond: "The time has come for us to be more inter-
ested in *how* the *Commedia* works than in *what* it says" (p. 46).

Typical of this antihermeneutic legislation against considering what
is being said—the central concern of hermeneutic effort, as Gadamer
makes clear—and the possible truth of what is being said is the con-
finement of "truth" to the horizon of a positive knowledge of how things
work. This critical move brings with it unawares the sort of epistemolog-
ical framework that had supplanted a hermeneutic paradigm, in certain
decisive ways, for example, in Descartes, and that dominates everywhere
in the age of science and technology. It puts the detached, self-reflective
subject in the position of judging what is truly going on. Knowledge is
only our self-conscious cognition of how things really work, not a re-

35. Teodolinda Barolini, "Detheologizing Dante. For a 'New Formalism' in Dante Stud-
ies," *Quaderni d'italianistica* 10 (1988), p. 43. This article reappears as the first chapter of *The
Undivine Comedy,* but I quote from the article, where certain formulations are a little starker and
help to clarify the difference between Barolini's "formal" criticism and hermeneutics.

sponse to anything or anyone else. It is deaf to all but its own clear and distinct perceptions.

Although it vaunts its neutrality, the question "How does the poem work?" practically has built into it the answer "Like clockwork." It is only when we face the question of truth as a question that claims us as readers of the *Commedia* that the problem of relating poetry and theology really becomes acute. So long as we take both poetry and theology as simply forms of culture appearing in Dante's poem, we can treat them philologically or "scientifically," and the question is simply how do they work, together or apart from or against each other, not what, finally, is the meaning of the poem and what it reveals.

That the project of the *Commedia* is to reveal theological truth may be said to be fairly widely accepted even among specialists. It is, moreover, widely agreed that this, and what follows from it, is integral to what makes Dante's poem so exceptional. Nevertheless, we as critics are content on the whole to leave Dante's theological affirmations opaque, treating them as natural enough for someone of Dante's time and temperament, but not seriously allowing that they could have any claim upon us in reading his poem today. Barolini's summons to a pragmatic approach really does little more than ratify what has become the silent consensus and implicit norm, if not the outright coercively secular morality in Dante studies, increasingly professionalized and specialized due to nearly irresistible trends in the academic institution.

I do not pretend that Dante criticism should be based on different premises, and surely not that it should become pious. I simply wish to show that, as in the case of Scripture, there may yet be more to be gleaned from this text after formal analysis and after the historical-critical method of criticism has performed its necessary and often quite exciting work of elucidation and has garnered its harvest of interesting information. This fact is enough to justify the pursuit of a criticism that situates itself within a horizon of the question of truth posed by the poem, which so animates meaningful readings of it sustained down through centuries of critical inquiry. This is in fact what the criticism we value most has always done, sometimes in spite of its own pretenses to scientific objectivity. I submit that we have not fully entered into the experience of Dante's poetry until we have let it claim its truth upon us and that this requires our making ourselves susceptible to it as truth, as opening the horizon of a world that can become our world and be true for us, or possibly so.

In a work such as the *Divine Comedy,* experience mediated by art and interpretation, whatever properly inspired, supernaturally graced experiences Dante may be supposed to have had or to have thought he had, can itself become revelatory, opening a dimension of religious transcen-

dence and truth. This amounts of saying that Dante's experience as crys-
tallized in the poem was neither necessarily mystical nor merely terrestrial
or technical, but was above all else (and as potentially including all these
forms of experience) hermeneutic, or, in other words, an experience in
poetic, and at the same time religious, interpretation. Dante's representa-
tions of a true and transcendent world can be understood, in a way per-
haps overlapping with other possible psychological or spiritual accounts,
as reworkings, on the basis of this sort of interpretive experience, of tradi-
tions available to him. The mystery of transcendence and the challenge
of truth are inherent in the experience of interpretation as such, and
Dante more than perhaps any other writer shows this.

So far as can ever be determined, no experience, certainly no religious
experience, is ever absolutely first; all are interpretations of antecedent
experiences memorialized in tradition, and proceed on the basis of—
even when in opposition to—tradition. The first thing to note about the
most evidently authentic accounts of supernaturally inspired experien-
ces is their derivativeness from the traditional assumptions, worldview,
and cultural heritage (not to mention personal biases and expectations)
of their protagonists.[36] All Christian visions are bound to be in some
degree interpretations of the Bible. The experiential framework set up
by that text and its world cannot but insinuate itself into the Christian's
every experience. For this reason alone, Christian mystical experience
per se turns out to be in a very considerable measure hermeneutic. This
obviously holds for the prototype, St. John's apocalypse, considering its
relation first of all to the Book of Ezekiel.

Characteristic of hermeneutic experience in general is its absorbed,
willing, believing participation in the traditions or mediated experience
that it takes up to interpret—at least to the extent of giving their full
range of possibilities a chance. Though compounded as well of critical
and suspicious moments, it is not fundamentally the experience of a
doubter enclosed within the Cartesian theater of the self; the self rather
surrenders to the experience and attempts to live in and through it, not
to measure all experience by some criterion of its own.[37] Because of this,
the difference between actually being the recipient of a transcendent vi-
sion and participating in such experience via the interpretation of tradi-
tion is attenuated and tends to disappear altogether. Dante enters into

36. The visions of Sister Teresa de Avila might be taken as a case in point. See, for example,
Edith Wyschogrod, *Saints and Postmodernism* (Chicago: University of Chicago Press, 1990). Cf.
also Benedicta Ward, *Miracles in the Middle Ages: Theory, Record and Event. 1000–1215* (Philadel-
phia: University of Pennsylvania Press, 1982).

37. George Steiner, *After Babel: Aspects of Language and Translation,* 2nd ed. (Oxford: Oxford
University Press, 1992), describes the first phase of the "hermeneutic motion" as necessarily
"an act of trust" (p. 312).

and exploits this kind of ambiguity, occasioning the sort of undecidability that we have seen reflected in the criticism.[38]

When we understand the *Commedia* and the world of the *Commedia* as an event of interpretation, rather than either as fiction pure and simple or as the transcription of reality, where the mediation in which alone a reality can be recognized as objective has been erased (and so much has been achieved by leading current criticism, notably, Barolini's), we become able to understand, and to make possible an experience of, its truth. Moreover, the *Commedia* can serve an exemplary function for us vis-à-vis the whole vast edifice of our tradition, which despite its plurivocity has a certain coherence and is readable as an in some sense unified construction, whose truth we have been losing.

Hermeneutic Experience and Truth: The Cases of Syncretism and Fallible Judgment

By close attention to the hermeneutical phenomenon and the features of it that have become more distinct through concentrated theorization in recent times, it may be possible among other things to sidestep the impasse between those who, traditionally, have insisted on the reality of the experience recounted in the poem and those for whom genuine understanding begins rather from an unambiguous recognition of its fictiveness. One strong indication of the interpretive essence of Dante's world and experience is the poem's syncretism; another comprises the judgments it advances on damnation and salvation of specific souls. Both have been great sources of scandal because they cannot in fact be reasonably accounted for except through clear awareness of the hermeneutic dimension and status of Dante's work, which tends inevitably to slip away and be eclipsed by more positive conceptions of truth. It is hard *not* to forget the hermeneutic complexity that conditions our every thought or experience, for we naturally crave facility, and, by consequence, "the divine vision darkens."

And so we, Dante's readers if not the scholars, become puzzled by—or can understand only as "ironic"—this purportedly "true" poem's unabashedly syncretistic eclecticism. Dante, of course, knew perfectly well how to distinguish between the representations of the other world as revealed in the Bible or as preserved in church tradition, the sole authoritative sources, and those of myth and classical literature. Yet he mixes both together indiscriminately in his "comedía." Does Dante really be-

38. On the possible ways of defining the *Commedia* in terms of prophetic vision, see further Emilio Pasquini, "Le metafore della visione nella *Commedia*," *Letture classensi* 16 (1987): 129–51; the essays on "visio" in *Lectura Dantis mystica. Il poema sacro alla luce delle conquiste psicologiche odierne* (Florence: Olschki, 1969); and P. Dinzelbacher, *Vision und Visionliteratur im Mittelalter* (Stuttgart: Hiersemann, 1981).

lieve in the existence of Cerberus, Geryon, and so on? Does he really expect Apollo to help him write the *Paradiso?* This would seem to contradict his recurrent strictures against belief in pagan divinities on the part of the ancient peoples endangered by their error ("Solea creder lo mondo in suo periclo . . . le genti antiche ne l'antico errore"—*Paradiso* VIII. 1 ff) in times of the false and lying gods ("ne' tempi de li dèi falsi e buggiardi"—*Inferno* II. 72).

What can turn such questions about Dante's truth claims into troublesome conundrums is the lack of a hermeneutic perspective on truth.[39] Dante's project is not to give a mirror image of the other world, but rather to interpret it. He recognizes that his possibilities as poet—and even as human being—are conditioned by the nature of interpretation. (Even apart from any conscious realization, Dante's poetic practice embodies such recognition.) Interpretation always involves a "forestructuring," determining in advance a possible field of objects on the basis of expectations that are just as liable to be false as true, but that nonetheless belong to the store of preconceptions and impressions that we bring to any experience and that guide our propensity to recognize and make sense of our perceptions, ordering them into meaningful experiential wholes. The classical heritage of myth about the underworld would inevitably form an important part of Dante's horizon of expectation.[40] Whether or not Dante believes that creatures such as Pluto and Phlegyas and the centaurs in some sense exist, what he represents for us is not the accurate picture, in the sense of a mirror image, of what is really in an objective space called the Inferno. Rather, he represents the ensemble of factors that play into the process of interpretation through which alone a place such as the Inferno can be experienced.

Dante's is an interpretive ontology having the unity of a world, blending classical and Christian worlds together into a unified experiential order. This takes place, however, not on an objective plane, but in a hermeneutic space, a space created by interpretation—that as such, we might add, reveals the nature of space per se. (This is why Kant, at least in one respect, with his transcendental deduction of space as a synthetic a priori form of intuition, is an important progenitor of the modern hermeneutic revolution.) The whole Inferno is to be found in—and as—a hermeneutic space for which Dante makes ontological claims. Likewise, his Para-

39. Such a perspective is of course sometimes strongly present in the criticism, for example in Auerbach's "Figura," but here we attempt to work out its theoretical presuppositions, which elsewhere remain only implicit.

40. A concept of horizon of expectation ("Horizonterwartung") is developed by Hans Robert Jauss, *Ästhetische Erfahrung und literarische Hermeneutik* (Frankfurt am Main: Suhrkamp, 1982). "Forestructuring" is a Husserlian term, here used in the sense its component parts suggest.

dise is explicitly a hermeneutic space of accommodation to the limits of human knowledge, which is sensuously conditioned. In this it is like Scripture, which "piedi e mano attribuisce a Dio e altro intende" ("attributes feet and hands to God and means something else"—*Paradiso* IV.44–45), attributing to the being of God what really originates in the epistemological conditions of any possible human conceiving of the divine. Dante's Purgatory, similarly, is constituted especially by the experience of liturgy, often in the form of clipped phrases that involve the reader in constructing the full experience without which this middle world of dreams and images would scarcely be realized at all. The signpost of this peculiar technique is *Purgatorio* II. 46–48, which describes the souls arriving by angelic ferry at the shore of the mountain singing "*In exitu Isräel de Aegypto . . .* con quanto di quel salmo è poscia scripto" ("*When Israel went out from Egypt . . .* with as much of that psalm as is written after"). In each case, interpretation is discovered as built into the making of the world that is experienced.

What is both ingenious and puzzling is Dante's representation of the structures of interpretation as all in the same plane with the objects that might be discovered in "a finite organical perception" within this topography.[41] The truth of such representation belongs to the sphere of interpretation rather than of any positively given fact. We might assume that Dante has presented everything as immediately given and present simply for dramatic effect, or for the effect, as critics put it, of "realism." Yet there is a sound epistemological rationale as well for this style of presentation. Initially, it is indeed impossible to distinguish between what is given objectively to perception and what belongs rather to the apparatus that makes perception possible. Experience as a synthetic unity presents a world entire. Only by reflection upon experience do form and content begin to be separated out from each other. Dante's poetic representations presuppose a great deal of reflection, but they still present a world as immediately and directly experienced. And yet this is not simply a world of objects but rather a world representing its own interpretive structures as well in vividly imagined and objectified form, even though such a procedure logically results in what could be called a "category mistake."

Clear recognition of the hermeneutic nature of Dante's world also can be reached through consideration of the judgments upon souls that it embodies. The poem emphatically warns against usurping the exclusive right of God to judge according to a wisdom and justice that surpass mortal understanding:

---

41. The language here, as that of the darkening of divine vision earlier, is Blake's, from *All Religions Are One*, pointing ahead to one momentous destination of Dante's legacy in the subsequent tradition of prophetic poetry.

"E voi, mortali, tenetevi stretti
    a giudicar: ché noi, che Dio vedemo,
    non conosciamo ancor tutti li eletti. . . ."
                          (*Paradiso* XX. 133–35)

("And you mortals, scrupulously refrain
    from judging: for we, who see God,
    do not yet know all the elect. . . .")

This is a reiteration of the warning already issued in the heaven of the Sun:

"E questo ti sia sempre piombo a' piedi,
    per farti mover lento com' uom lasso. . . .
Non sien le genti, ancor, troppo sicure
    a giudicar, sì come quei che stima
    le biade in campo prima che sien mature. . . .
Non creda donna Berta e ser Martino
    per vedere un furare, altro offerere,
    vederli dentro al consiglio divino;
ché quel può surgere, e quel può cadere."
                          (*Paradiso* XIII. 112–42)

("And let this make you always leaden footed,
    that you move slowly like a tired man. . . .
Let people not be too sure yet
    in judging, like one who counts the crops
    in the field before they are grown. . . .
Let not Madam Berta and Sir Martin believe
    because they see one rob, another give,
    that they see into the divine counsel,
since this one may rise, and that one fall.")

Can, then, Dante's supposedly historical and literally true vision really extend to knowing the condemnation or election of specific individuals? Is this not perilous presumption, if not blasphemy, on his part?

Dante's interpretations are powerful, we observed at the outset, owing to the way he invests himself in them. What they call for is an answering self-investment on the part of readers, for whom the poem's truth happens only within their projection of their own existence and their reinterpretation of Dante's interpretations. Only so do the things the poem represents become real events, rather than remaining statically self-identical in their condition as determinate representations. It is not as fully achieved representations that they are true and can be apprehended in their truth. As representations, they are only traces of an event of truth and interpretation, that is, of truth via interpretation, that has been experienced by Dante. Their apparent objectivity is without question presented with the utmost seriousness, yet must not be allowed to completely eclipse the dimension of interpretation in which alone the meaning of objective representations can be realized by readers and even by Dante himself.

The experience of Dante as traced in the poem opens a way for experience of truth and interpretation on the part of the reader. The truth experienced by the reader need not, indeed, very likely will not, entail the same judgments on historical personages as those of Dante. Such judgments in any case are always hazardous for human comprehension, since it is finite. The fact that Dante does offer definite, unequivocal judgments of particular individuals stands for the possibility that such knowledge might actually be granted, in specific instances of direct involvement: wonderfully, in an event of insight made religiously possible by divine grace or, psychologically, by caring without limit. Such an experience of insight may occur primordially as prior to all reflection on the inescapable finiteness of human thought, which would in theory exclude the possibility of genuine, definitive knowledge of particularity. But granted such a possibility, the concreteness of knowing the truth about individuals as in the eye of God, it can hardly be susceptible of being conveyed in objective, representational form. For the concrete content of such truth will be different as it occurs to and for each individual. How could anything concrete and particular be self-identical in the experience of various individuals? All experience it in relation to their own differentiated dispositions and situations. Hence, for example, not one but multiple gospels.

All the individuals punished, chastized, or rewarded can be experienced concretely by the reader as him- or herself. All the individual states of existence represented in the poem represent possibilities of existence for the reader personally. And their truth is to be attained precisely in this application. What Dante's poem objectively represents as taking place is not its truth, not the truth actually made to happen by the poem. Dante's images come into the reader's experience as objects of imagination or cognition, but they disclose their truth only to the extent that they are incorporated into a process of projection and reflection that concerns the reader's own being in its moral and historical individuality. The reader's applications of the images will vary widely from Dante's own. What Dante reveals about Muhammad as that personage was construed by him and his culture might be revealing for a present-day reader in relation to the possibility, closer to home, of him or her falling into the sin of sowing discord.

While the experience conveyed by the *Commedia* should fundamentally be understood as interpretive experience, this poem especially brings into view the opening toward truth and transcendence that can characterize such experience. This is a crucial and difficult point for us today, when truth and transcendence have become so suspect, their credibility weakening along with that of the whole religious and metaphysical edifice that—at least we are used to supposing—wielded hegemonic authority in the Middle Ages. Indeed, it has been possible for theorists to take for granted that the dimensions of truth and transcendence are precisely what hermeneutic thought needs to overcome in order to remain viable in the contemporary intellectual climate. Jean-Luc Nancy proposes that interpretation has replaced truth in the modern context,[42] and, indeed, this seems plausible if we take a scientific model of knowledge, which is supposedly *not* interpretive, as normative for determining truth. John Caputo bases his "radical hermeneutics" on the premise that "Hermeneutics wants to describe the fix we are in, and it tries to be hardhearted and to work 'from below.' It makes no claim to have won a transcendental high ground or to have a heavenly informer."[43]

If truth and transcendence have come to seem unattainable for us, I submit that this is because we have forgotten their intimate connection .with interpretation. This forgetting can be traced to too facile a belief in the fictions that interpretation (beginning even at the level of grammar, as Nietzsche reminds us) itself, as a matter of course, generates. So long as the fictions participate in the real interpretive experience they are produced by, as fluid expressions of it, they enrich and complete interpretation, giving it fullness and a face ("la vertià ch' ha faccia di menzogna"). When they are taken in and for themselves, as reality in their own right, the whole experience of which they are an articulation and projection having dropped out of the picture, they are obviously spurious. At this point, symbolic fictions can either be enforced by a *sacrificio intellecti,* which may of course be motivated by reminiscence of an intimation of their authentic origin (a frequent predicament in institutional religion), or they can be altogether thrown off as sheerest falsehood. This is precisely the situation modernity has arrived at with its polarization between religious and secular outlooks. Dante had in view a truth that embraced and united the two. I have attempted to show that, whatever the formulas in which it is expressed, it is fundamentally a truth of interpretation—at least so far as concerns what is of enduring value in it—for whoever receives it.

42. Jean-Luc Nancy, *Le partage des voix* (Paris: Galilée, 1982): "Il s'agit de s'interroger sur 'l'interprétation' . . . comme substitut moderne de la 'verité'" (p. 9).

43. John Caputo, *Radical Hermeneutics: Repetition, Deconstruction and the Hermeneutic Project,* p. 3.

FIVE

Resurrected Tradition and Revealed Truth

1. DANTE'S STATIUS

*I*n *Purgatorio* XXI–XXII, Dante leads into the climactic scene of recognition between Virgil and Statius, the first-century Roman poet, through a powerful allusion to the Gospels, specifically, to Luke, chapter 24, which recounts Christ's meeting after his resurrection with two disciples on their way to Emmaus, outside Jerusalem. The analogy, drawn quite explicitly to Luke's text ("sì come ne scrive Luca"), pervades Dante's text down to its stylistic inflections. Luke's "Et ecce duo ex illis ibant ipsa die in castellum . . . nomine Emmaus" echoes in the styleme— "Et ecco"—with which Dante's Statius is suddenly beheld:

> Et ecco, sì come ne scrive Luca
> che Cristo apparve a' due ch'erano in via,
> già surto fuor de la sepulcral buca,
> ci apparve un'ombra, e dietro a noi venìa. . . .
> *(Purgatorio* XXI. 7–10)

> (And behold, even as Luke writes
> that Christ, already risen from the grave,
> appeared to two who were on the way,
> a shade appeared, and came along behind us. . . .)

The "Et ecco" fixes attention upon the unexpected apparition to Dante and Virgil of the shade of Statius, catching up from behind on the way up the mountain of Purgatory, as something miraculous to relate, like the rising of Christ from the tomb ("surto fuor de la sepulcral buca"). The resurrectional thrust of the figure of Statius, the one soul in the *Commedia* actually witnessed rising up "surto," to paradisiacal life, will be seen to transfigure the body of literary tradition that he symbolically carries with him. In his recreation of Statius, Dante unearths, bringing to the light of language, the grounds in history of the transcendent truth of Christ. This truth is revealed through literature understood radically as poetic interpretation.

Beyond effects at the verbal surface, the far-reaching significance of the allusion for the meeting Dante arranges between Virgil and Statius turns on the initial nonrecognition by the pilgrims to Emmaus of their Lord. Luke 24:15–16 reads: "And it came to pass, that, while they communed together, and reasoned, Jesus himself drew near, and went with them. But their eyes were holden that they should not know him." Statius's "ombra" similarly approaches Dante and Virgil incognito—he will in fact be asked who he is ("Ora chi fosti?"—*Purgatorio* XXI. 79) only in the second half of the canto—and they take no notice of him as he comes along behind ("e dietro a noi venía"), so that the newly arriving shade must speak first ("né ci addemmo di lei, sì parlò pria"—*Purgatorio* XXI. 12). Commentators go so far as to point out the analogy here with the Lukan model. Allen Mandelbaum, for instance, comments: "Two disciples of Jesus on their way to Emmaus, absorbed in thought and talk, did not realize that they were being accompanied by 'Christ, new-risen from his burial cave,' until He spoke to them."[1] However, it is actually not upon his speaking, nor even immediately in response to his expounding of Scripture, that the two disciples finally recognize Jesus. Only at a later moment is he known by them, precisely *at the breaking of bread*: "And it came to pass, as he sat at meat with them, he took bread, and blessed it, and brake, and gave to them. And their eyes were opened, and they knew him; and he vanished out of their sight" (Luke 24.30–31). The fact that recognition comes about in connection specifically with the action of breaking bread is confirmed at the end of the sequence when the two disciples report back to the others in Jerusalem what had transpired on their way, "and how he was known to them in breaking of bread" (Luke 24.35).

Luke's words are a verbatim rehearsal of the words spoken at the consecration of the Eucharist, of which the earliest written version, reflecting the primordial rite, appears to be that in 1 Corinthians 11.24: He "took bread, and when he had given thanks, he brake it, and said, Take, eat; this is my body, which is broken for you." As such they evoke a precise liturgical *Sitz-im-Leben* of the early (and perduring) Church, in which Christ was recognized as present in the midst of his disciples in the celebration of the sacrament. Luke's understanding of what happened on the way to Emmaus is penetrated by this daily experience of the appearing, that is, of the flesh and blood presence, of the Lord to the faithful. This continuing experience shows up in Luke's text, at least when it is considered from a literary point of view, as reflected back into the sequence recapping the encounter on the road to Emmaus.

---

1. Allen Mandelbaum, *The Divine Comedy of Dante Alighieri: Purgatorio* (New York: Bantam, 1984), p. 369.

For Luke, it is in the life of the Church, nourished by the celebration of the sacrament, that the true identity of Jesus of Nazareth as the risen Lord is fully revealed. This event of true understanding is apprehended by Luke through an ongoing, living experience of Christ supervening upon him and his fellows "in the way." It is, more exactly, by its happening all over again in the present moment of the celebration of the Eucharist that the apparition in the past along the road can be recognized as Christ, truly the one who was dead and is now alive. If it does not continue to happen in the present, the religious truth revealed in the past becomes opaque and reduces to reported facts, news items that can be reasoned over, but without direct experience and recognition of their manifest truth, in the same way as the pilgrims to Emmaus reasoned with him but failed to recognize the true identity of the Lord, whom they took to be a stranger.

Luke's text indirectly demonstrates how the truth of Christ is revealed in the present experience of believers, each journeying along their personal way. For Christian truth must be lived. The recurring encounter with Christ sought by Luke and his community in the eucharistic rite, insofar as such ritual repetition coincides with the recognition of Jesus in the breaking of bread after some laying open of the Scriptures, just as in the Emmaus pericope, brings with it a cross-fertilization with context that involves a principle of multiplication and dissemination of experiences of the miracle, the resurrected Christ. The event is not, or is not only or essentially, a self-identical object, a historical "fact," to be passively accepted "on faith," as the news, become dogma, is handed on from one generation of believers to another. On the contrary, the miraculous event is only apprehended by those who are within it participatively, recognizing Christ for themselves in his meeting with them personally, making them witnesses to his resurrection.[2] And to this extent the event is always different, really new, and disseminatory.

Dante similarly emphasizes how Statius's recognition of the Christian truth latent in Virgil's text stems from his own personal experience in a world in which Christ is made present, is literally disseminated, in Christian worship and preaching (that is, by "new preachers"):

2. Luke's sense of the witness to the Resurrection of Jesus as based on the Church's always contemporary experience rather than exclusively on evidence concerning a past *factum* expresses itself again in his "latter treatise," the Acts of the Apostles. In recounting the choice by lot of Matthias to fill Judas Iscariot's place, Luke reports Peter's announcing that "Beginning from the baptism of John, unto that same day that he was taken from us, must one be ordained to be a witness with us of his resurrection" (Acts 1.22). There would be no eyewitnesses in an empirical sense to choose from, but this is evidently not what is meant by "witness." The same inference is called for by the conflation in this passage of the Resurrection with the whole of the gospel story.

"Già era 'l mondo tutto quanto pregno
 de la vera credenza, seminata
  per li messaggi de l'etterno regno;
e la parola tua sopra toccata
 si consonava a' nuovi predicanti;
  ond' io a visitarli presi usata."
          (Purgatorio XXII. 76–81)

("Already the world was completely impregnated
 with the true faith, sown
  by the messages of the eternal kingdom;
and your word, touched on above,
 chimed with the new preachers;
  whence I took to visiting them.")

The word of Virgil "touched on above" ("la parola tua sopra toccata"), quoted by Statius a few lines earlier (*Purgatorio* XXII. 70–72), is a passage from Virgil's fourth eclogue (verses 5–7) hyperbolically celebrating the advent of a "new progeny"—probably the birth of a son to Roman consul Gaius Asinius Pollio[3]—as inaugurating a return of the Golden Age. Christian interpreters, with a certain disregard for its author's intention and context, or at least with inverisimilar assumptions in this regard, traditionally read the passage as a prophecy of the birth of Christ. And so Statius reads it too. But the way Statius describes his coming to this intelligence of the text lays decisive emphasis on the "consonance" between such a meaning and the gospel message sounding in the air around him and authenticated by the witness of Christian lives ("i lor dritti costumi"), even to the point of their extinction in martyrdom ("quando Domizian li perseguette").

 Were it not for the contemporary experience of Christianity by which he is directly and personally touched, it seems safe to assume, adhering to Statius's own narrative logic, that the Christian prophetic meaning of Virgil's poetry, particularly of the fourth eclogue, would have remained just as closed to him as it had been to Virgil himself. Statius is able to understand Virgil better than Virgil understood himself thanks to his own experience, strongly determined, it would seem, by certain contextual advantages belonging to his own historical situation in an era of grace. The word of the gospel living and active within the Christian community and its preaching opens the way for Statius's Christian understanding of the pagan poet's text. The important point once again, as in Luke, is that the true meaning of a revelatory event or text is only one that can be lived and applied in the present, in the dimension of a happening of

---

3. Such information can be found, for example, in Sapegno's commentary.

truth, for individuals actually engaged in understanding their own existence in its light.[4]

The way in which Statius's understanding of the truth of Virgil's poetry springs out of his own historically determinate situation has been highlighted by Dante, not only through the reference in XXII. 76–87 to preaching and persecution under Domitian, but also in the exceptionally detailed, historically specific autobiography presented by Statius in *Purgatorio* XXI. 82–102 as preparation for the unveiling of his conversion in Canto XXII.[5] Statius responds to the question of who he was by situating his biography in exact historical terms, hinting at the significance for it of contemporary events: "Nel tempo che 'l buon Tito con l'aiuto / del sommo rege" (XXI. 82–83). The events of his own life, pivotally, his being drawn to Rome and honored as a poet, and the chronology of his works (XXI. 92–93), also go into making up the abundantly circumstantial biographical context for his conversion.

So far as can be determined on the basis of documentary evidence, Dante seems to have invented Statius's conversion,[6] evidently in order to

4. Perhaps Dante's simile does not say enough for us to be sure that he understood the significance of the Lukan pericope in just this way. Yet such a reading does come very close to the sort of understanding of history and its making, i.e., of its openness to the present of interpretation and to being remade through reading, that (as we have already seen in chapter 4, section 1) Dante momentously discovers and that, particularly here, he develops in his extraordinary interpretation of the biography of Statius. Dante's sense of history as an interpretive construction would have enabled him to understand intuitively and poetically this premise of the Lukan witness to the Resurrection regardless of whether he would have accepted it reflectively and dogmatically, whereas for us, given our modern, objectivist historical sense, the same point emerges only with what may seem rather subtle exegesis. In any case, however Dante understood Luke, the reaction of the present upon the historical past remains a crucial distinctive feature of his poetic-interpretive practice.

5. Cf. Ettore Paratore, "Stazio," *Enciclopedia Dantesca* (Rome: Istituto dell'Enciclopedia Italiana, 1976): "In Pg XXI è contenuta una biografia di S[tazio] che, per ampiezza e precisione di notizie (salvo l'errore sulla città natale), è un *unicum* nel poema, in cui di solito non ci si attarda sui particolari biografici dei personaggi incontrati" ("*Purgatorio* XXI contains a biography of Statius that for amplitude and precision of information [except for the error on his birth place] is unique in the poem, which usually does not linger on the biographical particulars of the personages encountered"—p. 420).

6. Paratore summarizes critical opinion with regard to Statius's conversion as concurring that Dante made it up ("avrebbe favoleggiato per conto suo tutto"). He emphasizes the contrast between the documentary biography in Canto XXI and the apparently pure invention of Statius's Christianity in Canto XXII: "Se in Pg XXI abbiamo una precisa presentazione della figura e dell'opera di S[tazio], nel XXII troviamo invece sviluppato quel complesso di notizie che con la vera biografia di S[tazio] non han da fare né punto né poco, e che costituiscono il sorprendente di più introdotto da D[ante]" ("If in *Purgatorio* XXI we have a precise presentation of the figure and work of Statius, in XXII we find developed instead that complex of data that have nothing to do with his true biography, and that make up the surprising 'something more' introduced by Dante"—Paratore, "Stazio," p. 420). However, some possible evidence for an antecedent tradition of Statius's Christianity is discussed by Giorgio Brugnoli in "Statius Christianus," *Italianistica*

present his own experience of conversion, assisted by Virgilian poetry, in historically objectivized form.[7] Poetically, this works in basically the same way as the "history" (suspending the question of what history is) of an encounter along the road to Emmaus, whatever else it may do as history, does to objectify in story form, as a discrete event, the faith experience of recognizing Christ in one's midst at the breaking of bread in the Mass. Just as in Luke it is the ongoing experience of salvation in the Eucharist that makes possible, at least in the particular manner memorialized by the text, the recognition that the resurrected Lord had been accompanying the disciples all along the way, even in the darkest hour when they least suspected it, so it is Dante's own experience of being led toward salvation by Virgil's poetry that makes possible his recognition in Statius's life of a scenario of conversion coinciding with poetic biography.

Dante appears in effect to admit that his attribution of a Christian conversion to Statius lacks documentary historical foundation by also inventing a tradition of Statius's Christianity's having been kept secret ("ma per paura chiuso cristian fu' mi"—*Purgatorio* XXII. 90), which serves as an alibi for the unlikely circumstance that such a putatively biographical fact should have remained unknown for so many centuries before being declared openly by Dante. This provides an additional hint of what is rather transparent in any case, that the life story of Statius transfers to itself and emblematizes what the whole *Divine Comedy* testifies was an overwhelmingly significant experience for Dante himself, namely, his own encounter with Virgil's text as integral to his embrace of Christian revelation and, specifically, of a personal Christian-prophetic vocation.

If Statius transforms the meaning of Virgil's text by understanding it in relation to his own situation and exigencies, then, Dante does practically the same thing with Statius's biography, the text of tradition regarding the later Roman poet's life. Dante's self-consciousness about the hermeneutic process and its accommodation even of invention and ma-

---

17 (1988): 9–15 and "Lo Stazio di Dante e Benvenuto," in *Benvenuto da Imola,* ed. P. Palmieri and C. Paolazzi (Ravenna: Longo, 1991), pp. 127–37.

7. So, for example, Fausto Montanari, "Il Canto XXII del *Purgatorio,*" in *Lectura Dantis Romana* (Turin: Società editrice internazionale, 1965), p. 5: "nel caso di Stazio, io credo, è bene sottintendere un tacito riferimento alla biografia di Dante: l'estesa descrizione di come Virgilio abbia elevato Stazio, e l'abbia salvato spiritualmente, io credo che si spieghi bene come chiara crittografia di ciò che Virgilio ha operato nei riguardi di Dante: egli è stato maestro di poesia e di vita morale; lo ha avviato poi alla salvezza spirituale" ("[I]n the case of Statius, I believe, it is well to understand a tacit reference to the biography of Dante: the extended description of how Virgil elevated Statius and raised him spiritually, I believe, is to be explained as a clear cryptograph of that which Virgil had effected with respect to Dante: he was the teacher of poetry and moral life; he set him on the way to spiritual salvation.") Recently, Riccardo Scrivano has taken up once again the widely diffused idea that "Statius is nothing but an autobiographical projection of Dante." "Stazio personaggio, poeta e cristiano," *Quaderni d'italianistica* 12 (1992): 196.

nipulation of tradition in the unfolding of truth, that is, in the expression of the truth presently experienced in and through that tradition as resurrected and relived, is even more strident with respect to another Virgilian text interpreted by Statius, this time not the eclogue's prophecy of a new birth but rather a moral sentence in the *Aeneid* concerning greed or prodigality.

Virgil's text—"Quid non mortalia pectora cogis, / auri sacra fames?" —in its original context in the *Aeneid* (III, 56–57), literally denounces the cursed hunger for gold, but Dante's Statius translates "sacra fame d'oro" and evidently understands the outburst as inveighing against the opposite vice, a lack of restraint in spending, which should be checked by *sacred* (not Latin *sacer,* blasphemous) hunger for gold. The meanings the phrase may have both in Virgil and for Statius are extremely controverted; the crux has provoked much ingenious scholarship, generally scandalized by the inaccuracy and exerting itself to find any conceivable justification for the apparently willful mistranslation of Virgil's lines.[8] But what remains clear in any case, to us and to Dante alike, is that the meaning of the lines can shift radically relative to the situation in which they are understood.[9] Statius's interpretation demonstrates how Virgil's text can be incorporated into his own life and, quite apart from considerations of philological "correctness" as the criterion of interpretation, disclose a life-giving, salvific meaning.

The important point made by the passage in this context representing Statius as numbered surprisingly among the redeemed is that Statius gathers a morally good and edifying meaning out of Virgil's text—one that saves him from being perpetually damned to the fourth circle of Hell

8. A relatively recent attempt to untie the classic knot is Paolo Balden's "Stazio e le possibili 'vere ragioni che son nascose' della sua conversione. *Purgatorio* XXII. 40–41," in *Lettere italiane* 38 (April–June 1985): 149–65. Balden claims to have found a satisfactory interpretation of the miscitation of Virgil by Statius—"Perchè non reggi tu, o sacra fame / de l'oro, l'appetito de' mortali?"—that accounts for Virgil's silence and evident approval of Statius's use and understanding of his words: Priam's prodigality toward Polimnestor would indirectly be the cause of the latter's insatiable greed. From my point of view, the crux of the evident mistranslation is itself far more significant than any solution that normalizes it.

9. This is confirmed by Ronald Martinez's philologically rigorous reading of the passage as Dante's demonstration that, removed from its original context, Virgil's text is intrinsically polysemic, embodying a process of semantic change even with no variation at the level of the signifier. This displaces the whole problematic of the "correct" translation: "Dante non ha tradotto né correttamente né erroneamente, ha tradotto con il fine di dimostrare che il significato di un testo si può trasformare senza mutarne le parole, secondo un processo tutto interno, al livello del significato e non del significante" ("Dante did not translate either correctly or erroneously, but rather with the purpose of demonstrating that the signified of a text can be transformed without changing the words, in accordance with a wholly internal process, at the level of the signified and not of the signifier"). "La *sacra fame dell'oro* (*Purgatorio* 22, 41) tra Virgilio e Stazio: Dal testo all'interpretazione," *Letture classensi* 18 (1989): 179.

("sentirei le giostre grame"—*Purgatorio* XXII. 42)—regardless of his philological probity or accuracy. Indeed, the irrelevance of letter-correct philology in this context of understanding the moral meaning and saving truth of tradition gains a sharper point from the critical readings stressing the egregiousness of the error. Such letter-blind, but spiritually clairvoyant, "applied" reading was not lacking in august precedents. Augustine, in *De doctrina christiana,* had proposed a similarly pragmatic exegetical criterion for determining legitimate meanings of Scripture based on whether or not they were conducive to engendering *caritas* ("ut huic aedificendi charitati sit utilis").[10]

In this way, Dante remains innocent of the illusory ideal, invented by the humanists, of an objective meaning of a traditionary text to be ascertained by disinterested philological method, and rather probes the way in which the moral commitment and historical situation of the interpreter inform and make its meaning possible. Statius's understanding of the truth of Virgil's text is revealed not as a scientifically warrantable knowledge of a positively determined historical object but rather as itself a contingent, historically determined event. It is because of Statius's prodigality at the juncture in his personal history where he happens to encounter Virgil's text that the meaning of the text can be understood and taken to heart as an admonition against this excess. Thus the text occasions for him an event of moral illumination, exposing his sin and lighting the way to its correction. The truth of the text comes out through its dynamic engagement with Statius's historically evolving existence, rather than by some sort of pure adherence to what Virgil in a remote past might be supposed to have meant. The text's meaning is disclosed as a function of what Statius lives in the present of his decision for moral conversion.

An analogous interpretive liberty must be taken, in turn, to discover the salvific sense of Statius's own poetry. Seen from a merely and disinterestedly historical point of view (that is, as something over and done with in the past), or, in other words, through the optics of the Muse of history, namely Cleo, Statius's works fail to make manifest any Christian meaning, as Virgil remarks:

> "per quello che Clïò teco lì tasta,
>   non par che ti facesse ancor fedele
>   la fede, sanza qual ben far non basta."
>   (*Purgatorio* XXII. 58–60)

10. Augustine, *De doctrina Christiana* 1, 35, xxxvi. Note that to Statius, similarly, everything Virgil says is a sign of love: "Ogne tuo dir d'amor m'è caro cenno" (*Purgatorio* XXII. 27).

> ("For by the notes which Cleo strikes from you there,
>   it does not appear that the faith yet made you faithful,
>   without which doing good is not enough.")

Statius's answer, however, situating his outwardly pagan literary work in relation to his Christian life, hints that his oeuvre may have a hidden meaning. The account of his two-fold conversion experience (moral and Christian-prophetic) ends by pointing out an unsuspected allusion in his own work to a sacrament, namely, baptism, recognizable as such, however, only retrospectively, in Dante's text, where it is inserted into the silver poet's biography and into the general context of return to the innocence of the Golden Age:

> "E pria ch' io conducessi i Greci a' fiumi
>   di Tebe poetando, ebb' io battesmo;
>   ma per paura chiuso cristian fu'mi,
> lungamente mostrando paganesmo."
>
> (*Purgatorio* XXII. 88–89)

> ("And before I led the Greeks to the streams of
>   Thebes in poetry, I was baptized;
>   but out of fear I was a hidden Christian,
> a long time making show of paganism.")

Statius's leading the Greeks, by his pen, to the river, stated in conjunction with the disclosure that he himself had crossed the river of salvation through baptism, takes on the connotation of a possible Christian allegorical meaning buried in his own ostensibly pagan and historical poem. Does Statius's poem in this veiled manner figure a baptism of Gentiles? That, indeed, is precisely what his own life story, as told by Dante, of an outwardly pagan but secretly Christian poet, does. In any case, this hint represents an opening of the past to redetermination by interpretation in the present (and thereafter, by the same process, in the future). This new context brings out the true meaning of the past in a way for which Dante makes Statius into a veritable emblem.

Dante intimates through another nuance the intrinsic openness of Statius's oeuvre to interpretation by calling attention to its incompleteness, when Statius is given to say that he died while the *Achilleid* was in progress ("in via"—XXI. 93—like the pilgrims to Emmaus in XXI. 8). This leaves the final meaning of Statius's work, hidden from all merely historical knowledge concerning the mortal man, to emerge rather from the way Dante reads him, through his own faith. This incompleteness of history is the hermeneutic condition for Statius's being recognized as one risen up from the river and baptized into the true faith. Once again a sacrament, this time not the Eucharist but baptism, yet still a ritual manifestation and repetition of Christ's death and resurrection (see Rom. 6.3 ff), serves as the enabling paradigm for Dante's retrospective reading of the true, which is to say the Christian, meaning of a pagan text, this time not Virgil's but Statius's. It is Dante's reading of him that in effect baptizes Statius into Christianity, empowering this meaning buried in his life and works to be disclosed in truth, that is, according to what *had* to be their ultimate truth for Dante.

That Statius's understanding and explication of Virgil's texts (like Dante's, in turn, of Statius's life and works) should be produced by their application to his own historical-existential situation, in such a way as to give those texts new and different meaning, retraces what has been recognized as a normative pattern for hermeneutic experience in general by Gadamer in his contemporary "recovery" of the fundamental hermeneutic problematic.[11] Under the heading of "Application" ("Anwendung"), taking a cue from scriptural exegesis, Gadamer remarks that "the text, whether law or gospel, if it is to be understood properly—i.e. according to the claim it makes—must be understood at every moment, in every concrete situation, in a new and different way. Understanding here is always application" (Gadamer, *Truth and Method,* p. 309).

The claim the text makes, according to Gadamer, is a claim to say something true, a point fundamental to the whole project of *Truth and Method,* no less than to the readings of Virgil by Statius and of Statius by Dante, both concerned quintessentially with truth, specifically with the truth of Christian revelation as found refracted in these authors' texts. Needless to say, this is a truth that makes a claim, demanding conversion in Dante's and Statius's cases as a response. The way the truth in question exceeds all that any philological method or historical science can ascertain is vigorously thrown into relief by Dante's unflinchingly self-assured, albeit flagrantly unscientific, interpretations, vouched for only by his own poetic vision and religious witness.

Gadamer argues, in effect, that the historical situatedness of every act of understanding legitimates appropriations based on application to one's own present reality, for it shows this to be an inescapable, even if often convert, condition of any understanding at all coming about. It is thus that the very truth of Virgil's texts can be declared to be the Christian prophetic or moral one: not only does Statius happen to understand them within this perspective; the texts are not understood in their truth at all apart from some such existential application and appropriation.

Somewhat disturbingly, however, the "different" understanding necessarily built into the hermeneutic process seems to bring with it no clear criteria for distinguishing between genuinely understanding and unscru-

---

11. *Truth and Method,* pt. 2, 2, 2.

pulously instrumentalizing a text. Dante seems to have underscored this eventuality by making Statius's interpretation, especially of the moral ex-postulation from the *Aeneid,* as blatantly contradictory to the evident sense of the text as possible. Indeed, objective criteria for "true" interpretation are in no wise forthcoming for Gadamer's unmethodological hermeneutics, any more than for Dante's grasping in faith the divine meaning of his seminal texts. In effect, such criteria are shown by Gadamer not to be possible, or at any rate not possibly certain, where the experience of truth in the interpretation of tradition is concerned. We have seen that Dante goes so far as to suggest that the disclosure of the profound truth of a text may be produced even by misprision.

And yet, even so, as Dante represents it, this is not to throw interpretation open to the wanton and irresponsible arbitrium of purely subjective assertion and "impressionistic" reading. The interpretive liberties granted by Dante to Statius in the interest of the truth that is disclosed only in application are, on the contrary, displayed as being used responsibly: indeed, they are deployed literally in response. Statius describes how he was reached by Virgil's poetry, already a century-old text, as if it had been spoken to him in conversation—"when you said" ("quando dicesti")—and as if Virgil had acted directly in person to reorient the direction of his life: "You first sent me towards Parnassus" ("Tu prima m' inviasti / verso Parnaso"—XXII. 64, 70).

Not an object, not even Truth in the abstract, the phenomenon experienced by Statius—the reality that comes over him—in his encounter with Virgil's text is that of being personally addressed: he is a 'Thou' vis-à-vis and 'I'. This structure of personal address, so fundamental to the presentation of Dante's own poem to its reader, is highlighted through the personal pronoun, used both with reference to and within the Virgilian text that alerts Statius to the error opposite from avarice, literally calling to him in his own existential situation with its specific risks:

> "E se non fosse ch' io drizzai mia cura,
>   quand' io intesi là dove *tu* chiame,
>   crucciato quasi a l'umana natura:
> 'Perché non reggi *tu,* o sacra fame
>   de l'oro, l'appetito de' mortali?'
>   voltando sentirei le giostre grame."
>
> (XXII. 37–42)

> ("And if it had not been that I set right my care,
>   when I understood the passage where *you* call,
>   as if vexed with human nature:
> 'Why don't *you* rule, O blessed hunger
>   for gold, the appetite of mortals?'
>   rolling I would feel the wretched jousts.")

The first "tu" conflates the poetic text with its author, who miracu-lously happens to be present before Statius as he speaks. An exceptional circumstance here, this may nonetheless illustrate, in idealized form, a normative condition for reading truly. The authorial presence calls through the text with a voice of moral outrage ("crucciato"), at least as it is understood by Statius in the event of understanding ("quand' io intesi"). The hearing of the address within the text is accompanied by a caring ("drizzai mia cura") on the part of the 'I' who hears, hence in a dimension of concern that is perhaps equally a condition and a con-sequence of the enunciatory event of the address calling for moral con-version. Statius has to take a message addressed to humankind ("l'umana natura") in a particular way, applying it to his own life as addressed to him personally, for it to yield its truth to him.

In this way, paradoxically, the personal appropriation that makes a truth integral to Statius's own existence into the point for him of a text already of distant provenance also is what enables the text to speak as a free and independent agency, a genuine otherness, that addresses Statius and claims him by the truth it announces. The event of appropriation, which superficially considered seems to grant the interpreter a free hand, actually appropriates him to what he is interpreting, pressing his being into the service of responding to a call. This call addresses Statius from the text in the person of its author. Thus the sequence suggests how personal appropriation and even philologically indefensible applications of a text can be genuinely responsive to those texts and even honor their "authority," perhaps more than (or alongside and together with) howso-ever philologically painstaking and scientifically "objective" an interpre-tation.

In Statius, Dante has compellingly illustrated how the truth of what is said in a text (and even of what happens, as on the road to Emmaus) depends on the event of reading itself, that is, on open, ongoing interpre-tation / application, not only on what happened once upon a time. The exigencies of the reader together with the circumstances in which the event of reading takes place are not only built-in biases and barriers to understanding the original meaning; they are the conditions under which the experience of truth handed down in tradition can happen, if it hap-pens at all. Naturally, conditions contemporary to interpretation of a tra-ditionary text from the past may become impediments to understanding too, and so need to be checked or placed in abeyance, but this is second-ary with respect to their necessary, constitutive role in the happening of any truth whatsoever, as the event of truth and its mediation by tradition is brought forth by Dante no less than by Gadamer.

The fact that Dante's poem is able to bring out a truth of history closed to previous ages, such as the conversion of Statius, or that Statius is able to interpret, retrospectively, the messianic meaning of Virgil's text, or again that Luke and other disciples can recognize Jesus as truly the resurrected one who accompanied them all along the way, after the fact, in the celebration of the Eucharist, opens to view a dimension of time as effectually intrinsic to truth. In each case, the truth remains sealed until interpretation, in a contextually specific way, brings it to the light of day in an event of disclosure. Truth, even when referred to and involving the past, always involves also a dimension of happening in the present. Dante was keenly aware of this, as we are perhaps in a position to fully appreciate once again today with the help of recent developments and recuperations in our theoretical understanding of interpretation.

Historicity and Transcendence

The particular historical circumstances in which Statius comes to understand Virgil's prophetic text—or the personal moral exigencies he brings to what he reads as a gnomic text—actually make possible the revelation in these texts of a truth that must remain extraneous to what was intended and understood in the same texts within their own historical context, even by Virgil himself. Dante accentuates at once the blindness of Virgil to the true meaning of his own text—this is done indirectly by sounding the note of Virgil's eternal exile—and the truth that he nevertheless luminously conveys:

> "Facesti come quei che va di notte,
>   che porta il lume dietro e sé non giova,
>   ma dopo sé fa le persone dotte. . . ."
>
> (XXII. 67–69).

> ("You did as one who goes by night,
>   who carries the light behind and benefits not himself,
>   but after himself makes people wise. . . .")

The contrast between Virgil's horizon and Statius's own could not be more dramatic, as their divided fates serve to remind us. The fact that Statius comes to Christianity through Virgil, a historical circumstance of a blatantly improbable kind, constitutes a provocation and a reminder of the specific genesis of his understanding, its particular historical conditionedness, which cannot be erased or substituted for by any more evidently appropriate kind of occasion. The shining of a divine, absolute truth in human understanding is possible only on the condition that it be disclosed in partial, accidental, conditioned ways that bring to light understanding and its finitude together with truth and its universality.

This is how Dante in his treatment of Statius highlights the historicity of understanding. Modern technological reality tends to flatten out and annul time and space, the mediums through which we move toward understanding. Instant, unrestricted availability of information through telecommunications and on-line computer systems obscures the way that something can be truly and humanly understood only when the time is ripe, by and for individuals on their life's journey, along which every step and turn brings new possibilities into their horizon. Truth becomes an objective digital configuration of information that the right technology enables us to possess. What is eclipsed is the historicity of hermeneutical experience, the finite limiting circumstances of an individual's historical existence that are the very conditions which enable truth, even with its claim to universality, as in Christian revelation, to be disclosed. What Dante is vindicating in his treatment of Statius is, in the first place, the historicity of understanding.

But having placed such emphasis on the limits imposed by historical conditionedness, Dante also follows this ineluctable finitude of interpretation through to its extraordinary consequences: they include such possibilities as a new, resurrected life of meaning and transcendent truth. For radical openness to the historicity of truth paradoxically brings with it radical openness to truth's transcendence of its own historical occasions. "History" itself becomes relativized as a form of disclosure, that is, as a determinate way of occurring of truth. This is perhaps the crucial insight the religious tradition Dante represents and realizes has to offer to a self-styled "postmetaphysical" modernity, clinging one-sidedly to the revelation of historical relativity, while letting slip out of mind that by the same logic this too can be only relatively true, not substantially more correct than assertions of the revelation of absolute truths. The submission to a truth so absolute as to show up how relative and contingent, occasioned perhaps even by mistakes, his own or anyone else's experience of it is saves Dante from the absolute assertion that no such truth can exist.

The affirmation that Virgil was essential to Statius's finding of the faith—as paradoxical as this must be in a context where Virgil's own perdition is harped on determinedly and pathetically—brings Christian truth and tradition into intrinsic relation with its negation, with paganism, the tradition also of the "false and lying gods." Dante pries into the event of conversion, his own as much as Statius's, or again that of the "natura umana," and finds that it is inextricably bound up with and dependent upon a historical crossroads with what is ostensibly outside the plan of salvation. Faith is generated by what does not belong to faith but is kept without, consigned to eternal exile ("l'etterno essilio"), in the phrase from Virgil's own greeting of Statius:

> "Nel beato concilio
> ti ponga in pace la verace corte
> che me rilega ne l'etterno essilio."
>
> (XXI. 16–18)

> ("May the true court which consigns me
> to eternal exile place you in peace
> in the blessed assembly.")

The glaring irony of Virgil's exclusion from salvation, insistently evoked at just this juncture where Virgil, for his having borne the light showing the way to Christ, is apotheosized as the prophet to whom Statius owes the salvation of his soul, demonstrates as starkly as possible the evident contradiction between history with its casualties and the transcendent, saving meaning that literally rises up ("surge") from it. The *skandalon* of the Resurrection, of the mortal body condemned to death, which nevertheless takes on new life as a glorious body, thus becomes the miraculous and enigmatic sign presiding over Dante's treatment of Christian truth and pagan tradition in the Statius cantos. The Resurrection is the symbol par excellence of historicity *and* transcendence affirmed together in their seeming contradictoriness. In the mystery of the Resurrection, the body in its determinate, historical individuality is conceived as inextricably belonging to a life that is glorified and exalted, transcending the conditions of history, finitude, mortality.

Statius stands for the positive relationship between historicity and transcendence, between the extraneous occasion in pagan poetry and the revealed truth of religion reached thereby, that Dante interprets with such tenacity. Dante weds revealed truth indissolubly to the historical conditions under which it is realized, while at the same time transfiguring those very conditions so that they can be seen to belong to an order transcending nature and history, even to a plan preceding history. This conjunction of seeming opposites is built into cantos XXI and XXII in all sorts of subordinate ways, resonating with the central thematics embodied in the paradox of resurrection, that is, of a finite, contingent body bearing eternal life, or, analogously, of a timely, chance occasion's being intrinsic to an experience of truth apprehended as eternal.

Statius's first discourse, a long exposition about how the mountain of Purgatory stands above the processes of nature causing perturbations in mundane existence—

> "Cosa non è che sanza
> ordine senta la religione
> de la montagna, o che sia fuor d'usanza.
> Libero è qui da ogne alternazione:

di quel che 'l ciel da sé in sé riceve
esser ci puote, e non d'altro, cagione."
                                (XXI. 40–45)

("The religion of the mountain suffers
    nothing that is without order
    or that departs from custom.
This place is free from every change:
    that which heaven from itself into itself
    receives, and nothing else, can here be a cause.")

—explains that natural contingency is transcended in the realm of salvation above the three-step passage into Purgatory proper. This exclusion of contingency from the environment is the counterpart in the domain of nature to the transcendence of contingency in history experienced by all who finally have been saved and culminating in the visions of Paradise, where history is contemplated as reflected in God, that is, from the point at which all times are present (*Paradiso* XVII. 17–18).

And yet, although Statius's explanation affirms that contingency is transcended in the part of the mountain where they stand, this very explanation is called forth by a cataclysmic event leaving Dante and Virgil practically in a state of shock. Indeed, above the threshold of Purgatory, shattering eruptions of earthquake and lightning seem to be integral to the life of the saved. The life of the spirit is itself an eruption as this canto and the poem generally present it. The difference obtaining on that side of salvation to which Dante goes over is that external events are transparent to spirit, their very suddenness an immediate manifestation of an unfathomable, incalculable divine rationale and fateful meaning.

The way that chance historical or biographical fact may be comprehended retrospectively as depending upon a providential plan determined by transcendent motives can now be understood to have been hinted at, for example, in the description of the times of "good Titus," who is mentioned as having avenged the Jews' killing of Christ by destroying Jerusalem with the help of God ("Nel tempo che 'l buon Tito, con l'aiuto / del sommo rege, vendicò le fóra / ond' uscì 'l sangue per Giuda venduto"—XXI. 82–84). Even such violent explosions of history are transfigured in retrospect as serving a divine purpose. Statius's migration from Toulouse to Rome ("tolosano, a sé mi trasse Roma") becomes a providential calling from a place far outside the circle of destiny to the cultural and spiritual capital of the empire.

Nevertheless, Dante refuses to forget, even after such transfigurations, the role of what could not but appear at the time to be casual circumstances as indispensable to the necessary happenings of true destiny. Statius's remark, for instance, that he would have willingly postponed his assent to heaven for the chance to have lived in Virgil's time—

> "E per esser vivuto di là quando
>   visse Virgilio, assentirei un sole
>   più che non deggio al mio uscir di bando."
>
> (XXI. 100–102)

> ("And to have lived there when
>   Virgil lived, I would assent to a sun
>   more than I owe before my release from banishment.")

—apparently breaks out of the teleological logic and hierarchy of values otherwise governing all that happens in this context of the exceptionless religious order of the mountain. It is incongruous that at this very moment of his emancipation from all worldly desire, purified for the desire of God alone, Statius should be tethered by such a human hankering.[12] This stray desire turning back toward earthly life, however, happens to be miraculously fulfilled in this very moment, as Statius is face to face with the poet he had so longed to meet. Chance is here transfigured as destiny. Such collapsing together of errant contingency with the significantly necessary is likewise ciphered into the episode in the smile that this very remark happens to bring to Dante's face. It provokes an observation that accidental eruptions of emotion in bodily expression can be most revealing of truth:

> ché riso e pianto son tanto seguaci
>   a la passion di che ciascun si spicca,
>   che men seguon voler ne' più veraci.
>
> (XXI. 106–8)

> (for laughter and weeping are so closely adherent
>   to the passion from which each springs,
>   that they follow the will least in the most truthful.)

This smile, notwithstanding its spontaneous and inopportune quality (or even just because of it), is transfigured by an eschatological light. The uncontrollable smiling shows up as a "lampeggiar di riso" ("lightning smile"—XXI. 114), reflecting the lightning (or sunlight) that flashes in the face of Jesus transfigured on Mt. Tabor, as well as in those of the angels of apocalypse. The holy shout given up as the mountain quakes in celebration of the liberation (of Statius's soul)—

---

12. Giovanni Cecchetti, "The Statius Episode: Observations on Dante's Conception of Poetry," *Lectura Dantis: A Forum for Dante Research and Interpretation* 7 (1990): 106.

> Tremaci quando alcuna anima monda
> sentesi, sì che surga o che si mova
> per salir sù; e tal grido seconda.
>
> (XXI. 59–61)

> (It trembles here when any soul feels itself
> cleansed, so as to rise or set out
> to climb upward; and such a shout seconds.)

—is likewise eschatological in derivation and finds its echo in the poetic apocalypse toward which the whole of *Purgatorio* crescendoes, prefiguring how the blessed shall rise wearing a new body and voice:

> Quali i beati al novissimo bando
> surgeran presti ognun di sua caverna,
> la revestita voce aleluiando. . . .
>
> (*Purgatorio* XXX. 13–15)

> (Just as the blessed at the new banns
> will rise ready, each from his cavern,
> the reclad voice singing alleluia. . . .)

All the sudden, spontaneous gestures thematically highlighted in the canto, with its portrayal of the uncontainable emotions of Statius and of Dante, expressed, respectively, in a vain impulse to embrace Virgil and in the involuntary smile, are not merely natural phenomena happening by chance; they are here unveiled as playing a part in the fulfillment of a deeper scheme. In the final perspective of the poem, human and historical occasions are transfigured in a plan preordained from eternity. This paradoxical compenetration of superior fate and its chance occasion is expressed again another way in the syntax of Virgil's question, "qual sole o quai candele / ti stenebraron?" (XXII. 61–62), placing the divine source of all illumination, symbolized by the sun, alongside the apostolic bearers and disseminators of tradition in history, the candles, in a parallel construction.[13]

Dante refuses to forget or elide the historical occasions of eternal salvation—Virgil being the chief exemplar of sparking salvation history while remaining unilluminated by it—and contemplates their utterly surprising coincidence with the work of providence, grace. The personal address that opened Christian revelation to Statius came unforgettably from Virgil. Dante cannot overemphasize the importance for eternal salvation of this historical circumstance:

13. See Cecchetti, "The Statius Episode," p. 109: "In the *Commedia*, the sun is a constant metaphor of God . . . ; here it signifies grace or an inspiration of Grace, and the 'candele' have the sense of human teachings that can lead to the sun; but the disjunctive *o* places the two sources of spiritual light on the same level, as far as their effective benefits are concerned."

"Per te poeta fui, per te cristiano."
(*Purgatorio* XXII. 73)

("By you I became poet, by you Christian.")

And in so doing he suggests, moreover, that the conjunction of the necessary and the contingent in salvation is somehow intimately related to poetry.

What is the meaning of this deep-seated connection, this parallelism or virtual coinciding, between poetry and Christianity, in which the whole significance of the cantos about Statius is felt to be concentrated? Poetry constitutes the historical means by which Statius was led to the Christian truth that transcends history. Dante probes the interconnectedness and coincidence of the two. Virgil is expressly recognized as engendering Statius not only as poet but also as Christian. Virgil guides Statius in the art of poetry and also lights for him the way to faith. But how to get from the one to the other? Between the two lies an abysslike mystery. That a history without Christ, subject to all the chance perturbations that disturb nature below the gate of Purgatory proper, should nevertheless be the indispensable ground for revealing—and therefore also for discerning—the divine order of things is the ordinarily inscrutable riddle that Dante ponders in these cantos. Dante states, with confidence itself somewhat miraculous, the necessity to revelation of historical contingency and recalcitrance, the intrinsic relation to a condition that is always already loss, embodied monumentally in Virgil. The miraculous is that human life, historically conditioned as it inextricably is, should give rise to a transcendent meaning symbolized by the resurrection of the body. In accordance with this miracle, human life is claimed by the revelation of an eternal truth that Dante insists rises out of and is to be understood on the basis of the contingent character of human existence.

"La divina fiamma"

How, then, does Dante mediate this tension between the chance happenings of history and the significances of a divinely preordained destiny, in other words, the contradiction between historicity and transcendent truth, both of which are decisively affirmed here as throughout the *Commedia*? The answer the work gives and *is,* of course, is poetry. By understanding the revelation of transcendent truth as inherently poetical in so far as it touches us, on the one hand, and history as poetically made in a way involving but also possibly exceeding all human making, on the other, both historicity and transcendent truth can be understood together as mutually implicated aspects of religious revelation. The way in which Dante shows the much vaunted historicity of his poem, as well as of human lives and even of world events, to be a poetical-hermeneutical construct was dealt with at some length in section 1 of chapter 4. The inherent poeticality of religious truth, on the other hand, even when it is revealed as eternal or transcendent, emerges as the chief point and astonishing affirmation of the encounter with Statius as considered in this chapter.

At the very heart of the Statius saga lies poetry harboring the potential for transcendence toward a divine source. Statius says to Virgil:

> "Tu prima m'inviasti
> verso Parnaso a ber ne le sue grotte
> e prima apresso Dio m'alluminasti."
>   (XXII. 64–66)

> ("You first sent me
> towards Parnassus to drink in its grottoes
> and first next to God enlightened me.")

From Parnassus to God; the one follows hard upon the other. This is the same sublime sequencing as operates in "Per te poeta fui, per te cristiano" (XXII. 73), where poetry conducts, via the thin stroke of a comma splice, from the human to the divine.

The continuity and even the coinciding of the human and the divine, as in the Incarnation, Dante understands to be humanly attainable essentially in and by poetry. In fact Statius the poet, in essence a Christian Virgil, is Dante's most overt *figura Cristi*.[14] In Statius, Dante realizes the peculiar vocation of poetry to raise humans to the level of the divine, to bestow on human activity and making an immortal dimension of significance. Poetry's potential proximity to the divine, to which it offers humans a sort of access, was promoted in the ancient cult of poetry, signally, by none other than Statius himself in, for example, the envoi addressed by the poet to his own work at the end of the *Thebaid,* with its homage to the "divine Aeneid" of Virgil: "Vive, precor; nec tu divinam Aeneida tempta, / sed longe sequere et vestigia semper adora" (XII, 816–17). This tribute echoes in the words with which Dante's Statius celebrates the *Aeneid,* including the same word "divina" together with a metaphor that we have already seen is also applied to the saving word sown by the gospel message, that of the "seed" ("seme"):

> "Al mio ardor fuor seme le faville,
>   che mi scaldar, de la divina fiamma
>   onde sono allumati più di mille;
> de l'Eneïda dico, la qual mamma

---

14. According to Cecchetti, Statius is the only such figure in the poem.

fummi, e fummi nutrice, poetando:
sanz' essa non fermai peso di dramma."

(XXI. 94–99)

("Seeds of my ardor were the sparks,
    which warmed me, of the divine flame
    by which more than a thousand are illumined;
  of the *Aeneid,* I say, which a mother
    was to me, and to me was nursemaid in making poetry:
    without it I would not have been worth a drachm.")

Poetry as a sacred flame ("divina fiamma"), as a seed ("seme") of salvation or divine spark ("favilla"), as mother providing vital nourishment (made phonetically palpable in the infantile "mm" humming doubled and thrice-resounded through the second *terzina*), becomes the living link between the human and the divine, the historical and the transcendent. While Virgil's poetry becomes natural mother to Statius, the natural here is continuous with the spiritual, like the "sete natural" ("natural thirst") of the Samaritan woman, alluded to along with the Emmaus pilgrims at the beginning of the whole sequence, satiated by "grazia" (XXI. 1–3). In poetry, that is, in "making," it is possible to discern the human as divine, nature as grace.

Fleshed out in these as well as in other ways, "Per te poeta fui, per te cristiano" runs the path to poetry together with that leading to revealed Christian truth. Is this convergence just Statius's own personal case or, behind this, just Dante's peculiar experience? Granted, one need not become a poet like the two of them in order to embrace the faith. Yet their life story, in the context of Dante's poem revealing the nature of the Christian experience of truth in general, takes on an emblematic significance. It is, to be sure, presented as belonging to an individual life history, but it is also representative of something essential in the relations between poetry and revelation. As we have seen, first with reference to the experience of the pilgrims to Emmaus, religious truth is revealed within a participatory act (such as ritual repetition in the Eucharist), a consenting that also is a making and a making possible, a voluntary or free movement of faith that at the same time is understood as given by grace.

Communication and memorialization of religious experience is itself inherently poetic, and, consequently, religious revelation is itself a "making" that involves human spontaneity and creativity embraced within the event of divine self-disclosure. Luke notes that the resurrected Lord might have passed by the disciples on the way to Emmaus, but something within them, a disposition rendering possible the experience they are to have of him, makes them wish to detain him: "And they drew nigh unto the village, whither they went: and he made as though he would have gone farther. But they constrained him, saying, Abide with us" (Luke 24.28–29). Again, after Jesus had been revealed to them and then vanished from their sight, "they said to one another, Did not our heart burn within us, while he talked with us by the way, and while he opened to us the scriptures?" (Luke 24.32)

This burning heart, as interior correlative to the presence of the Lord and his opening of prophetic tradition, registers something essential about the locus of the event of truth. While it is localized in external space, that is, in the real presence of the Lord in their midst along the way to Emmaus, this putatively objective phenomenon is perceived in its true identity only by a burning heart and a soul so disposed that it bids the stranger to stay. The heart so burning functions as a metonymy for faith as the condition of religious understanding. In some sense, faith "makes" its object, even while understanding itself as being induced by a higher maker. As in all poetry, something objective is made that helps communicate an experience of what is not properly objectifiable at all.

Here we touch upon the poetic making at the heart of religious experience. There is always something obscure in the miraculous, in Christ's surging up from the "sepulcral buca," in his suddenly being beheld ("Ecco") by the pilgrims to Emmaus, in Statius's coming up *from behind,* overtaking Virgil and Dante. The Resurrection itself is never witnessed; there is no account in the Gospels of the event's actually transpiring, only that of the disciples' experiences, after the fact, of their resurrected Lord. The mystery is always reached through interpretation directed backward to what is unknowable in itself and can be spoken of at all only in terms of the interpretative experiences arising from it. The compenetration of these natural experiences of making, and the mystery/miracle that animates and transfigures them, gives the human acts the character of something miraculous in their own right. Dante suggests later, when examined on faith, that even if there had been no miracles such as the Bible attests, the fact of the faith's universal spread would be miracle enough to prove its veracity:

> "Se 'l mondo si rivolse al cristianesmo,"
>   diss' io, "sanza miracoli, quest' uno
>   è tal, che li altri non sono il centesmo."
>   (*Paradiso* XXIV. 106–8)

> ("If the world converted to Christianity,"
>   I said, "without miracles, this one alone
>   is such, that the others are not one-hundredth of it.")

This argument is obviously specious from a logical standpoint, but is quite accurate as a description of an aspect of the effectual working of revelation in history, by virtue of its clairvoyance concerning the miracle potentially transpiring in interpretation itself.

What is obscure in religious experience is that which resists objectification, that which does not belong to the order of objective experience at all, the supernatural and otherworldly. And yet religious experience and witness, since time immemorial, has continually sought objectifications to serve its need for self-expression. In doing so, it has operated poetically. The human making that makes communicable the experience of what transcends representation intrinsically belongs to religious experience, and it is played out to its fullest extent, reaching a plenum of expression, in the religious poem of Dante. Dante makes the poetically objectified other world of religious experience the very "argument" of his work.

The faculty of poetic making is what brings out in human beings their status as not simply being within the world but as able to transcend it in making a new and different world. (In so doing, of course, they also transcend themselves, so that the doing is no longer in any simple, static sense "theirs.") For the activity of making brings into evidence the transcendental coordinates that determine everything within the world. Modern hermeneutic theory agrees with Dante in appreciating the guiding role of art in pointing up a dimension of reality transcending the reality of objects.[15] But to a large degree, in conformity with a modern, secular worldview, contemporary hermeneutic theorists resist theological interpretation of this reality, such as is found in Dante. Yet vital hermeneutic insight is regrettably lost by this alienation of what traditionally has been thought and symbolized as the theological dimension of interpretation.

Human making itself is never an object, or never merely such; even the objects it produces bring into play and into question the coordinates in terms of which objects can be determined. Human making or poetry in this sense concerns what transcends all that is within the world. The world itself in the making of *poiēsis,* therefore, is necessarily presented as "new." Poetry as interpretive making is the human act by which the world is discovered in its newness as what asks to be characterized, by virtue of its unworldly, extraworldly nature, as a divine event.

"Secol si rinova"

The world as new and other, precisely, the "other world" as Dante presents it, or, in other words, a world transcending what we know as the world and what comes to pass in recorded history, is the perennial theme

---

15. Cf. Heidegger's "The Origin of the Work of Art" and part 1 of Gadamer's *Truth and Method.*

of poetry that comes to climactic expression in the Virgilian prophecy cited by Dante as divinely inspired. What Dante has divined to be the message at the core of poetry, distilled into the "divine" verses by the *Aeneid*'s author that for him summed up the meaning of all ancient poetry, is precisely the proclamation of the renewal of the world, of the advent of a new progeny, of the universe set right again:

> "'Secol si rinova;
> torna giustizia e primo tempo umano
> e progenie scende da ciel nova.'"
>
> *(Purgatorio* XXII. 70–72)

> ("'The world grows new again;
> justice returns and the first human age,
> and a new progeny descends from heaven.'")

We can begin to understand poetry in accordance with its hermeneutic meaning, its fundamentally interpretive character as "making," by following this hint about its essential content. Poetry represents the world as new. Its central message is that of the dawn of a new age, for by its representations, with their distance from the actual world, it makes possible a happening of the world as new. Our relation to the world—and thereby the world itself—is made different through poetry. This sense of Dante's finds a theoretical counterpart in Gadamer's theory of hermeneutic experience as essentially an experience of the new, or rather as any experience whatever being experienced *as* new.[16]

This openness to the new, at the same time a return to the old, is the defining characteristic of hermeneutic experience as Gadamer describes it, essentially the experience of tradition as new. Not itself any specific experience, hermeneutic experience depends on the capacity to receive new experience, which also means to experience as new all that has been traditionally experienced, as at once other and one's own, and as the opening of a horizon upon the unknown of the future: "The nature of experience is conceived in terms of something that surpasses it. . . . The truth of experience always implies an orientation toward new experience. That is why a person who is called experienced has become so not only *through* experiences but is also open *to* new experiences" (Gadamer, *Truth and Method,* p. 355).

So construed, in its projection of a new world, or of the world as new, the structure of hermeneutic experience coincides with the vital substance of poetry as Dante understood it. Dante repeatedly reverts, as if to poetry's most essential myth, to the promise of the renewal of the

---

16. *Truth and Method* 2.3.b. In addition, see Gadamer, "Zum Begriff des 'Neuen,'" in *Neure Philosophie* II, *Gesammelte Werke,* vol. 4 (Tübingen: J. C. B. Mohr, 1987).

Golden Age ("secol si rinova"). This mythic reign of natural justice under Saturn, as it was dreamt by the ancient poets, is identified in the Edenic paradise at the apex of the *Purgatorio* as an obscure version of the original place of innocence in the biblical revelation of the Garden of Eden:

> "Quelli ch'anticamente poetaro
>   l'età dell'oro e suo stato felice
>   forse in Parnaso esto loco sognaro."
>   (*Purgatorio* XXVIII. 141)

> ("Those who of old sang
>   the age of gold and its happy state
>   perhaps with their Parnassus dreamed of this place.")

But this old is at the same time the image of the new. At the end of Canto XXII the whole sequence winds up with an allusion to the first age, figured by the poets as good as gold ("Lo secol primo quant' oro fu bello"), nourished in natural simplicity on nectar and acorns, as adumbrating the return to nature of John the Baptist, who ate locusts and wild honey, and who ushers in the new age openly revealed in the gospel: "Quanto per lo Vangelio v'è aperto"—XXII. 148–54.

The world *is* new to the extent that it is in and through *poiēsis*. For it is the "making" that is constantly emerging in poetry that makes the world and makes worlds possible for human experience. This essential creativity and regenerative power links poetry with religious renewal, specifically, with Christian redemption of the world in the kingdom of God and of the individual soul in the resurrected life. Dante asserts, moreover, the world-renewing power of poetry in highlighting the classic Golden Age myth, coinciding with the Edenic "truth" of Scripture, as the quintessential argument of poetic tradition.

Dante's whole journey through the *Purgatorio* is structured as a return to the origin of human existence, to the Garden of Eden as well as to the state of original justice that man enjoyed there. It throws into epic relief the historical nature of understanding in unveiling the advent of the new as the return of the old. Whatever is presented to us is understood in terms of these coordinates. Understanding is intrinsically a recapitulation of the past and at the same time an openness to the new. Only by this structure is recognition possible on the one hand and receptivity on the other—which together may be taken as the essential component functions of understanding, its double sine qua non, even for the understanding of revealed religious truth.

The itinerary of Dante's poem could hardly make it clearer that the return to the golden time before and after historical time is possible only in time, through history, and specifically through history understood as *poiēsis*. Dante has to work his way through Hell and Purgatory (and so also through the *Inferno* and *Purgatorio*), through both "temporal fire and eternal," assuming the whole burden of history with all its entrapments, in order to arrive at the Garden. Salvation entails not simply being lifted out of time into eternity, but rather a process of purgation working through time, where alone grace can reach him and bear him "a l'etterno dal tempo."

Thus Dante resurrects the tradition of a Golden Age, which was so central a myth for pagan poetry, letting it coalesce with the mount of inspiration of classical poetry in general, Parnassus (cf. *Purgatorio* XXII. 65, XXVIII. 141, XXXI. 141), and proceeds to interpret the originary identity of this resurrected tradition with the revealed truth of the biblical Garden of Eden. We have seen many times that the guiding insight of the *Purgatorio,* pivoting on the Statius encounter, is this correspondence between, indeed this coincidence of, the interpretive resurrection of tradition and the revelation of transcendent truth. The Emmaus pericope itself, we saw, is contrived so as to suggest how the real presence of Christ is revealed in the reliving of experiences preserved and disseminated in tradition. In that text, revealed truth in the strict sense of Scripture shows itself as in essence resurrected tradition. Dante's insistence on how even pagan tradition, when given new life through Christian interpretation, can be understood to lead to revealed truth underscores yet more conspicuously how revelation works precisely through the resurrection of tradition achieved in and by hermeneusis.

Art and Immortality

Gadamer's philosophical hermeneutics, for all its emphasis on the finite historical conditionedness of understanding, also aims to render intelligible such a "suprahistorical value" ("übergeschichtlichen Wert") as "the classical."[17] Hermeneutic consciousness and self-reflection make possible a rehabilitation of this concept, from merely being a term descriptive of a historical period and style to the normative status that belongs to it in the hermeneutic experience of truth. In this sense, the "classical" work of art serves as a touchstone of values such as beauty and truth, prescinded from mere fluctuating standards of taste. As normative, whatever deserves to be called "classical" is transhistorical because it is always already operative before historical reflection begins; it is a constitutive, structuring part of the tradition within which all such reflection necessarily is carried out. The classic, before it begins to be consciously examined, becoming an

---

17. *Truth and Method,* p. 287. Cf. further p. 288: "When we call something classical, there is a consciousness of something enduring, of significance that cannot be lost and that is independent of all the circumstances of time—a kind of timeless present that is contemporaneous with every other present."

object, always already shapes reflection on aesthetic values through the binding power and authoritativeness of the standards it embodies.

Thus the classical is defined by Gadamer, following and adapting Hegel, as "self-significant" and "self-interpretive." By its power of interpreting itself, the classic reaches into the present and addresses it. In so doing, the classical precedes, encompasses, and anticipates latter-day interpretations within its own already-in-progress self-interpretation: "[T]he classical preserves itself precisely *because* it is significant in itself and interprets itself; i.e. it speaks in such a way that it is not a statement about what is past—documentary evidence that still needs to be interpreted—rather, it says something to the present as if it were said specifically to it" (Gadamer, *Truth and Method*, p. 290). This specifically suggests how the hermeneutic theory of the classic finds in the instance of the *Commedia* as classic, with its highlighting of the address to the interpreter, an exceptionally acute and self-conscious instantiation.

Moreover, Dante has purposefully woven an ideal of the poetic classic as resistant to time together with his model of Christian salvation and resurrected life in the Statius cantos. Statius's remark that "poet" is the name that most endures and honors ("il nome che più dura e che più onora"—XXI. 85) gestures toward a transhistorical value in literature parallel to the eternal truth of the word of the gospel. This parallelism achieves lapidary form in the line in which Statius gives credit for his discovery of enduring, preserving, saving value in both the literary and the religious domains at once to that greatest of classics, in Dante's view, Virgil: "Per te poeta fui, per te cristiano" ("Through you I became poet, through you Christian").

Purgatorio XXI–XXII intimates that *poiēsis* fundamentally is a means by which humans may participate in immortality. Though immortality is certainly a gift from the transcendent Lord of life, it does not come to humans as an object wrapped up neatly in a package. It comes to them, or rather is given, through their own making, through an active involvement with what transforms them in their activity of self-transcendence. Taken in its etymological sense of "making," frequently employed in the Middle Ages and perhaps implicitly by Dante himself in *De vulgari eloquentia* II. iv, poetry can encompass the nature of all art. It is in this sense, ultimately, that art becomes so fundamental to the experience of all of Purgatory, issuing in the rising up to an eternal life.

Art, and, quintessentially, poetry, is how humanity participates in creating enduring forms. To the extent human beings aspire to what they interpret as some eternal form of existence, the hermeneutic nature of interpretation dictates that they can attain it only by participating in its making. All of the *Purgatorio* illustrates how human effort—the "tanto labore" (XXI. 112) of Virgilian resonance—contributes to the work of redemption through purifying and edifying. Salvation does not merely fall out of the sky. Even with its unconditional transcendence of all merely human possibilities, it must nevertheless be received, nurtured, and "seconded" (see Virgil's discourse on love: *Purgatorio* XVII. 82 ff) within the human sphere. The integrity of the secular order in coordination with the divine dispensation is well recognized as one of the determinative constants in the work of Dante as "poet of the secular world." Hence, also the argument with regard to human freedom—and its need to be guided and disciplined—in *Purgatorio* XVI. 73 ff, so thematically as well as numerically central to the *cantica*. This freedom is eminently exercised in the art of poetry, where self-fashioning through interpretation opens possibilities for freedom vis-à-vis one's whole world of experience.

The *Purgatorio* teaches that a genuine participation in divine reality is fashioned over time by assiduous human effort, and poetry is exalted as the model for this human endeavor of self-fashioning in the divine image. This is the great message particularly of the Statius cantos, as Giovanni Cecchetti and others have so well appreciated. In the symbol of Statius, a poet in the genealogical line that in Dante's conception engenders the highest poetry, "poetry becomes the means for guiding humanity on the road to salvation and immortality in the broadest and deepest sense."[18]

Because salvation is realized through a making that transpires essentially in time—and all the images of action and endurance of souls in Purgatory depict this temporal dimension of sanctification—there is also, inevitably, loss. Time—at least in human experience as we know it—even while serving as the medium of redemption and reformation, at the same time distances and deletes, and Dante agonizes over its losses. Virgil, in the economy of the *Commedia* as a whole, tragically symbolizes this concomitant loss inherent in the temporal nature of human existence.

In the person of Statius, by contrast, the discipline of poetry (not to the exclusion, naturally, of penance) is manifestly fused into the efforts by which the soul frees itself from Purgatory and struggles its way from time into eternity. Of course, the delusion of achieving immortality through poetry or through any other human endeavor has also been acutely exposed and damned in several of the most haunting and unforgettable episodes of the poem. In *Inferno* XV, Brunetto Latini's teaching of how man eternalizes himself ("come l'uom s'eterna") through humanistic works such as his *Tesoro* is seen to have blown up in his eternally charcoaled face. Similarly, the prologue scene, especially as Freccero teaches that it be read, demonstrates the futility of all efforts to attain

18. Cecchetti, "The Statius Episode," p. 96. Christopher Kleinhenz similarly emphasizes "the transcendent power of poetry" in "The Celebration of Poetry: A Reading of *Purgatorio* XXII," *Dante Studies* 106 (1988): 21–41.

through the power of human intellect, that is, philosophically, the re-
deemed state symbolized by the top of Mount Purgatory; rather, the
pilgrim has to go down into Hell, along the other way ("altro viaggio"),
that of conversion, completely and unconditionally surrendering all his
human resources to the divine. And again Ulysses, sailing with the exclu-
sive guidance of human virtue and knowledge ("virtute e canoscenza"),
with all his stirring rhetoric, belongs to the same constellation of false star-
seekers.

Yet none of these powerful scenes discourages Dante from entrusting
his own journey to salvation to an irreducibly poetic itinerary. Centrally,
in the Statius episode, together with the concentration on poetry thence-
forward to the end of the *Purgatorio,* Dante emphasizes rather the contin-
uum between the human activity of "making" and the divine.[19] In this
conjunction, Dante shows himself willing to embrace the ancient pagan
cult of poetry and poet ("il nome che più dura e che più onora") as
attaining to immortality, sublating the ancient immortality of fame into
the eternal life of Christian resurrection. Although he has shown poetry,
its meaning and truth, to be historically determined in absolutely decisive
ways, he also sees it as leading beyond the temporal order, "a l'etterno
dal tempo."

This opening upon something infinite and immortal begins precisely
in the historical situatedness that characterizes the act and event of poetry.
Dante's exaltation of poetry as a way of communicating with divinity and
as a vehicle to immortality is no mere reiteration of the idealizing cli-
chés and self-deceptions he himself devastatingly critiques. Rather, in the
phenomenon of poetry he is contemplating the central mystery of the
Christian religion, the mystery of the Incarnation. This is the mystery of
a transcendent God existing as a historical man in order that humans
might again share in the divine life. The central motif of the Resurrec-
tion, of the body's rising up to life again, through its affirmation of the
necessarily and eternally incorporated nature of human life, is in fact a
corollary of the Incarnation. Both in this life and for the next, the making
and interpreting that poetry essentially is constitutes a historically con-
crete nexus between the human and the divine.

This connection becomes comprehensible only when we learn to
view poetry as interpretation and to understand interpretation herme-
neutically as an event involving humanity with its other, with what
utterly transcends it, ultimately, divinity. Poetry of the sublime sort trea-
ted here by Dante is not essentially only a human activity—although it

---

19. In a significant exception at the very end of the *cantica* (XXXIII. 85–90), helping to
maintain its balance, Beatrice reproves Dante's adherence to a "school" whose doctrine is as far
from the divine way as heaven is from the earth, echoing the topos from Isaiah (55.9) of humilia-
tion of all things human before God.

unmistakably takes up and includes the human, even as condemned, as in Virgil—so much as a participation in an event of the divine. This stupendous possibility is developed by Dante in the episodes involving poetry in the *Purgatorio* in the wake of the Statius cantos, signally, where he describes himself as one who writes poetry by taking dictation interiorly from an inspiring Love ("quando / Amor mi spira, noto"—XXIV. 52–53). Poetry's potential for vehiculating transcendence toward a specifically Christian divinity is implied in the Trinitarian underpinnings of the poetics Dante intimates in these famous verses defining his "dolce stil novo."[20] Since this is a lyric poetics, its full consideration belongs to a discussion of language as essentially lyrical in the *Paradiso,* to be undertaken separate cover.[21]

The openness of human, historical existence to transhistorical value, as in the classic as theorized by Gadamer, has been understood throughout literary and philosophical tradition in terms of the phenomenon of *poiēsis.* It is the nature of *poiēsis* to be open to transcendence. The making involved in poetry involves the agent in an event that transcends conscious control and the boundaries of the activity of an ego, making that very agent into something other, transcending the self through relation to what transcends it. This is the aspect of the ontology of "making" in art that has been explored by Gadamer, particularly under the rubric of "play." The game involves its players in the happening of an event that reaches beyond them, remaking them and bestowing on them an augmented being.

It is worth considering, then, how poetry becomes the specific preoccupation of the cantos immediately ensuing upon the climactic meeting with Statius and, more generally, how it becomes the pervasive theme of the second *cantica* all along its itinerary from time to eternity, punctuated as it is by the meetings with Dante's poetic progenitors. This leitmotif

20. The topic has been skillfully pursued by Mazzotta in *Dante. Poet of the Desert,* p. 192 ff, and by R. L. Martinez in "The Pilgrim's Answer to Bonagiunta and the Poetics of the Spirit," *Stanford Italian Review* 3 (1983): 37–63.

21. Without yet attempting to develop the *Commedia*'s positive implicit theory of transcendence of time through language, it is nonetheless possible at this stage to allude to the essential role that poetic language is destined to fulfill of bridging the gap of static, logical incompatibility between historical contingency and something eternal, transcendent, predestined from the foundation of the world. The truth revealed in and through time as Dante understands it is nevertheless a truth that transcends time. And in his applied, poetic reflection upon language as interpretation in the *Paradiso* he probes the conditions of interpretation that make possible such an apprehension, or rather happening, of a truth apprehended as itself transhistorical and even "eternal." From this point it becomes evident how it is specifically through poetic language that Dante strives to attain to eternity. This quest is to be followed out concretely in the sequel to this volume, under the title *The Veil of Eternity. Language and Transcendence in the Paradiso.*

emerges early on in the *Purgatorio* in scenes with the singer of Dante's own verses, Casella, in Canto II, and then the troubadour, Sordello, in Canto VI. But most importantly, the cantos following XXI and XXII, including Dante's encounters with nearly contemporary and earlier poets (Forese Donati, Bonagiunta da Lucca, Guido Guinizzeli, Arnaut Daniel), further develop the eloquent hint given in XXI–XXII about poetry's being a theological hermeneutic or vehicle of the divine Word.

The meeting with Forese among the penitent gluttons in Canto XXIII revises and redeems Dante's earlier, scarcely edifying exchange of insults, in the form of a scathing *tenzone,* with this poet and relative. Therewith it participates in the general purification of poetry under way throughout the *Purgatorio.* Dante first hears from the midst of the gluttonous the words, both wept and sung, *"Labïa mëa, Domine."* These words concentrate on personal possession of the external organ, namely, the lips, not only for this degrading sin but also for its purification by prayer. They exemplify poetry, moreover, specifically in the form of liturgy—and therefore of participation in divinity or in making God-like, an integral feature of Purgatory at every ascending stage. This quotation from Psalm 50 is apt to suggest, furthermore, how Dante's own lyric poetics can be seen in the end to converge upon sacred poetry. For the complete verset of the Vulgate that this incipit invokes—"Labia mea, Domine, aperies; et os meum anuntiabit laudem tuam"—alludes to the poetry of praise Dante discovered as the keynote for his *dolce stil novo.* In this praise style, Dante finds for his poetry "new and nobler matter than in the past" ("materia nuova e più nobile de la passata"—*Vita nuova* XVII).[22] Together with the meeting with Bonagiunta da Lucca in Canto XXIV, with its formulation of the religious inspiration of his poetry of love, as mentioned above, this makes up another important link in Dante's sacralization of his poetic vocation.

In a further step, the poetic genealogy through vernacular poets, particularly Guido Guinizzeli and Arnaut Daniel, in Canto XXVI, following Statius's explanation in XXV of the direct inspiration of the soul into the six-month-old fetus, helps to develop the analogy between God's creation of man and poetic creation (the inspiration of sense into the growing body of language). However, in order that it may be so glorified, secular love poetry must be purged of the lust that also motivates it by the punishment of these poetic progenitors in purgatorial flames on this last ledge of Purgatory. This then makes it possible to conceive, as in

---

22. Dante's "redemption" of his own love poetry in the *Purgatorio* is brought out through examination of the verbal microstructure of *Inferno* II and V in comparison with *Purgatorio* II and XXIII-XXVI, specifically with regard to their stilnovistic inflections, by Barolini in *Dante's Poets.*

Dante's poetry, the incarnation of divine love in history through the living language of the vernacular.

In Canto XXVII, Dante crosses into the earthly paradise, where nature and grace coalesce and where art, consequently, is effortless and redeemed. Here, in the "divina foresta," nature is divinized through art, as in the song of the birds, which has become a natural liturgy ("con piena letizia l'ore prime, / cantando"—XXVIII. 14–18). Moreover, in Canto XXIX Dante is regaled with the high artifice of an allegorical spectacle representing individually, with poetic fancy, the very books of the biblical revelation. Their iconic substitutes parade before him with the pomp of a triumph (the traditional pageant celebrating the return of a victorious general to Rome), thus fusing secular and sacred in poetic vision. In the concluding cantos (XXXII. 103–5, XXXIII. 52 ff) poetic allegory is finally expressly employed as the medium of divine prophecy in the visions Dante is commissioned to write down "in pro del mondo" ("on the world's behalf").

But first the theme of poetic representation as veiled theological revelation builds to a climax in the person of Beatrice, entering dramatically, "velato sotto l'angelica festa" ("veiled under the angelic festival"), in Canto XXX. 65. The progressive unveiling of her beauties begins here (especially in XXXI. 136–45) to be established as a metaphor for revelation—to be pursued throughout the *Paradiso*. Her advent supervening upon Virgil's disappearance from the scene,[23] trailing funereal strains (*"Manibus, oh, date lilia plenis"*—XXX. 21), shows love to be stronger than death in what is perhaps a more audacious troping of the meaning of a famous Virgilian text, that presaging Dido's doom ("Adnosco veteris vestigia flammae," translated in XXX. 48), even than those wrought by Statius. Out of a tradition bounded by death and damnation, poetry rises as revelatory of divine, immortal life. Beatrice, whose bodily death Dante's earlier love poetry lamented, now reappears as the embodiment of the personal resurrected Christ of his own life, as suggested by the liturgical tag *"Benedictus qui venis!"* (XXX. 19) that fetes her entrance.

These examples indicate Dante's pervasive concentration on how poetry achieves a specifically religious transcendence, programmatically in the Statius episode and with undiminishing intensity to the end of the *cantica*. The parallel endeavors of poetry and religion, of the disciplines of artistic refining and spiritual-moral cleansing, become one and the same thing in the redemptive event of the *Purgatorio*. Moreover, the

---

23. Exegesis of this passage, for example by Jeffrey Schnapp, in "Introduction to *Purgatorio*," in Rachel Jacoff, ed., *The Cambridge Companion to Dante*, recalls that what in Virgil were the funerary flowers of Marcellus "are now revealed as the eternal lilies of the Virgin Mary: flowers which signify not meaningless loss, but the resurrection of the dead for all eternity" (p. 204).

theme of poetry's redemptive power reflects specularly upon the redemption in act in Dante's poetry itself, highlighting that ontological and performative dimension, beyond the merely representational, that has been insisted upon throughout this study as crucial to the project of the *Commedia* and its "originality."

The *Purgatorio* shows quite emphatically the way in which the knowledge even of divine revelation is the effect of history. Centrally, in the Statius cantos, the consciousness of Christian faith, which lies at the heart of the work, is analyzed in terms of pagan tradition as the historical ground on which the experience of conversion "rises"—the whole *cantica* being resurrectional in tenor and conception, verbally keyed to variegated inflections of "surto," starting from *Purgatorio* I. 7: "la morta poesì resurga" ("let dead poetry rise up"). Dante's creation of Statius recognizes the necessary continuity of Christian life with the life of the past deposited in tradition, but at the same time reveals its deeply mysterious coinciding with a new, "eternal" life that transcends all that is merely past.

In retrospect, the resurrection of pagan tradition through its incorporation into the truth of Christian revelation can be seen to have been programmed into the *Purgatorio* from its very first canto. To open this *cantica* and realm, Dante invokes Calliope to rise up among the now "sacred Muses" ("e qui Calliopè alquanto surga"—I. 9). In doing so, he also alludes indirectly (through reference to the Pierides) to her song about Persephone's cyclical death and rebirth in Ovid's *Metamorphoses* V. And the first person he encounters here, in the shape of Cato, represents the rebirth of a now baptized and sanctified paganism. This paragon of pagan virtue, who died famously and freely at Utica, left there "the garment that on the great day will be so bright" ("la vesta ch'al gran dì sarà sì chiara"—I. 75). With this assurance of his eventual bodily resurrection to glory, Cato appears in the realm of Christian salvation transformed into a patriarchal figure, a Roman Moses.

In like manner, the whole second realm ("il secondo regno"—I. 4), that of Purgatory, is presented from the outset as a revival of pagan Rome now resurrected and redeemed. The patron goddess and mother of the imperial dynasty descended from Aeneas glows over the opening scene just before dawn. In so appearing, Venus not only anticipates the sun, a pagan divinity whose rising course Dante and Virgil are directed to follow on their ascent toward true divinity. She also veils Pisces (I. 21), a symbol in primeval Christianity for *Iesus Christus,* the initials of whose name abbreviate the Greek word "ichthys" for fish. Of course, "the lovely planet" ("lo bel pianeto"—I. 19) also adumbrates Dante's love, Beatrice, who is to appear at the climax of the *cantica,* Christlike at the center of its revelations. She, unlike his own Marcia, condemned to Limbo and seeming to represent the inevitable sacrificial exclusion in this economy of redemption of the pagan, is honored by Cato.[24]

At this point, we have followed the first two of three stages of reflection on a divine hermeneutic (or hermeneutic of the divine) built into Dante's poem. A rupturing of the aesthetic-mimetic, or mythic, surface of art—the veil—was seen to be the upshot of the hermeneutic injunction in *Inferno* IX. Undisguised as aesthetic illusion, the poem was brought into intrinsic relation with historical existence through its narrative temporality's being grafted onto the temporality of the existence of its reader. Once it is exposed in this way as an event rooted in existence and history, a hermeneutic perspective on all its representations as interpretive and historical in nature is expressly opened for understanding the poem. What is remarkable about Dante's poem is the extent to which this historical and interpretive consciousness has been incorporated into the work itself.

If the *Inferno* shows the necessity of transcendence breaking into time conceived as a closed circle of fate—the endless cycle of repetition the damned are condemned to and what St. Augustine proposed as the shape of history for pagans, deprived of the Incarnation; and if the *Purgatorio* illustrates how religious revelation is actually constructed in and across time, poetically, and is realized through the historically conditioned unfolding of tradition; then the *Paradiso* completes this journey of poetic, historical, and theological interpretation by the transcendence of time through language toward the vision of divinity.

2. HERMENEUTICS, HISTORICITY, AND SUPRAHISTORICAL TRUTH

In the Statius cantos, as we have seen, Dante underscores how the Christian truth of Virgil's text—at least insofar as the latter can be disclosed as messianic—is actually produced by an event distant in time and especially in culture, not to mention in inspiration, from the original production of the text. This emphasis, in effect, acknowledges that the truth in question is of the nature of an event, ineradicably determined by time. Today we would willingly take this to mean, furthermore, that there is no truth inherent in Virgil's text, especially none of the kind Dante elicits from it, and consequently conclude that there is no preestablished truth standing ready for the disclosure that comes to Statius when he under-

---

24. These and other suggestions concerning *Purgatorio* I are further pursued by Victor Turner in "African Ritual and Western Literature: Is a Comparative Symbology Possible?" in *Blazing the Trail: Way Marks in the Exploration of Symbols,* ed. Edith Turner (Tucson and London: University of Arizona Press, 1992).

stands himself in terms of Virgil's texts. This would be, supposedly, to do away with any metaphysical ghosts lurking behind the event itself in its sheer contingency, producing an "effect of truth," as a certain postmodern critique puts it.

Even hermeneutic thinkers, who still wish to allow for a genuine experience of truth in art, philosophy, and other humanistic disciplines, agree at least that any truth that is disclosed must necessarily be changing and time-bound, even though they may also concede that it is problematic how this can be compatible with "truth." The consensus against claims to a truth that is transcendent with respect to time and history, widely shared among hermeneutic thinkers today, is voiced, for example, by Jean Grondin, in a statement purporting to define a norm for "philosophical hermeneutics": "Philosophical hermeneutics holds that the pretension to a timeless truth springs directly from a denial of one's own temporal character." Metaphysics and its aspiration to timeless truth is precisely what hermeneutics at first overcomes or leaves behind: "Die philosophische Hermeneutik lässt sich zunächst die metaphysische Obsession des Überzeitlichen." [25]

In concert with this view, across a wide spectrum of disciplines and intellectual constituencies today it has become virtually a dogma of modern hermeneutic theory that there can be no such thing as transcendent or timeless truth. The "revelation" of the historical conditionedness of all thinking and claims to knowledge is taken as tantamount to the demise of all transcendental notions and of every way of thinking that forgets or denies or abstracts from the contingent, perspectival, history-bound occurring of any cognition whatever. This line of argument has been continuously asserted in philosophy at least since its clamorous, if belated, inauguration in Nietzsche's "death of God" pronouncement.

But this exclusion of suprahistorical, metaphysical truth does not necessarily belong to the hermeneutic phenomenon as such. Rather, it expresses, parochially, the spirit of the modern age, secular and earthbound. The energies of hermeneutic activity over the vast arc of human experience, as recorded, for example, in myth and ritual, have bulked largely in the direction of discerning what has been understood to be divine truth or revealment manifesting itself in the sublunar sphere. This direction was ambiguously present in Heidegger's hermeneutic thought, too, increasing in intensity in the later Heidegger in the interrogation of a disclosure enfolding gods and mortals.[26] And Gadamer himself, to whom

25. Jean Grondin, *Einführung in die philosophische Hermeneutik*, p. 15. Even theological thinkers like David Klemm typically concur that in hermeneutics "understanding does not purport to reach transtemporal truth." *Hermeneutical Inquiry*, vol. 2 (Atlanta: Scholars Press, 1986), p. 2.

26. The term "hermeneutic" is largely silenced in the later Heidegger. But in "Aus einem Gespräch von der Sprache: Zwischen einem Japaner und einem Fragenden," in *Unterwegs zur*

"philosophical hermeneutics" professes allegiance, expressly leaves open
the possibility of a "suprahistorical 'sacred' time" ("überzeitliche 'heile'
Zeit"—*Truth and Method*, p. 122) such as Dante's work strives to let hap-
pen, as well as probing the possibilities of such transhistorical phenomena
as the beautiful and the classical.

Dante represents the putative truths of Christian faith as revealed in a
timely way that makes unique interpretive events belong intrinsically to
these truths. Nevertheless, Dante still vindicates the Christian truth as
transcendent, as beyond historical contingency; he propounds it in a lan-
guage of the eternal: "la *vera* credenza, seminata / per li messaggi de l'et-
terno regno" ("the *true* faith sown / by messages of the *eternal* kingdom").
Dante fully embraces the historicity of truth and at the same time its
transcendence. In doing so he participates in what Christian tradition un-
derstands as the revelation of God incarnate. The resources of hermeneu-
tics, as discovered anew through Dante's poetry, have helped us to think
through, and especially to apprehend poetically, the possibility of such a
paradox. We have seen, and must now reflect on, how Dante's treatment
of the problem opens perspectives and possibilities for hermeneutic think-
ing that today are by and large overlooked or even ruled out as impos-
sible a priori, in what often amounts to a form of intellectual coercion
not to think "the eternal."[27]

Thinking the eternal proves difficult for hermeneutic thinkers because
the language of the eternal seems necessarily to presuppose some sort of
preconstituted truth that at certain opportune junctures in history can
come to be known for what it in any case *is* apart from historical happen-
ings; this would seem, moreover, to fall short of the Heideggerian insight
into truth as alētheic, as nothing but the happening of a disclosedness of
beings.[28] But the difference between this "alētheic" conception and a
rhetoric of preconstituted truth—what is often taken as some kind of
ultimate, "substantive" difference—is actually without decisive impor-
tance once we are no longer trying literally to say what truth is, but
instead are simply letting it happen, via the cooperation of *poiēsis,* in its
own time and way. Truth is discovered in a timely fashion, but when it
happens, the way the experience of truth is represented or objectified
might just as well reify it, since no statement can do otherwise. What is

Sprache, it is hinted that the term drops out of use because it designates what slips into name-
lessness and so coincides with the unnameable essential source of appearing, which all Heideg-
ger's thought is about. See especially pp. 121–23.

27. Even Ricoeur brackets the question in *Temps et récit* 1 (Paris: Seuil, 1983), pp. 19–20.

28. To quote once again from "The Origin of the Work of Art": "But truth does not exist
in itself beforehand, somewhere among the stars, only to descend later among beings. This is
impossible for the reason alone that it is after all only the openness of beings that first affords
the possibility of a somewhere and of a place filled by present beings" (p. 61).

important is not that the statement tell the truth about truth—as if that, as opposed to speaking from within the truth, were even possible—but that it feed back into the experience of interpreting truth, helping to make the condition of openness to, and of the letting happen of, truth freshly possible. This end might more effectively be served by reactualization, as in ritual, of community-constituting memories and beliefs or even by the reiteration of foundational insights formulated as dogma than by howsoever exacting philosophical ratiocination. To think truth definitively as "event" or "happening" is still to confine it within the metaphysics of a concept, a concept perhaps with certain advantages but also representing a certain loss or impoverishment with respect to the concept of the eternal.

Indeed, only if we, quite erroneously, take "historicity" as some positive object of knowledge is it exclusive of eternity and transcendence. Understood dynamically as precisely what always remains ungraspable because inhabited by flux—and, as Dante has concretely shown, by the dynamism of interpretation itself—precisely historicity becomes the key to recognizing how truth is disclosed as what transcends the historical occasions of its own disclosure. Have we ever definitely understood the nature of this radical openness and indeterminacy that inescapably characterizes all our experience and our very existence? Certainly not by fixing a label such as "historicity" to it, in however modest a mood and illusion-wary a way the notion may be defined. After all, what is "historicity"? What is "event"? The very terms of hermeneutic philosophy are not self-evident; their intelligibility is itself circumscribed by an event in which they are employed and alone can occur intelligibly. It is no good one-sidedly emphasizing "Geschichtlichkeit" (historicity)—though this may give us the feeling that we have discovered the right orientation to living as earthly beings, unlike those metaphysics-beclouded medievals—for "Geschichtlichkeit" as some sort of essential property is no more intelligible per se than "the eternal." Indeed, we cannot but suspect that the one, as it turns out, is always already thought in and through the other.

What hermeneutic thought has to try to think is historicity *as* transcendence. It is precisely the historical, time-conditioned event-character of human existence that opens it toward what cannot be determined as merely worldly or historical. In its ineradicably temporal constitution, human existence is constantly transcending itself and every achieved, objective form of existence within the world. The radical experience of this historicity has always been fraught with the paradox that what is encountered within the eye of the tornado of constant flux is apprehended and articulated as the very opposite of flux, and has been described throughout Christian and other traditions as the "eternal." This

is the experience of the still point of the turning world. It is often charac-
terized as "the mystical."[29] Frequently, proponents of hermeneutics de-
clare the complete independence of hermeneutics from anything mysti-
cal in nature. But this forced circumscription cuts hermeneutics off from
certain of the deep springs of meaning in human experience, the inter-
pretation of which is thereby regrettably impoverished and constricted.

The ground-breaking insight into the historicity of our knowing,
when formulated as a proposition and advocated as the general principle
of hermeneutic thought, betrays this very insight. It becomes closed to
instances of suprahistorical knowledge such as metaphysics and religious
revelation purport to realize and ends up legislating against all claims of
"transcendence," whereas its own purpose, in accordance with its radical
motivations, rather must be to understand the sense that such claims can
have—that is, the sense they have had and do have historically for vast
segments of humanity, understood together with and through the mean-
ing they can have for the interpreter who asks this question.

Thus the first obvious problem with too one-sidedly embracing her-
meneutics as ushering in the good news of a definitive break with "any
'transcendental' standpoint beyond historical consciousness" (Donald
Marshall, "Truth, Tradition, and Understanding") is that it is also charac-
teristic of hermeneutic thinking to engage in genuine, self-questioning
dialogue with all other points of view. Even in emphasizing the historical
nature of all culture and understanding, hermeneutics must nevertheless
still consider claims to transhistorical or transcendent knowledge about,
for example, the "other" world of religious discourses, which have been
and are in fact advanced historically. To reduce any form of culture or
thought to preconceived "historical" terms while inevitably taking one's
own notion of history as positively given would be to traduce the herme-
neutic ethos. However often hermeneutic thinking has hit upon and
rested with that term "historicity," the term itself must remain open to
being historically defined. For this reason, hermeneutics cannot even de-
fine itself so as to exclude openness to any form of transcendent knowl-
edge or revelation. All it can establish in advance, in accordance with its
own guiding rule and spirit, is that it will approach such claims out of its
own historically grounded and specific experience, given its understand-
ing of what "historical" means in the present tense and tension of its
own thinking.

Rather than taking "historicity" as a new fixing of the real status of
all possible knowledge in the human situation, anticipating with this con-
cept a priori all the possibilities that will ever be confronted, the term

29. For example, in the concluding paragraphs, on "das Mystische" (6.45, 6.522; cf.
6.4311), of Wittgenstein's *Tractatus Logico-Philosophicus* (London: Routledge, 1922).

can and deserves to be interpreted with the emphasis on the historical character of existence as a continual transcending of itself toward what exceeds it. Historicity as the self-transcending, open structure of human, temporal existence is what estranges every objective order of the world, including history itself. History as a fixed order of events within the past is upset by historicity, which entails the openness of the event of history and therefore resists all definitive ordering.

Not the objective order of things always and ever the same as themselves for a subject, but the unattainability, the unfixability of things for an existing knower immersed in historical flux, always arriving on the scene too late to find things except as always already there, is what is expressed most immediately in acknowledging or conceptualizing a givenness and an order of things as "eternal." For precisely in realizing the constantly self-transcending character of historical existence, what has been experienced is the miraculous givenness of beings and of an order or gathering beyond all objective, worldly, historical experience. What comes here to experience (and to language) is the openness and the transcending inherent in and subtending historicity, the miraculous givenness of things in their relatedness even beyond the limits of all historically imposed orders of objects (indeed, as their enabling condition). This is what so often has been called "eternal."

Most all of Heidegger's energy concentrated on truth as immanent in the coming to pass of beings—and as nothing else.[30] To make his point— that truth *is* only as transpiring in time (in some sense a restatement of the insight that truth is revealed only as incarnate in history)—he felt compelled to deny any possibility of transcendent or eternal truth—truth "somewhere in the stars." This seemed necessary in order to focus attention on truth as really and truly happening in the event of disclosedness of beings. For if he let truth be something preconstituted in a Platonic heaven, then all that happens historically, it seemed, could at best be only an appearance, expression, annunciation, and so on, of it. But this is not actually so, no matter how naturally the denial of preconstituted truth is attracted to the affirmation of the eventhood of truth as a way of apprehending and driving home the latter conception. Once the "truth" of the eventhood of truth has been firmly grasped and established, we are ready to look into it a little further and see its own internal insecurity and instability. The possibility that truth may indeed exist somewhere in the heavens from all eternity may then be seen to emerge from the phenomenon of the event of truth itself, and, indeed, just this possibility

---

30. George Steiner has emphasized Heidegger's attempt to articulate "an ontology of pure immanence" and its ultimate, inevitable failure in *Martin Heidegger* (Chicago: University of Chicago Press, 1989), p. xviii.

has been passionately envisaged by poets and thinkers from the dawn of virtually every known civilization. This is a further step that hermeneutic theory in modern and postmodern times has rarely had the lucidity and resoluteness to take. It is true that it opens a door to intractable dogmatisms—but this, too, more than ever in an era of the return of religious fundamentalisms, needs to be understood in its genuine possibility, rather than being alienated as incomprehensible, unintelligent behavior.

What is absolutely astonishing is that the early Church did have the lucidity and resoluteness to proclaim, as at Chalcedon in 453, that Jesus Christ, its Truth, was unequivocally a historical man and yet also fully God eternal. It could hardly have made any harder sense. Predictably, heresies continued to proliferate. But somehow, through it all, the absolute paradox of the Incarnation—which complements the numerical paradox of the Trinity—was preserved in the experience of faith. The Christian revelation had embraced the historicity of truth together with its eternity. It proclaimed that truly God had come into history and become human. And although by the schemata of the imagination that come to be called "logic" this precluded the divinity's being an eternal being, that too was nevertheless uncompromisingly affirmed as true—known at an existential level, by faith, with respect to which formalizable logic is superficial.

Even purely philosophical hermeneutics has never ceased to interrogate itself about the possible or necessary universality of truth in the wake of the full disclosure of its ineluctable historicity. Any effort to communicate with others—other countries, cultures, languages—presupposes that insight generated in one specific historical situation may also be valid for others, in their diverse situations, outside that original context. Thus any such effort is predicated on a belief that thought is not reducible to the historical conditions under which it is formed, but can reach out and meet and connect with alien contexts and conditions. This degree of universality of the truth formulated under specific circumstances, and the transcendence of those circumstances that communicability implies, suggests the basic hermeneutic experience that contemporary theorists feel the need to be able to account for and that work such as Dante's validates in terms of a full-blown theology of interpretation.

Grondin's recent Gadamerian presentation of philosophical hermeneutics identifies as the central problem of philosophy since Hegel the problem of how truth in any universal or binding sense is compatible with historicity: "Its problem is the question concerning the possibility of a binding truth (einer verbindlichen Wahrheit) and therewith of a conclusive philosophy within the horizon of a self-consciously historical world. Are all truths or moral principles dependent on their historical context?" (Einführung in die philosophische Hermeneutik, p. 14). The specter of historical relativism and even of "historichen Nihilismus" poses a skeptical challenge that "philosophical hermeneutics," as represented by Grondin, deems itself called into the lists to meet. What has become clear through our study of Dante's hermeneutic practice, as exemplary of a vast tradition's, is how the problem of a communicable and *binding* truth is best understood in terms of responding to what we are responsible to, and how this means in the last instance to someone who addresses us.

The decisive test of one's hermeneutic openness, of the relinquishing of one's securities in the submission to time and change in human existence, is the readiness to be spoken to by an other. Finding oneself face to face with a divinity who commands and disposes one is discovered in the Bible as the ultimate hermeneutic experience of human beings and their communities. Old Testament religion is an especially rich resource for studying this primordial hermeneutic disposition to "hear God."[31] All types of human rites and religious obeisance, as forms of controlled submission to time and contingency, have in general stemmed from this—recognizing the divine power and its claims upon humans.

The aim of the hermeneutic quest, accordingly, can normally be defined as that of encountering otherness. This holds even for the renegade, poststructuralist hermeneutics like deconstruction. In fact, rather ironically, "otherness" has taken on an aura of holiness in the discourse of deconstruction. But, to those who are willing to believe, it seems that no demarche of openness to the other, except maybe those of other world religions, comes so close to realizing this goal as the Judeo-Christian tradition, centered on an encounter with "the living God" who disposes all subjects antecedently to their conception of him or even of themselves.

Western humanity learned the meaning of its historicity first and foremost from the Bible. This book is written out of the heart-rending historical experience of a people repeatedly subjugated, bearing in the acutest degree the suffering and "negativity" of all genuine experience, according to the Gadamerian/Hegelian definition (*Truth and Method,* p. 353 ff). The fact that this tradition also tenders a revelation of eternity is the more marvelous. Fixing and dictating the contents of this revelation for historically distinct peoples is excluded by the very logic of the present argument. But openness to transcendence of one's own time-bound experience, as illustrated exemplarily by Dante, has shown itself to be a possibility that can be embraced.

It belongs to the argument of the present book to suggest that if mo-

---

31. See, for example, Gerhard von Rad, *Theologie des Alten Testaments* (Munich: Kaiser, 1965–66).

dernity can learn a greater hermeneutic openness in this direction it can unlearn some of its precious, hard-earned cynicism, compounded of philosophical skepticism, ideological suspiciousness, and closed-mindedness when not downright deadness toward the "spiritual," which even in the midst of its breakthroughs can suffocate and imprison it. All this partakes in illusion, too, as does everything human, hermeneutically considered. For, as Dante so compellingly teaches, it is in being surpassed that any human cognition whatever furthers the journey toward truth.

A New Hermeneutic Horizon for Religious Revelation in Poetic Literature?

*T*his project opened on a wager that hermeneutic thought and Dante owed each other a lot, though the reciprocal debt had perhaps not been fully realized, nor certainly exploited. What are the returns, in sum, on the account that was opened by this wager and on the two-fold investment it entailed? What insights of hermeneutic thought, medieval or modern, have lent an enriched fund of intelligibility and challenge to the *Commedia* and perhaps profited in turn by the transaction?

Medieval theories of interpretation per se have not been extensively dealt with in this study, for by and large they are instrumental to the exegetical task and do not explicitly pursue the speculative implications of the phenomenon of interpretation. Speculative insight into how interpretation constitutes reality as it can be humanly experienced is, however, powerfully active in certain strains of metaphysical thinking (for example, in debates over speculative grammar in the thirteenth and fourteenth centuries[1]) and operates especially vigorously, as has been the argument of this book, in Dante's poetic praxis of address to the reader.

That truth or the disclosure of reality, and this for Dante includes the ultimate eschatological reality of Christian belief, should take the form of an event that intrinsically involves the one to whom the disclosure is made, that is, the interpreter or reader, is a thesis—the mainspring of speculative hermeneutics—that receives constant confirmation and conspicuous application throughout Dante's poem. The exposure of structures of interpretive involvement permeates the work and its styles in more, and more subtle, ways than can be exhaustively examined. The poet's personal involvement in all that his poem discloses and the

---

1. An orientation to this literature can be obtained from Jan Pinborg, "Die Logik der Modistae," in *Medieval Semantics: Selected Studies on Medieval Logic and Grammar*, ed. S. Ebbesen (London: Variorum, 1984), and from R. H. Robins, *Ancient and Medieval Grammatical Theory in Europe with Particular Reference to Modern Linguistic Doctrine* (London: Bell, 1951). See, further, Gian Carlo Alessio, "La grammatica speculativa e Dante," in *Letture classensi* 13 (1984): 69–88.

inscription of the reader and of the event of reading into the text of the poem—both macroscopically in the structure of direct address and in filigrain in various forms of continuous implicit address, as well as in a generally diffused presentation of objective states of souls as modalities of their own self-understanding—mark and achieve what is a thorough-going hermeneutic understanding of reality as itself an event of understanding.

That any revelation of truth or event of understanding should be an event of someone who understands, and that interpretation is internal to this event rather than working on any sort of object from the outside, is the common principle that animates Dante's work and hermeneutic thought alike, appropriating them to one another. Dante's poem compellingly demonstrates this self-reflexive structure of mutual implication between truth and understanding. This is particularly brought out by the poem's hermeneutic imperatives, the addresses, as specularly doubling the protagonist's interpretive predicament back upon the reader's, with which it is discovered to coincide. By this means, Dante impressively realizes the participatory potential of poetry to render theological revelation effective in personal experience and in history.

In ways examined in this study, the *Commedia* works out our being within our world and reality rather than outside and over against it taken as object. Moreover, we have seen that this makes it possible for the things in the world and even and especially our own artifacts, our "poiē-mata," so to speak, to become vehicles of a word that addresses us, in a way they could not when they were limited to being objects within our epistemological framework, as has been the prevailing way of treating them in modern times obsessed by the powers and possibilities of technological control. For what speaks, means, intends, addresses can no longer be grasped as any objectified entity: all objects are translated into the infinity of the medium, language, which itself in turn must not be objectified and totalized as "all there is," but rather should be let be as on the way to what transcends it. Thus we are not led inevitably to the conclusion, merely because it is never possible to present in positive, objective form a subject who is speaking, that therefore the phenomenon of address is nothing but illusion. Rather, it is only consistent with full cognizance of the finiteness of our knowledge to allow whatever might answer to the notion of author or source of the address to recede to a position of transcendence.

Communicating takes a little faith, even though the fashion of doubting all that cannot be positively demonstrated all too often still passes for intellectual rigor in our secularly minded culture. The hermeneutic point of view takes all the positive objects of our knowledge as nothing but mediations, and yet leaves open the possibility—arguably the necessary possibility—of their reference to transcendent being.[2]

We can opt for a "demystified" view that would dissolve subjectivity, along with all such purported realities, like divinity, that are not objectively given in experience, as so many metaphysical illusions. This, however, involves maintaining dogmatically that the effects of subjectivity, or the faith in a transcendent God, have no ultimate ground or referent just because any object that can ever be positively presented is already within the mediations of hermeneutics and therefore not graspable as an independent principle or self-sufficient subject. But to say on this basis that there can be no metaphysical entities is to take the mediations not *as* mediations but as the real thing, the only thing there is, which is once again to betray the very insight that hermeneutics has fostered. It is to forget or neglect the hermeneutic distance that makes our dealings have to do most directly with things that are defined and rendered objects of knowledge and discourse by being defined and known, and that therefore are mediations rather than "things themselves." Rejection of the possibility of a transcendent truth and world simply translates the world of appearances into a real world come back to haunt us, even while it triumphantly announces an end to the shadowy "other" world of metaphysics.[3] It has forgotten the point of the language of the other world's coming into being in the first place as a sign of the structure of understanding as always unable to fully objectify what it understands, including itself.

Alternatively, we can let subjectivity float free, above and beyond all its positive instances, such as in "man," and allow that these may be partial images of a possible true Subject. That such a Being should reveal itself through the world's religions or specifically as the Trinity or the Incarnate Son is not impossible. It can even become an absolutely compelling form for symbolizing the mystery of transcendence built into the hermeneutic nature of our experience. Conviction becomes possible only from within

2. A point of view with strong affinities to the one developed here is argued for by George Steiner in *Real Presences* (Chicago: University of Chicago Press, 1989). Steiner underscores the "tenor of trust which underlies, which literally underwrites the linguistic-discursive substance of our Western, Hebraic-Attic experience" (p. 89). Steiner's overarching thesis, "that any coherent understanding of what language is and how language performs, that any coherent account of the capacity of human speech to communicate meaning and feeling is, in the final analysis, underwritten by the assumption of God's presence" (p. 3), which he illustrates in wide-ranging and eclectic ways, is supported by my essay through a concentrated revisiting of one crucial juncture in our cultural heritage.

3. Cf. Nietzsche, *Ecce Homo* (sec. 2), trans. W. Kaufman: " 'The true world and the apparent world'—that means: the mendaciously invented world and reality." *On the Genealogy of Morals and Ecce Homo* (New York: Random House, 1966).

the specific historical mediations in which one finds oneself involved (and in which one first finds oneself), and Dante's poem demonstrates the crucial role poetry can assume in mediating such a revelation. In this, Dante is only continuing to develop a poeticality intrinsic to the religious revelation of the Bible.

The hermeneutic outlook, far from having been invented toward the turn of the eighteenth century, is one of the perennial orientations of philosophy and of the experience of reality in general. It was discovered by Heidegger in the Greeks, for whom the world was not an object but an opening, the Open ("die Lichtung"), in which "man" found himself disclosed together with his world.[4] But even more pertinent to Dante's hermeneutic consciousness is the historical and relational understanding of human existence in the Bible. Knowing in the Bible is above all a being involved with. Knowledge of God and God's knowing his people cannot be prescinded from the covenant and commitment, personal and communal, that bind the parties together in a relationship.

This direct dependence of all we know and believe on what we are comes to articulation even in the untheoretical texts on which Christianity is founded. That the knowledge of God is bound up with an ontological condition is stated more or less explicitly throughout the New Testament, perhaps nowhere more suggestively than in John's words: "[I]t doth not yet appear what we shall be: but we know that, when he shall appear, we shall be like him; for we shall see him as he is" (1 John 3.2). Being like God and knowing him truly are inseparable. John measures the degree of a person's knowledge by the quality of his being, so that being and its modes become the criterion of genuine knowing: "He that loveth not, knoweth not God; for God is love" (1 John 4.8). The rationally baffling formula "God is love" becomes more understandable when we consider that God's being can be known to us only through our own possibilities of being, among which Christians recognize love as the highest. St. John's grasp of the unity of being and knowing is so simple and clairvoyant that there is simply no theoretical problem for him; he blends the orders of being and knowing together unproblematically, again, for example, in accusing of hypocrisy those who claim to have fellowship with God yet walk in darkness "and do not the truth" (1 John 1.6).[5]

4. See, for example, Heidegger, "The End of Philosophy and the Task of Thinking," in *Basic Writings*, pp. 373–92; originally published in *Zur Sache des Denkens* (Tübingen: Max Niemeyer Verlag, 1969), pp. 61–80.

5. This insight into genuine knowing as a doing has a counterpart in contemporary hermeneutic philosophy that has been worked out especially in connection with pragmatism and Aristotelian "phronesis." See, for example, Gadamer, *The Idea of the Good in Platonic-Aristotelian Philosophy*, trans. P. C. Smith (New Haven: Yale University Press, 1986).

At stake in the problem of hermeneutics is the possibility of communication and of a revelation of meaning or truth, not only among human beings but also primordially of and from God as what transcends them, or from Being as such. The Christian religion responds to this problem fundamentally through the idea of Incarnation, and Dante incorporates the logic of this idea as a light of understanding in his work as poet and prophet. We have seen how Dante's poem works incarnationally to reveal its truth in the lives of those who can embody it, the readers, and in the history of interpretations of Christian revelation. Inextricably connected with the notion of Incarnation is the other great doctrine of the Christian religion, that of the Trinity. The second and final part of this meditation on the hermeneutic logic or theo-logic of the *Commedia* will bring out the self-reflexive structures of Dante's poetry, particularly that of the *Paradiso,* that incorporate a dynamic of self-transcending. It will explore how the self-reflexive verbal structures that characterize poetry, especially lyric, become at the same time a reflection of a divine transcendence. Whereas for postmodernity, self-reflexivity has become a structure of self-enclosure upon the self in its intricate self-deceptiveness and ultimate emptiness, for Dante and his culture self-reflexivity could also, and more profoundly, be understood as the reflection of transcendence, even as the image of a Trinitarian divinity.[6]

The theory of interpretation here argued for by the freeing of key insights, rather than in any exhaustive, systematic fashion, can be unveiled in its subtleties only as evoked by the minute inflections of the poetry as it does its work of interpreting, projecting speculative horizons of a suggestiveness and complexity beyond the capacity of theoretical statements to articulate. The present labor of searching out the broad horizons of the interpretive phenomenon of religious truth in poetic literature hopefully has made us more ready and able to take in what the poetry itself reveals about this truth in its effectual working. Thus it may be possible to light upon the significant nuances of the poetry that can make a work like the *Divine Comedy* happen for us in the power of its truth as an event of religious revelation.

6. Thus a program for reading the *Commedia* as a whole in relation to the speculative questions of hermeneutics will have been outlined by the present work together with this sequel. It may be seen in preview as moving from the individuation of the constitutive role of the reader in the *Inferno,* and from the historicity of interpretation in *Purgatorio,* as exemplified by Statius, to the problematic of language and transcendence in the *Paradiso,* focusing especially on the heaven of Jupiter. Dante's poetic odyssey and hermeneutic theory alike (as later Heidegger and part 3 of *Truth and Method*—"Linguistic Ontology"—both attest) culminate in reflections on language and its possibilities for reflecting totality and disclosing truth.

Core Bibliography of
Recurrently Cited Sources

Alighieri, Dante. *La Commedia secondo l'antica vulgata.* Ed. G. Petrocchi. 4 vols. Società Dantesca Italiana. Milan: Mondadori, 1966–67.

————. *Convivio.* Ed. C. Vasoli. Vol. 5, bk. 1, pt. 2 of *Opere minori.* Milan: Ricciardi, 1988.

————. *De vulgari eloquentia. Epistole.* Ed. Pier Vincenzo Mengaldo et al. Vol. 5, bk. 2 of *Opere minori.* Milan: Ricciardi, 1973.

————. *Vita nuova.* Ed. D. De Robertis. Vol. 5, bk. 1, pt. 1 of *Opere minori.* Milan-Naples: Ricciardi, 1979.

Augustine. *St. Augustine's Confessions.* 2 vols. Loeb Classical Library. Cambridge: Harvard University Press, 1912.

————. *De doctrina christiana libri quattuor.* Ed. Guilelmus M. Green. Corpus Scriptorum ecclesiasticorum, vol. 80. Vindobonac: Hoelder-Pichler Tempsky, 1963.

Auerbach, Erich. "Dante's Addresses to the Reader." *Romance Philology* 7 (1953–54): 268–79.

————. *Dante als Dichter der irdischen Welt.* Berlin: Walter de Gruyter, 1929. Trans. Ralph Manheim under the title *Dante: Poet of the Secular World* (Chicago: University of Chicago Press, 1961).

————. "Figura." In *Neue Dante-studien.* Istanbul, 1944. Trans. R. Manheim under the title *Scenes from the Drama of European Literature, Six Essays* (New York: Meridian, 1959).

Barański, Zygmunt. "La lezione esegetica di *Inferno* I: Allegoria, storia e letteratura nella *Commedia.*" In *Dante e le forme dell'allegoresi.* Ed. M. Picone. Ravenna: Longo, 1987.

Barolini, Teodolinda. *Dante's Poets: Textuality and Truth in the* Comedy. Princeton: Princeton University Press, 1984.

————. "Detheologizing Dante. For a 'New Formalism' in Dante Studies." *Quaderni d'italianistica* 10 (1988): 35–53.

————. *The Undivine Comedy: Detheologizing Dante.* Princeton: Princeton University Press, 1993.

Bori, Cesare. *L'interpretazione infinita: L'ermeneutica cristiana antica e le sue trasformazioni.* Bologna: il Mulino, 1987.

Bultmann, Rudolph. *New Testament & Mythology and Other Writings.* Ed. S. M. Ogden. Philadelphia: Fortress Press, 1984.

Caputo, John. *Radical Hermeneutics: Repetition, Deconstruction and the Hermeneutic Project.* Bloomington: Indiana University Press, 1987.

Caesar, Michael. *Dante: The Critical Heritage. c. 1314(?)–c. 1870.* New York: Rutledge, 1989.

Cecchetti, Giovanni. "The Statius Episode: Observations on Dante's Conception of Poetry." *Lectura Dantis* 7 (1990).

Charity, A. C. *Events and Their Afterlife: A Dialectics of Christian Typology in the Bible and in Dante.* London: Cambridge University Press, 1966.

Contini, Gianfranco. "Dante come personaggio-poeta della *Commedia*." In *Varianti e altra linguistica: Una raccolta di saggi (1938–68).* Turin: Einaudi, 1970.

Culler, Jonathan. "Apostrophe." *diacritics* 7 (1977): 59–69.

Curtius, Ernst Robert. *Europäische Literatur und lateinisches Mittelalter.* Bern: A. Francke, 1948. Trans. W. Trask under the title *European Literature and the Latin Middle Ages* (New York: Bollingen, 1952).

De Sanctis, Francesco. *Lezioni sulla* Divina Commedia. Ed. Michele Manfredi. Bari: Laterza, 1955.

Dragonetti, Roger. *Aux frontières du langage poétique.* Ghent: Romanica Gandensia, 1961.

Ebeling, Gerhard. *Wort und Glaube.* 3 vols. Tübingen: J. C. B. Mohr, 1960–75. Trans. J. Leitch under the titles *Word and Faith* (Philadelphia: Fortress, 1963) and *God and Word* (Philadelphia: Fortress, 1967).

Freccero, John. *Dante: The Poetics of Conversion.* Ed. Rachel Jacoff. Cambridge: Harvard University Press, 1986.

Funk, Robert W. *Language, Hermeneutic, and the Word of God: The Problem of Language in the New Testament and Contemporary Theology.* New York: Harper & Row, 1966.

Gadamer, Hans-Georg. *Wahrheit und Methode.* Tübingen: J. C. B. Mohr, 1960. Trans D. Marshall and J. Weinsheimer under the title *Truth and Method.* 2nd ed., rev. (New York: Crossroad, 1989).

Gmelin, Hermann. "Die Anrede an den Leser in Dantes Göttlicher Komödie." *Deutsches Dante-Jahrbuch* 29–30 (1951): 130–40.

Grondin, Jean. *Einführung in die philosophische Hermeneutik.* Darmstadt: Wissenschaftliche Buchgesellschaft, 1991. Trans. J. Weinsheimer under the title *Introduction to Philosophical Hermeneutics* (New Haven: Yale University Press, 1994).

Heidegger, Martin. *Basic Writings.* Ed. David Krell. New York: Harper & Row, 1977.

———. *Early Greek Thinking.* Trans. Krell and Capuzzi. New York: Harper & Row, 1975.

———. *Sein und Zeit. Gesamtausgabe I. Abteilung: Veröffentlichte Schriften 1914–70* Vol. 2. Frankfurt: Klostermann, 1977. Trans. J. Macquarie and E. Robinson under the title *Being and Time* (New York: Harper & Row, 1962).

———. *Unterwegs zur Sprache.* Pfullingen: Verlag Günter Neske, 1959. Trans. P. Hertz under the title *On the Way to Language* (New York: Harper & Row, 1971).

———. *Der Ursprung des Kunstwerkes.* Stuttgart: Reclam, 1960; originally a 1935–36 lecture published in *Holzwege* (Klostermann: Frankfurt am Main, 1950). Trans. A. Hofstadter under the title "The Origin of the Work of Art," in *Poetry, Language, Thought* (New York: Harper & Row, 1971).

———. *Vorträge und Aufsätze.* Pfullingen: Neske, 1954.

———. "Vom Wesen der Wahrheit" (1930). In *Gesamtausgabe I. Abteilung: Veröffentlichte Schriften 1914–70.* Vol. 9, *Wegmarken.* Frankfurt am Main: Klostermann, 1977. Translated under the title "On the Essence of Truth," in *Basic Writings.*

Hollander, Robert. "Dante *Theologus-Poeta.*" In *Studies in Dante.* Ravenna: Longo, 1980.

Holy Bible. Authorized (King James) Version, 1611. London: Oxford University Press. Translation occasionally modified in accordance with *The Greek New Testament.* 2nd. ed. New York: United Bible Societies, 1968.

Jacoff, Rachel. *The Cambridge Companion to Dante.* Cambridge: Cambridge University Press, 1993.

Jeanrond, Werner. *Text und Interpretation als Kategorien theologischen Denkens* in *hermeneutische Untersuchungen zur Theologie* 23. Tübingen: J. C. B. Mohr, 1986. Trans. T. J. Wilson under the title *Text and Interpretation as Categories of Theological Thinking* (Dublin: Gill and Macmillan, 1988).

Kirkpatrick, Robin. *Dante's Inferno: Difficulty and Dead Poetry.* Cambridge: Cambridge University Press, 1989.

Löwith, Karl. *Meaning in History.* Chicago: University of Chicago Press, 1949.

Lubac, Henri de. *Exégèse médiévale.* Paris: Aubier, 1961.

Marshall, Donald G. "Truth, Tradition, and Understanding." *diacritics* 7 (1977): 70–77.

Mazzotta, Giuseppe. *Dante. Poet of the Desert: History and Allegory in the "Divine Comedy."* Princeton: Princeton University Press, 1979.

Nardi, Bruno. *Dante e la cultura medievale.* 2nd ed., rev. Bari: Laterza, 1949.

Nova Vulgata Bibliorum Sacrorum. Rome: Libreria Editrice Vaticana, 1979.

Ormiston, Gayle, and Alan Schrift, eds. *Transforming the Hermeneutic Context: From Nietzsche to Nancy.* Albany: State University of New York Press, 1990.

Padoan, Giorgio. "La 'mirabile visione' di Dante e l'Epistola a Cangrande." In *Il pio Ennea, l'empio Ulisse.* Ravenna: Longo, 1977.

Patrologiae Cursus Completus: Series Latina. Ed. J. P. Migne. Paris, 1844–64.

Pépin, Jean. *Dante et la tradition de l'allégorie.* Montréal: Institut d'Études Médiévales, 1970.

Picone, Michelangelo, ed. *Dante e le forme dell'allegoresi.* Ravenna: Longo, 1987.

Ricoeur, Paul. *Le conflit des interprétations: Essais d'herméneutique I.* Paris: Seuil, 1969.

———. "What is a Text? Explanation and Interpretation." In D. Rasmussen, *Mythic-Symbolic Language and Philosophical Anthropology: A Constructive Interpretation of the Thought of Paul Ricoeur.* The Hague: Martinus Nijhoff, 1971. Partial translation of "Qu'est-ce qu'un texte? Expliquer et comprendre. In *Hermeneutik und Dialektik.* Vol. 2, *Sprache und Logik: Theorie der Auslegung und Probleme der Einzelwissenschaften,* ed. R. Bubner, K. Cramer, and R. Wiehl (Tübingen: J. C. B. Mohr, 1970), pp. 181–200.

———. *Du text à l'action: Essais d'herméneutique II.* Paris: Seuil, 1986.

Schleiermacher, Friedrich D. E. *Hermeneutics: The Handwritten Manuscripts.* Ed. H. Kimmerle. Trans. J. Duke and J. Forstman. Montana: Scholars Press, 1977.

Singleton, Charles S. *Dante Studies I: Elements of Structure.* Cambridge: Harvard University Press, 1957.

———. "The Irreducible Dove." *Comparative Literature* 9 (1957): 129–35.

———. "The Vistas in Retrospect." *Atti del congresso internazionale di studi danteschi* 20–27 (April 1965). Later published in *Modern Language Notes* 81 (1966): 55–80.

Spitzer, Leo. "The Addresses to the Reader in the *Commedia.*" *Italica* 32/3 (1955): 143–65.

Stazio, Publius Papino. *Opere*. Ed. A. Traglia and G. Aricò. Turin: Unione Typi-grafico-editrice, 1990.

Tambling, Jeremy. *Dante and Difference*. Cambridge: Cambridge University Press, 1988.

Thomae Aquinatis Sancti. *Opera omnia*. New York: Musurgia, 1949.

Thompson, David. *Dante's Epic Journey*. Baltimore: Johns Hopkins University Press, 1974.

Vattimo, Gianni. *Arte e verità nel pensiero di Martin Heidegger*. Turin: Giappichelli, 1966.

Vergilius, Marco Publius. *The Aeneid*. Ed. J. W. Mackail. Oxford: Clarendon Press, 1930.

Index

243